A CONFESSION AND WHAT I BELIEVE

A CONFESSION AND WHAT I BELIEVE

By

LEO TOLSTOY

TRANSLATED, WITH AN INTRODUCTION, BY AYLMER MAUDE

GYAN

ISBN : 978-81-212-9054-8(HB)

First Published in 1882
ndian Reprint in 2018

Published by

Gyan Publishing House
5, Ansari Road
Daryaganj, New Delhi-110002
Phone: 9811692060
E-mail: books@gyanbooks.com

Printed at: G. Print Process, Delhi.

CONTENTS

INTRODUCTION

A FEW words of introduction are necessary to this volume which contains two of Tolstoy's most remarkable works. Between the completion of *Anna Karenina*, early in 1877, and the resumption of his literary activity in the year 1885, with his popular Tales, Tolstoy devoted himself to religious reflection and to a close study of the Gospels and of dogmatic theology, although the latter subject repelled him. Apart from a retranslation of the Gospels with voluminous notes, the works contained in this volume are almost the only literary productions of his that appeared between his forty-ninth and fifty-seventh year, that is to say during eight of the years when his powers were at their zenith

An attempt was made in Russia to suppress these books, but they circulated clandestinely in large numbers, in hectographed copies and also in volumes printed abroad and smuggled into the country. No adequate reply to Tolstoy's terrific onslaughts upon Church and State was produced, and within a single generation, in Russia, the institutions he attacked had crumbled to dust.

These books have been translated into all civilized languages and have circulated far and wide. Nowhere have the views they contain been adequately met. On the contrary they have now become part of the air we breathe, and denunciations of Church and State, Parliamentary Government, Capital, and the institution of property, as well as of law and order in general, have become commonplaces of democratic rhetoric, and those institutions are now in some circles regarded as offences against the people which must be swept away as a prelude to putting down the mighty from their seats, exalting the humble and meek, filling the hungry with good things and sending the rich empty away.

This is serious. Our country has not yet followed in the footsteps of Russia; but here too an axe is laid to the root of the tree. What is said in these works cannot be suppressed. It is closely interwoven with some of the profoundest truths humanity has known; but it will deal a death-blow to civilization unless it can be answered. Lowell well exclaimed:—

'Oh Lord, ef folks wuz made so's't they could see
The begnet pint there is in an idee!
Ten times the danger in 'em th' is in steel;
They run your soul thru an' you never feel,
But crawl about an' seem to think you're livin',
Poor shells o' men, nut wuth the Lord's forgivin',
Till you come bunt ag'in a real live fect,
An' go to pieces when you'd ough' to ect!'

If the attack here made with power, conviction, and effect on the moral basis of our lives cannot be, and is not, convincingly met, it will continue to eat into the piles on which our house stands, and the whole order of our lives will crumble into dust.

A Confession is the most important of Tolstoy's autobiographical writings, and will bear comparison with the most famous confessions ever penned; but it soon merges into a consideration not of his own life alone, but of the life of us all, to whom a brief existence ending in inevitable death has been given here on earth.

The conclusion he reaches in *A Confession* and in *What I Believe* is, that personal life lived for one's own ends must be a misfortune to any one intelligent enough to realize the facts; and that the only escape is to merge one's life with that of 'the son of man': that light of reason manifest in all humanity, which will endure when our personal career is ended, and which comes to us from a source outside ourselves. Life, he says, is a blessing for him who identifies himself with the son of man in the task of establishing the kingdom of God on earth, here and now. Life is a misfortune for him who seeks his personal welfare, which is an effort death inevitably baffles.

Tolstoy's interpretation of Christ's five commandments differs very considerably from that given by the Church, but he introduces an intelligible and practical meaning which most of us had never suspected till we read his books. Together with much that is profoundly true and immensely important, Tolstoy announces and elaborates a theory of non-resistance, and expounds a doctrine of Christian anarchy which, plausibly as he states it, appears to be as gross a superstition as any of those he attacks.

If his theory be right (and he claims for it

Christ's authority), nothing can, and nothing should, save our industrial, political, or national existence from destruction. If, however, Christ meant this, it is curious that he did not say more than a few words of doubtful interpretation on a matter to which Tolstoy found it necessary during the last thirty years of his life to devote many volumes. Furthermore, Christ said, 'Render unto Cæsar the things that are Cæsar's,' bidding us apparently give some recognition to government to which, Tolstoy says, we should give none. Even if Christ meant what Tolstoy says he meant, if this conflicts, as it does, with our reason, conscience, and experience of life, it is still our duty to reject it. For, as Tolstoy has said, we select Christ's teaching and prefer it to other teachings, and call it divine, because it appears to us reasonable and true. If, on the contrary, after being interpreted by Tolstoy, it turns out to be plainly false, we must reject Christ's authority rather than substitute falsehood for truth.

We here face a stupendous problem, which only those who read this book carefully are likely to realize fully.

The amazing fact remains that Tolstoy's works, which have had a large circulation the world over, greatly influencing the lives of many people, and paving the way for a complete collapse of the fabric of Russian civilization, have, on this practical and crucial matter of non-resistance, met with no adequate reply. At any rate I know of no reasoned rejoinder to

Tolstoy's teaching that shows a proper appreciation of the force of his case and meets it on its merits, except the reply to him given in the second volume of my *Life of Tolstoy* (and briefly recapitulated in the subsequently published *Leo Tolstoy*). Here again a strange thing happened : Just as Tolstoy's doctrine had been before the world for over twenty years practically unanswered, so my reply, when it appeared, passed uncontroverted. The book itself was well received and appreciatively noticed, but that crucial matter, the repudiation of the theory of Non-Resistance, was nowhere mentioned. Even Tolstoy himself (who was by that time probably too old, too ill, and too harassed to deal with the matter) only said, when I submitted it to him, 'I have only one thing to object to in your article, namely, that it destroys my position at its roots.' I never knew what he really meant by that remark, but I feel sure he was too wedded to the view he had made his own to be seriously shaken by anything that could be said against it.

It is usually no part of a translator's duty to controvert the views expressed in a work he is translating, especially if he be in cordial agreement with a great part of it. But having devoted attention to this particular problem for over thirty years, and having, by close participation in the Tolstoy colony at Purleigh, and in the Dukhobor migration to Canada, as well as by personal intercourse with Tolstoy, his family, and his associates, had unusual opportunities of studying the effects of his teaching in actual life, I feel that it would hardly be fair to the reader to pass by the perplexities I have myself lived through without an occasional foot-note to indicate the joints in Tolstoy's armour.

Finally, I venture to suggest that if our spiritual leaders believe that there is anything in our existing institutions, industrial, legal, religious, or national, which deserves defence, they should produce some reply to the indictment formulated in this book, and should publish the same before it is here, as already in Russia, too late to save the existing structure.

I do not suggest a wholesale acceptance or repudiation of Tolstoy's teaching, the difficult but necessary task is to *discriminate* and to sift the wheat from the chaff.

AYLMER MAUDE.

GREAT BADDOW,
CHELMSFORD,
November 6, 1920.

NOTE

FOOT-NOTES by Tolstoy are marked L. T.; for the rest the translator is responsible.

A CONFESSION

AN INTRODUCTION TO A CRITICISM OF DOGMATIC THEOLOGY AND AN EXAMINATION OF THE CHRISTIAN TEACHING.

A CONFESSION

I

I WAS baptized and brought up in the Orthodox Christian faith. I was taught it in childhood and throughout my boyhood and youth. But when I left the second course of the university, at the age of eighteen, I no longer believed any of the things I had been taught.

Judging by certain memories, I never seriously believed, but merely relied on what I was taught and on what was professed by the grown-up people around me; and that reliance was very unstable.

I remember that before I was eleven, a boy, Vladimir Milyutin (long since dead), a grammar school pupil, visited us one Sunday and announced as the latest novelty a discovery made at his school. The discovery was that there is no God, and that all we are taught about Him is a mere invention (this was in 1838). I remember how interested my elder brothers were in this news. They called me to their council, and we all, I remember, became very animated, and accepted the news as something very interesting and quite possible.

I remember also that when my elder brother, Dmitry, who was then at the university, suddenly, in the passionate way natural to him, devoted himself to religion and began to attend all the Church services, to fast and to lead a pure and moral life, we all—even our elders—unceasingly held him up to ridicule and called him, for some unknown reason, 'Noah.' I remember that Musin-Pushkin, the then curator of Kazan University, when inviting us to a dance at his house, ironically persuaded my brother (who was declining the invitation) by the argument that even David danced before the Ark. I sympathized with these jokes made by my elders, and drew from them the conclusion that though it is necessary to learn the catechism and go to church, one must not take such things too seriously. I remember also that I read Voltaire when I was very young, and that his raillery, far from shocking me, amused me very much.

My lapse from faith occurred as is usual among people on our level of education. In most cases, I think, it happens thus: a man lives like everybody else, on the basis of principles not merely having nothing in common with religious doctrine, but generally opposed to it; religious doctrine does not play a part in life, in intercourse with others it is never encountered, and in a man's own life he never has to reckon with it. Religious doctrine is professed far away from life and independently of it. If it is encountered, it is only as an external phenomenon disconnected from life.

By a man's life and conduct, then as now, it was and is quite impossible to judge whether he is a believer or not. If there be a difference between a man who publicly professes Orthodoxy and one who denies it, the difference is not in favour of the former. Then, as now, the public profession and confession of Orthodoxy was chiefly met with among people who were dull and cruel, and who considered themselves very important. Ability, honesty, reliability, good-nature and moral conduct were more often met with among unbelievers.

The schools teach the catechism and send the pupils to church ; and Government officials must produce certificates of having received Communion. But a man of our circle, who has finished his education and is not in the Government service, may even now (and formerly it was still easier for him to do so) live for ten or twenty years without once remembering that he is living among Christians and is himself reckoned a member of the Orthodox Christian Church.

So that, now as formerly, religious doctrine, accepted on trust and supported by external pressure, thaws away gradually under the influence of knowledge and experience of life which conflict with it, and a man very often lives on, imagining that he still holds intact the religious doctrine imparted to him in childhood, whereas in fact not a trace of it remains.

S., a clever and truthful man, once told me the story of how he ceased to believe. When he was already twenty-six, he once, on a hunting expedition, at the place where they put up for the night, by habit retained since childhood, knelt down in the evening to pray. His elder brother, who was at the hunt with him, was lying on some hay and watching him. When S. had finished and was settling down for the night, his brother said to him: 'So you still do that?'

They said nothing more to one another. But from that day S. ceased to say his prayers or go to church. And now he has not prayed, received Communion, or gone to church for thirty years. And this not because he knows his brother's convictions and has joined him in them, nor because he has decided anything in his own soul, but simply because the word spoken by his brother was like the push of a finger on a wall that was ready to fall by its own weight. The word only showed that where he thought there was faith, in reality there had long been an empty place, and that therefore the utterance of words and the making of signs of the cross and genuflections while praying were quite senseless actions. Becoming conscious of their senselessness, he could not continue them.

So it has been and is, I think, with the great majority of people. I am speaking of people of our educational level, who are sincere with themselves, and not of those who make the profession of faith a means of attaining worldly aims. (Such people are the most fundamental infidels, for if faith is for them a means of attaining any worldly aims, then certainly it is not faith.) These people of our education are so placed that the light of knowledge and life has caused an artificial erection to melt away, and they have either already noticed this and swept its place clear, or they have not yet noticed it.

The religious doctrine taught me from childhood disappeared in me as in others, but with this difference, that as from the age of fifteen I began to read philosophical works, my rejection of the doctrine became a conscious one at a very early age. From the time I was sixteen I ceased to say my prayers and ceased to go to church or to fast, of my own volition. I did not believe what had been taught me in childhood, but I believed in something. What it was I believed in I could not at all have said. I believed in a God, or rather I did not deny God; but I could not have said what sort of God. Neither did I deny Christ and his teaching, but what his teaching consisted in I again could not have said.

Looking back on that time, I now see clearly that my faith—my only real faith—that which, apart from my animal instincts, gave impulse to my life—was a belief in perfecting myself. But in what this perfecting consisted, and what its object was, I could not have said. I tried to perfect myself mentally—I studied everything I could, anything life threw in my way; I tried to perfect my will, I drew up rules which I tried to follow; I perfected myself physically, cultivating my strength and agility by all sorts of exercises, and accustoming myself to endurance and patience by all kinds of privations.

And all this I considered to be the pursuit of perfection. The beginning of it all was, of course, moral perfection; but that was soon replaced by perfection in general: by the desire to be better, not in my own eyes or those of God, but in the eyes of other people. And very soon this effort again changed into a desire to be stronger than others: to be more famous, more important and richer than others.

II

SOME day I will narrate the touching and instructive history of my life during those ten years of my youth. I think very many people have had the same experience. With all my soul I wished to be good; but I was young, passionate, and alone, completely alone when I sought goodness. Every time I tried to express my most sincere desire, which was to be morally good, I met with contempt and ridicule; but as soon as I yielded to nasty passions I was praised and encouraged.

Ambition, love of power, covetousness, lasciviousness, pride, anger and revenge—were all respected.

Yielding to those passions, I became like the grown-up folk, and I felt that they approved of me. The kind aunt with whom I lived, herself the purest of beings, always told me that there was nothing she so desired for me as that I should have relations with a married woman: '*Rien ne forme un jeune homme, comme une liaison avec une femme comme il faut.'*[1] Another happiness she desired for me was that I should become an aide-de-camp, and if possible aide-de-camp to the Emperor. But the greatest happiness of all would be that I should marry a very rich girl and so become possessed of as many serfs as possible.

I cannot think of those years without horror, loathing, and heartache. I killed men in war, and challenged men to duels in order to kill them; I lost at cards, consumed the labour of the peasants, sentenced them to punishments, lived loosely and deceived people. Lying, robbery, adultery of all kinds, drunkenness, violence, murder—there was no crime I did not commit, and for all that people praised my conduct, and my contemporaries considered and consider me to be a comparatively moral man.

So I lived for ten years.

During that time I began to write from vanity, covetousness, and pride. In my writings I did the same as in my life. To get fame and money, for the sake of which I wrote, it was necessary to hide the good and to display the evil. And I did so. How often in my writings I contrived to hide under the guise of indifference, or even of banter, those strivings of mine towards goodness, which gave meaning to my life! And I succeeded in this, and was praised.

At twenty-six years of age[2] I returned to

[1] Nothing so forms a young man, as an intimacy with a woman of good breeding.

[2] Tolstoy makes a slip here: he was twenty-seven.

Petersburg after the war, and met the writers. They received me as one of themselves and flattered me. And before I had time to look round I had adopted the views on life of the set of authors I had come among, and these views completely obliterated all my former strivings to improve. Those views furnished a theory which justified the dissoluteness of my life.

The view of life of these people, my comrades in authorship, consisted in this: that life in general goes on developing, and in this development we—men of thought—have the chief part; and among men of thought it is we—artists and poets—who have the greatest influence. Our vocation is to teach mankind. And lest the simple question should suggest itself: What do I know, and what can I teach? it was explained in this theory that this need not be known, and that the artist and poet teach unconsciously. I was considered an admirable artist and poet, and therefore it was very natural for me to adopt this theory. I, artist and poet, wrote and taught, without myself knowing what. For this I was paid money; I had excellent food, lodging, women, and society; and I had fame, which showed that what I taught was very good.

This faith in the meaning of poetry and in the development of life was a religion, and I was one of its priests. To be its priest was very pleasant and profitable. And I lived a considerable time in this faith without doubting its validity. But in the second, and especially in the third year of this life, I began to doubt the infallibility of this religion and to examine it. My first cause of doubt was that I began to notice that the priests of this religion were not all in accord among themselves. Some said: We are the best and most useful teachers; we teach what is needed, but the others teach wrongly. Others said: No! we are the real teachers, and you teach wrongly. And they disputed, quarrelled, abused, cheated, and tricked one another. There were also many among us who did not care who was right and who was wrong, but were simply bent on attaining their covetous aims by means of this activity of ours. All this obliged me to doubt the validity of our creed.

Moreover, having begun to doubt the truth of the authors' creed itself, I also began to observe its priests more attentively, and I became convinced that almost all the priests of that religion, the writers, were immoral, and for the most part men of bad, worthless character, much inferior to those whom I had met in my former dissipated and military life; but they were self-confident and self-satisfied as only those can be who are quite holy or who do not know what holiness is. These people revolted me, I became revolting to myself, and I realized that that faith was a fraud.

But strange to say, though I understood this fraud and renounced it, yet I did not renounce the rank these people gave me: the rank of artist, poet, and teacher. I naïvely imagined that I was a poet and artist and could teach everybody without myself knowing what I was teaching, and I acted accordingly.

From my intimacy with these men I acquired a new vice: abnormally developed pride, and an insane assurance that it was my vocation to teach men, without knowing what.

To remember that time, and my own state of mind and that of those men (though there are thousands like them to-day), is sad and terrible and ludicrous, and arouses exactly the feeling one experiences in a lunatic asylum.

We were all then convinced that it was necessary for us to speak, write, and print as quickly as possible and as much as possible, and that it was all wanted for the good of humanity. And thousands of us, contradicting and abusing one another, all printed and wrote—teaching others. And without remarking that we knew nothing, and that to the simplest of life's question: What is good and what is evil? we did not know how to reply, we all, not listening to one another, talked at the same time, sometimes backing and praising one another in order to be backed and praised in turn, sometimes getting angry with one another—just as in a lunatic asylum.

Thousands of workmen laboured to the extreme limit of their strength day and night, setting the type and printing millions of words which the post carried all over Russia, and we still went on teaching and could in no way find time to teach enough, and were always angry that sufficient attention was not paid us.

It was terribly strange, but is now quite comprehensible. Our real innermost concern was to get as much money and praise as possible. To gain that end we could do nothing except write books and papers. So we did that. But in order to do such useless work and to feel assured that we were very important people, we required a theory justifying our activity. And so among us this theory was devised: 'All that exists is reasonable. All that exists develops. And it all develops by means of Culture. And Culture is measured by the circulation of books and newspapers. And we are paid money and are respected because we write books and newspapers, and therefore we are the most useful and the best of men.' This theory would have been all very well if we had been unanimous, but as every thought expressed by one of us was always met by a diametrically opposite thought expressed by another, we ought to have been driven to reflection. But we ignored this; people paid us money, and those on our side praised us; so each of us considered himself justified.

It is now clear to me that this was just as in a lunatic asylum; but then I only dimly suspected this, and like all lunatics, simply called all men lunatics except myself.

III

So I lived abandoning myself to this insanity for another six years, till my marriage. During that time I went abroad. Life in Europe and my acquaintance with leading and learned

Europeans [1] confirmed me yet more in the faith in which I believed, of striving after perfection, for I found the same faith among them. That faith took with me the common form it assumes with the majority of educated people of our day. It was expressed by the word 'progress.' It then appeared to me that this word meant something. I did not as yet understand that, being tormented (like every live man) by the question how it is best for me to live, in my answer, 'Live in conformity with progress,' I was replying as a man in a boat would do if when carried along by wind and waves he replied to what for him was the chief and only question, 'whither to steer', by saying, 'We are being carried somewhere.'

I did not then notice this. Only occasionally —not by reason but by instinct—I revolted against this superstition, so common in our day, by which people hide from themselves their lack of understanding of life. . . . So, for instance, during my stay in Paris, the sight of an execution revealed to me the instability of my superstitious belief in progress. When I saw the head part from the body, and how they thumped separately into the box, I understood, not with my mind but with my whole being, that no theory of the reasonableness of our present progress could justify this deed; and that though everybody from the creation of the world, on whatever theory, had held it to be necessary, I knew it to be unnecessary and

[1] Russians generally make a distinction between Europeans and Russians.

bad ; and therefore the arbiter of what is good and evil is not what people say and do, nor is it progress, but it is my heart and I. Another instance of a realization that the superstitious belief in progress is insufficient as a guide to life, was my brother's death. Wise, good, serious, he fell ill while still a young man, suffered for more than a year, and died painfully, not understanding why he had lived, and still less why he had to die. No theories could give me, or him, any reply to these questions during his slow and painful dying. But these were only rare instances of doubt, and I actually continued to live professing a faith only in progress. 'All evolves and I evolve with it : and why it is that I evolve with all things will be known some day.' So I ought to have formulated my faith at that time.

On returning from abroad I settled in the country, and chanced to occupy myself with peasant schools. This work was particularly to my taste, because in it I had not to face the falsity which had become obvious to me and stared me in the face when I tried to teach people by literary means. Here, also, I acted in the name of Progress, but I already regarded Progress itself critically. I said to myself : 'In some of its developments Progress has proceeded wrongly ; and with primitive peasant children one must deal in a spirit of perfect freedom, letting them choose what path of progress they please.' In reality I was ever revolving round one and the same insoluble problem, which was : How to teach without knowing what to teach.

In the higher spheres of literary activity I had realized that one could not teach without knowing what ; for I saw that people all taught differently, and by quarrelling among themselves only succeeded in hiding their ignorance from one another. But here, with peasant children, I thought to evade this difficulty by letting them learn what they liked. It amuses me now, when I remember how I shuffled in trying to satisfy my desire to teach, while in the depth of my soul I knew very well that I could not teach anything needful for I did not know what was needful. After spending a year at school work, I went abroad a second time, to discover how to teach others while myself knowing nothing.

And it seemed to me that I had learnt this abroad, and in the year of the peasants' emancipation (1861) I returned to Russia armed with all this wisdom ; and having become an Arbiter,[1] I began to teach, both the uneducated peasants in schools and the educated classes through a magazine I published. Things appeared to be going well, but I felt I was not quite sound mentally, and that matters could not long continue in that way. And I should perhaps then have come to the state of despair I reached fifteen years later, had there not been one side of life still unexplored by me, which promised me happiness : that was marriage.

For a year I busied myself with arbitration work, the schools, and the magazine ; and I became so worn out—as a result especially of my mental confusion—and so hard was my

[1] To keep peace between peasants and owners.

struggle as Arbiter, so obscure the results of my activity in the schools, so repulsive my shuffling in the magazine (which always amounted to one and the same thing: a desire to teach everybody, and to hide the fact that I did not know what to teach), that I fell ill, mentally rather than physically, threw up everything, and went away to the Bashkirs in the steppes, to breathe fresh air, drink kumys,[1] and live a merely animal life.

Returning from there I married. The new conditions of happy family life completely diverted me from all search for the general meaning of life. My whole life was centred at that time in my family, wife and children, and therefore in care to increase our means of livelihood. My striving after self-perfection, for which I had already substituted a striving for perfection in general, i.e. Progress, was now again replaced by the effort simply to secure the best possible conditions for myself and my family.

So another fifteen years passed.

In spite of the fact that I now regarded authorship as of no importance, I yet, during those fifteen years, continued to write. I had already tasted the temptation of authorship : the temptation of immense monetary rewards and applause for my insignificant work ; and I devoted myself to it as a means of improving my material position, and of stifling in my soul all questions as to the meaning of my own life, or of life in general.

I wrote, teaching what was for me the only

[1] A fermented drink prepared from mare's milk.

truth, that one should live so as to have the best for oneself and one's family.

So I lived; but five years ago something very strange began to happen to me. At first I experienced moments of perplexity and arrest of life, as though I did not know how to live or what to do; and I felt lost and became dejected. But this passed, and I went on living as before. Then these moments of perplexity began to recur oftener and oftener, and always in the same form. They were always expressed by the questions: What's it for? What does it lead to?

At first it seemed to me that these were aimless and irrelevant questions. I thought that it was all well known, and that if I should ever wish to deal with the solution, it would not cost me much effort; just at present I had no time for it, but when I wanted to I should be able to find the answer. The questions, however, began to repeat themselves frequently, and more and more insistently to demand replies; and like drops of ink always falling on one place, they ran together into one black blot.

That occurred which happens to every one sickening with a mortal internal disease. At first trivial signs of indisposition appear, to which the sick man pays no attention; then these signs reappear more and more often and merge into one uninterrupted period of suffering. The suffering increases, and before the sick man can look round, what he took for a mere indisposition has already become more important to him than anything else in the world—it is death!

That was what happened to me. I understood

that it was no casual indisposition, but something very important, and that if these questions constantly repeated themselves, they would have to be answered. And I tried to answer them. The questions seemed such stupid, simple, childish questions; but as soon as I touched them and tried to solve them, I at once became convinced (1) that they are not childish and stupid, but the most important and profound of life's questions; and (2) that, try as I would, I could not solve them. Before occupying myself with my Samara estate, the education of my son, or the writing of a book, I had to know *why* I was doing it. As long as I did not know why, I could do nothing, and could not live. Amid the thoughts of estate management which greatly occupied me at that time, the question would suddenly occur to me: 'Well, you will have 6,000 *desyatinas*[1] of land in Samara Government and 300 horses, and what next?' . . . And I was quite disconcerted, and did not know what to think. Or, when considering my plans for the education of my children, I would say to myself: 'What for?' Or when considering how the peasants might become prosperous, I suddenly said to myself: 'But what does it matter to me?' Or when thinking of the fame my works would bring me, I said to myself, 'Very well; you will be more famous than Gogol or Pushkin or Shakespeare or Molière, or than all the writers in the world—and what of it?' And I could find no reply at all. The questions would not wait, they had to be

[1] The *desyatina* is about 2¾ acres.

answered at once, and if I did not answer them, it was impossible to live. But there was no answer.

I felt that what I had been standing on had collapsed, and that I had nothing left under my feet. What I had lived on no longer existed; and I had nothing left to live on.

IV

My life came to a standstill. I could breathe, eat, drink, and sleep, and I could not help doing these things; but there was no life, for there were no wishes the fulfilment of which I could consider reasonable. If I desired anything, I knew in advance that whether I satisfied my desire or not, nothing would come of it. Had a fairy come and offered to fulfil my desires I should not have known what to ask. If in moments of intoxication I felt something which, though not a wish, was a habit left by former wishes, in sober moments I knew this to be a delusion, and that there was really nothing to wish for. I could not even wish to know the truth, for I guessed of what it consisted. The truth was that life is meaningless. I had, as it were, lived, lived, and walked, walked, till I had come to a precipice and saw clearly that there was nothing ahead of me but destruction. It was impossible to stop, impossible to go back, and impossible to close my eyes or avoid seeing that there was nothing ahead but suffering and real death—complete annihilation.

It had come to this, that I, a healthy, fortunate

man, felt I could no longer live : some irresistible power impelled me to rid myself one way or other of life. I cannot say I *wished* to kill myself. The power which drew me away from life was stronger, fuller, and more widespread than any mere wish. It was a force similar to the former striving to live, only in a contrary direction. All my strength drew me away from life. The thought of self-destruction now came to me as naturally as thoughts of how to improve my life had come formerly. And it was so seductive that I had to be wily with myself lest I should carry it out too hastily. I did not wish to hurry, only because I wanted to use all efforts to disentangle the matter. 'If I cannot unravel matters, there will always be time.' And it was then that I, a man favoured by fortune, hid a cord from myself, lest I should hang myself from the crosspiece of the partition in my room, where I undressed alone every evening ; and I ceased to go out shooting with a gun, lest I should be tempted by so easy a way of ending my life. I did not myself know what I wanted : I feared life, desired to escape from it ; yet still hoped something of it.

And all this befell me at a time when all around me I had what is considered complete good fortune. I was not yet fifty ; I had a good wife who loved me and whom I loved, good children, and a large estate which without much effort on my part improved and increased. I was respected by my relations and acquaintances more than at any previous time. I was praised by others, and without much self-deception could consider that my name was famous. And far from being insane or mentally diseased, I enjoyed on the contrary a strength of mind and body such as I have seldom met with among men of my kind; physically, I could keep up with the peasants at mowing, and mentally I could work for eight and ten hours at a stretch without experiencing any ill results from such exertion. And in this situation I came to this—that I could not live, and, fearing death, had to employ cunning with myself to avoid taking my own life.

My mental condition presented itself to me in this way: my life is a stupid and spiteful joke some one has played on me. Though I did not acknowledge a 'some one' who created me, yet such a presentation—that some one had played an evil and stupid joke on me by placing me in the world—was the form of expression that suggested itself most naturally to me.

Involuntarily it appeared to me that there, somewhere, was some one who amused himself by watching how I lived for thirty or forty years: learning, developing, maturing in body and mind, and how—having with matured mental powers reached the summit of life from which it all lay before me, I stood on that summit—like an arch-fool—seeing clearly that there is nothing in life, and that there has been and will be nothing. And he was amused. . . .

But whether that 'some one' laughing at me existed or not, I was none the better off. I could give no reasonable meaning to any single action, or to my whole life. I was only surprised that I could have avoided understanding this from the very beginning—it has been so long known to all. To-day or to-morrow sickness and death will come (they had come already) to those I love or to me; nothing will remain but stench and worms. Sooner or later my affairs, whatever they may be, will be forgotten, and I shall not exist. Then why go on making any effort? . . . How can man fail to see this? And how go on living? That is what is surprising! One can only live while one is intoxicated with life; as soon as one is sober it is impossible not to see that it is all a mere fraud and a stupid fraud! That is precisely what it is: there is nothing either amusing or witty about it: it is simply cruel and stupid.

There is an Eastern fable, told long ago, of a traveller overtaken on a plain by an enraged beast. Escaping from the beast he gets into a dry well, but sees at the bottom of the well a dragon that has opened its jaws to swallow him. And the unfortunate man, not daring to climb out lest he should be destroyed by the enraged beast, and not daring to leap to the bottom of the well lest he should be eaten by the dragon, seizes a twig growing in a crack in the well and clings to it. His hands are growing weaker, and he feels he will soon have to resign himself to the destruction that awaits him above or below; but still he clings on. Then he sees that two mice, a black and a white one, go regularly round and round the stem of the twig to which he is clinging, and gnaw at it. And soon the twig itself will snap and he will fall into the dragon's jaws. The traveller sees this and knows that he will inevitably perish; but while still hanging he looks around, sees some drops of honey on the leaves of the twig, reaches them with his tongue and licks them. So I too clung to the twig of life, knowing that the dragon of death was inevitably awaiting me, ready to tear me to pieces; and I could not understand why I had fallen into such torment. I tried to lick the honey which formerly consoled me; but the honey no longer gave me pleasure, and the white and black mice of day and night gnawed at the branch by which I hung. I saw the dragon clearly, and the honey no longer tasted sweet. I only saw the unescapable dragon and the mice, and I could not tear my gaze from them. And this is not a fable, but the real unanswerable truth intelligible to all.

The deception of the joys of life which formerly allayed my terror of the dragon now no longer deceived me. No matter how often I may be told, 'You cannot understand the meaning of life, so do not think about it, but live,' I can no longer do it: I have already done it too long. I cannot now help seeing day and night going round and bringing me to death. That is all I see, for that alone is true. All else is false.

The two drops of honey which diverted my eyes from the cruel truth longer than the rest: my love of family, and of writing—art as I called it—were no longer sweet to me.

'Family' . . . said I to myself. But my family —wife and children—are also human. They are placed just as I am: they must either live in a lie or see the terrible truth. Why should they live? Why should I love them, guard them, bring them up, or watch them? That they may come to the despair that I feel, or else be stupid? Loving them, I cannot hide the truth from them: each step in knowledge leads them to the truth. And the truth is death.

'Art, poetry?' . . . Under the influence of success and the praise of men, I had long assured myself that this was a thing one could do though death was drawing near—death which destroys all things, including my work and its remembrance; but soon I saw that that too was a fraud. It was plain to me that art is an adornment of life, an allurement to life. But life had lost its attraction for me; so how could I attract others? As long as I was not living my own life, but was borne on the waves of some other life—as long as I believed that life had a meaning, though one I could not express—the reflection of life in poetry and art of all kinds afforded me pleasure: it was pleasant to look at life in the mirror of art. But when I began to seek the meaning of life, and felt the necessity of living my own life, that mirror became for me unnecessary, superfluous, ridiculous, or painful. I could no longer soothe myself with what I now saw in the mirror, namely, that my position was stupid and desperate. It was all very well to enjoy the sight when in the depth of my soul I believed that my life had a meaning. Then the play of lights—comic, tragic, touching, beautiful, and terrible—in life amused me. But when I knew life to be meaningless and terrible, the play in the mirror could no longer amuse me. No sweetness of honey could be sweet to me when I saw the dragon, and saw the mice gnawing away my support.

Nor was that all. Had I simply understood that life had no meaning I could have borne it quietly, knowing that that was my lot. But I could not satisfy myself with that. Had I been like a man living in a wood from which he knows there is no exit, I could have lived; but I was like one lost in a wood who, horrified at having lost his way, rushes about, wishing to find the road. He knows that each step he takes confuses him more and more; but still he cannot help rushing about.

It was indeed terrible. And to rid myself of the terror I wished to kill myself. I experienced terror at what awaited me—knew that that terror was even worse than the position I was in; but still I could not patiently await the end. However convincing the argument might be that, in any case, some vessel in my heart would give way, or something would burst and all would be over, I could not patiently await that end. The horror of darkness was too great, and I wished to free myself from it as quickly as possible by noose or bullet. That was the feeling which drew me most strongly towards suicide.

V

'But perhaps I have overlooked something, or misunderstood something?' said I to myself several times. ‘It cannot be that this condition of despair is natural to man!’ And I sought for an explanation of these problems in all the branches of knowledge acquired by men. I sought painfully and long, not from idle curiosity or listlessly, but painfully and persistently day and night—sought as a perishing man seeks for safety—and I found nothing.

I sought in all the sciences, but, far from finding what I wanted, became convinced that all who like myself had sought in knowledge for the meaning of life had equally found nothing. And not only had found nothing, but had plainly acknowledged that the very thing which made me despair—namely the senselessness of life—is the one indubitable thing man can know.

I sought everywhere; and thanks to a life spent in learning, and thanks also to my relations with the scholarly world, I had access to scientists and scholars in all branches of knowledge, and they readily showed me all their knowledge not only in books, but also in conversation, so that I had at my disposal all that science has to say on this question of life.

I was long unable to believe that it gives no other reply to life's questions than that which it actually does give. It long seemed to me, when I saw the important and serious air with which science announces its conclusions, which have nothing in common with the real questions of human life, that there was something I had not understood. I long was timid before science, and it seemed to me that the lack of conformity between the answers and my questions arose not by the fault of science, but from my ignorance, but the matter was for me not a game or an amusement, but one of life and death, and I was involuntarily brought to the conviction that my questions were the only legitimate ones, forming the basis of all knowledge, and that not I with my questions was to blame, but science if it pretends to reply to those questions.

My question—that which at the age of fifty brought me to the verge of suicide—was the simplest of questions, lying in the soul of every man from the foolish child to the wisest elder: it was a question without answering which one cannot live, as I had found by experience. It was: 'What will come of what I am doing to-day or shall do to-morrow—What will come of my whole life?'

Differently expressed, the question is: 'Why should I live, why wish for anything, or do anything?' It can also be expressed thus: 'Is there any meaning in my life that the inevitable death awaiting me does not destroy?'

To this one question, variously expressed, I sought an answer in science. And I found that in relation to that question all human knowledge is divided as it were into two opposite hemispheres, at the ends of which are two poles: the one a negative, and the other a positive; but that neither at the one nor the other pole is the answer to life's questions.

The one series of sciences seems not to recognize the question, but clearly and exactly replies to its own independent questions: that is the series of experimental sciences, and at the extreme end of them stands mathematics. The other series of sciences recognizes the question, but does not answer it; that is the series of abstract sciences, and at the extreme end of them stands metaphysics.

From early youth I had been interested in the abstract sciences, but later the mathematical and natural sciences attracted me, and until I put my question definitely to myself, until that question had itself grown up within me urgently demanding a decision, I contented myself with those counterfeit answers which science gives.

Now in the experimental sphere I said to myself: 'Everything develops and differentiates itself, moving towards complexity and perfection, and there are laws directing this movement. You are a part of the whole. Having learnt as far as possible the whole, and having learnt the law of evolution, you will understand also your place in the whole, and will know yourself.' Ashamed as I am to confess it, there was a time when I seemed satisfied with that. It was just the time when I was myself becoming more complex and was developing. My muscles were growing and strengthening, my memory was being enriched, my capacity to think and understand was increasing, I was growing and developing; and feeling this growth in myself it was natural for me to think that such was the universal law in which I should find the solution of the question of my life. But a time came when the growth within me ceased. I felt that I was not developing, but fading, my muscles were weakening, my teeth falling out, and I saw that the law not only did not explain anything to me, but that there never had been or could be such a law, and that I had taken for a law what I had found in myself at a certain period of my life. I regarded the definition of that law more strictly; and it became clear to me that there could be no law of endless development; it became clear that to say, 'in infinite space and time everything develops, becomes more perfect and more complex, is differentiated,' is to say nothing at all. Those are all words with no meaning, for in the infinite there is neither complex nor simple, no forward or backward, no better or worse.

Above all, my personal question, 'What am I with my desires?' remained quite unanswered. And I understood that those sciences are very interesting, very attractive, but that they are exact and clear in inverse proportion to their applicability to the question of life: the less their applicability to the question of life, the more exact and clear they are, while the more they try to reply to the question of life, the more obscure and unattractive they become. If one turns to the division of sciences which attempt to reply to the questions of life—to physiology, psychology, biology, sociology—one encounters an appalling poverty of thought, the greatest obscurity, a quite unjustifiable pretension to solve irrelevant questions, and a continual contradiction of each authority by others and even by himself. If one turns to the branches of science which are not concerned with the solution of the questions of life, but which reply to their own special scientific questions, one is enraptured by the power of man's mind, but one knows in advance that they give no reply to life's questions. Those sciences simply ignore life's questions. They say: 'To the question of what you are and why you live we have no reply, and are not occupied therewith; but if you want to know the laws of light, of chemical combinations, the laws of development of organisms, if you want to know the laws of bodies and their form, and the relation of numbers and quantities, if you want to know the laws of your mind, to all that we have clear, exact, and unquestionable replies.'

In general the relation of the experimental sciences to life's question may be expressed thus: Question: 'Why do I live?' Answer: 'In infinite space, in infinite time, infinitely small particles change their forms in infinite complexity, and when you have understood the laws of those mutations of form, you will understand why you live on the earth.'

Then in the sphere of abstract science I said to myself: 'All humanity lives and develops on the basis of spiritual principles and ideals, which guide it. Those ideals are expressed in religions, in sciences, in arts, in forms of government. Those ideals become more and more elevated, and humanity advances to its highest welfare. I am part of humanity, and therefore my vocation is to forward the recognition and the realization of the ideals of humanity.' And at the time of my weak-mindedness I was satisfied with that; but as soon as the question of life presented itself clearly to me, those theories immediately crumbled away. Not to speak of the unscrupulous obscurity with which those sciences announce conclusions formed on the study of a small part of mankind, as general conclusions; not to speak of the mutual contradictions of different adherents of this view, as to what are the ideals of humanity; the strangeness, not to say stupidity, of the theory consists in the fact that in order to reply to the question facing each man: 'What am I?' or 'Why do I live?' or 'What must I do?' one has first to decide the question: 'What is the life of the whole' (which is to him unknown and of which he is acquainted with one tiny part in one minute period of time). To understand what he is, man must first understand all this mysterious humanity, consisting of people such as himself, who do not understand one another.

I have to confess that there was a time when I believed this. It was the time when I had my own favourite ideals, justifying my own caprices, and I was trying to devise a theory which would allow one to consider my caprices as the law of humanity. But as soon as the question of life arose in my soul in full clearness that reply at once flew to dust. And I understood that as in the experimental sciences there are real sciences, and semi-sciences which try to give answers to questions beyond their competence, so in this sphere there is a whole series of most diffused sciences which try to reply to irrelevant questions. Semi-sciences of that kind, the juridical and the social-historical, endeavour to solve the questions of a man's life by pretending to decide, each in its own way, the question of the life of all humanity.

But as in the sphere of man's experimental knowledge one who sincerely inquires how he is to live cannot be satisfied with the reply—Study in endless space the mutations, infinite in time and in complexity, of innumerable atoms, and then you will understand your life'—so also a sincere man cannot be satisfied with the reply: 'Study the whole life of humanity of which we cannot know either the beginning or the end, of which we do not even know a small part, and then you will understand your own life.' And like the experimental semi-sciences, so these other semi-sciences are the more filled with obscurities, inexactitudes, stupidities, and contradictions the further they diverge from the real problems. The problem of experimental science is the sequence of cause and effect in material phenomena. It is only necessary for experimental science to introduce the question of a final cause, and it becomes nonsensical. The problem of abstract science is the recognition of the primordial essence of life. It is only necessary to introduce the investigation of consequential phenomena (such as social and historical phenomena) and it also becomes nonsensical.

Experimental science then only gives positive knowledge and displays the greatness of the human mind when it does not introduce into its investigations the question of an ultimate cause. And, on the contrary, abstract science is only then science and displays the greatness of the human mind when it puts quite aside questions relating to the consequential causes of phenomena and regards man solely in relation to an ultimate cause. Such in this realm of science, forming the pole of the sphere, is metaphysics or philosophy. That science states the question clearly: 'What am I, and what is the universe? And why do I exist, and why does the universe exist?' And since it has existed it has always replied in the same way. Whether the philosopher calls the essence of life existing within me, and in all that exists, by the name of 'idea,' or 'substance,' or 'spirit,' or 'will,' he says one and the same thing, that this essence exists, and that I am of the same essence; but why it is he does not know, and does not say, if he is an exact thinker. I ask: 'Why should this essence exist? What results from the fact that it is and will be?' . . . And philosophy not merely does not reply, but is itself only asking that question. And if it is real philosophy, all its labour lies merely in trying to put that question clearly. And if it keeps firmly to its task, it cannot reply to the question otherwise than thus: 'What am I, and what is the universe?' 'All and nothing'; and to the question 'Why?' by 'I do not know.'

So that however I may turn these replies of philosophy, I can never obtain anything like an answer—and not because, as in the clear experimental sphere, the reply does not relate to my question, but because here, though all the mental work is directed just to my question, there is no answer, but instead of an answer one gets the same question, only in a complex form.

VI

In my search for answers to life's questions I experienced just what is felt by a man lost in a forest.

He reaches a glade, climbs a tree, and clearly sees the limitless distance, but sees that his home is not and cannot be there; then he goes into the dark wood, and sees the darkness, but there also his home is not.

So I wandered in that wood of human knowledge, amid the gleams of mathematical and experimental science which showed me clear horizons but in a direction where there could be no home, and also amid the darkness of the abstract sciences where I was immersed in deeper gloom the further I went, and where I finally convinced myself that there was, and could be, no exit.

Yielding myself to the bright side of knowledge, I understood that I was only diverting my gaze from the question. However alluringly clear those horizons which opened out before me might be, however alluring it might be to immerse oneself in the limitless expanse of those sciences, I already understood that the clearer they were the less they met my need and the less they replied to my question.

'I know,' said I to myself, 'what science so persistently wishes to discover, and along that road there is no reply to the question as to the meaning of my life.' In the abstract sphere I understood that notwithstanding the fact, or just because of the fact, that the direct aim of science is to reply to my question, there is no reply but that which I have myself already given: 'What is the meaning of my life?' 'There is none.' Or: 'What will come of my life?' 'Nothing.' Or: 'Why does everything exist that exists, and why do I exist?' 'Because it exists.'

Enquiring for one region of human knowledge, I received an innumerable quantity of exact replies concerning matters about which I had not asked: about the chemical constituents of the stars, about the movement of the sun towards the constellation Hercules, about the origin of species and of man, about the forms of infinitely minute imponderable particles of ether; but in this sphere of knowledge the only answer to my question, 'What is the meaning of my life?' was: 'You are what you call your "life"; you are a transitory, casual cohesion of particles. The mutual interactions and changes of these particles produce in you what you call your "life." That cohesion will last some time; afterwards the interaction of these particles will cease, and what you call "life" will cease, and so will all your questions. You are an accidentally united little lump of something. That little lump ferments. The little lump calls that fermenting its "life." The lump will disintegrate, and there will be an end of the fermenting and of all the questions.'

So answers the clear side of science and cannot answer otherwise if it strictly follows its principles.

From such a reply one sees that the reply does not answer the question. I want to know the meaning of my life, but that it is a fragment of the infinite, far from giving it a meaning, destroys its every possible meaning. The obscure compromises which that side of experimental exact science makes with abstract science, when it says that the meaning of life consists in development and in co-operation with development, owing to their inexactness and obscurity cannot be considered as replies.

The other side of science—the abstract side—when it holds strictly to its principles, replying directly to the question, always replies, and in all ages has replied, in one and the same way: 'The world is something infinite and incomprehensible. Human life is an incomprehensible part of that incomprehensible "all."' Again I exclude all those compromises between abstract and experimental sciences which supply the whole ballast of the semi-sciences called juridical, political, and historical. In those semi-sciences the conception of development and progress is again wrongly introduced, only with this difference, that there it was the development of everything, while here it is the development of the life of mankind. The error is there as before: development and progress in infinity can have no aim or direction, and, as far as my question is concerned, no answer is given.

In truly abstract science, namely in genuine

philosophy—not in that which Schopenhauer calls 'professorial philosophy,' which serves only to classify all existing phenomena in new philosophic categories and to call them by new names—where the philosopher does not lose sight of the essential question, the reply is always one and the same—the reply given by Socrates, Schopenhauer, Solomon, and Buddha.

'We approach truth only inasmuch as we depart from life,' said Socrates when preparing for death. 'For what do we, who love truth, strive after in life? To free ourselves from the body, and from all the evil that is caused by the life of the body! If so, then how can we fail to be glad when death comes to us?

'The wise man seeks death all his life, and therefore death is not terrible to him.'

And Schopenhauer says:

'Having recognized the inmost nature of the world as *will*, and all its phenomena—from the unconscious working of the obscure forces of Nature up to the completely conscious action of man—as only the objectivity of that will, we shall by no means evade the consequence, that with the voluntary renunciation and surrender of the will, all those phenomena are also abolished: that constant stream and effort without end and without rest at all the grades of objectivity, in which and through which the world consists; the multifarious forms succeeding each other in gradation; together with the form will disappear all the manifestations of will; and finally also the universal forms of this manifestation, time and space, and its last fundamental form: subject and object, all are abolished. Where there is no *will* there is no presentation, and no world. Before us, certainly, nothingness alone remains. But what resists this transition to nothingness, our nature, is indeed only that same will to live (Wille zum Leben), which we ourselves are, as it is our world. That we abhor annihilation so greatly, or, what is the same thing, our desire to live, is simply another expression of the fact that we strenuously will life, and are nothing but this will, and know nothing besides it. Therefore that which remains after the entire abolition of will, for us who are so full of will, is certainly nothing; but conversely, to those in whom the will has turned and has renounced itself, this our world, which is so real, with all its suns and milky ways—is nothing.'

'Vanity of vanities,' says Solomon—'vanity of vanities—all is vanity. What profit hath a man of all his labour which he taketh under the sun? One generation passeth away, and another generation cometh: but the earth abideth for ever. . . . The thing that hath been, is that which shall be; and that which is done is that which shall be done: and there is no new thing under the sun. Is there anything whereof it may be said, See, this is new? it hath been already of old time, which was before us. There is no remembrance of former things; neither shall there be any remembrance of things that are to come with those that shall come after. I the Preacher was King over Israel in Jerusalem. And I gave my heart to seek and search out by wisdom concerning all that is done under heaven: this sore travail hath God given to the sons of man to be exercised therewith. I have seen all the works that are done under the sun; and behold, all is vanity and vexation of spirit. . . . I communed with my own heart, saying, Lo, I am come to great estate, and have gotten more wisdom than all they that have been before me over Jerusalem: yea, my heart hath great experience of wisdom and knowledge. And I gave my heart to know wisdom, and to know madness and folly: I perceived that this also is vexation of spirit. For in much wisdom is much grief: and he that increaseth knowledge increaseth sorrow.

'I said in my heart, Go to now, I will prove thee with mirth, therefore enjoy pleasure: and behold this also is vanity. I said of laughter: It is mad: and of mirth, What doeth it? I sought in my heart how to cheer my flesh with wine, and while my heart was guided by wisdom, to lay hold on folly, till I might see what it was good for the sons of men that they should do under heaven the number of the days of their life. I made me great works; I builded me houses; I planted me vineyards: I made me gardens and orchards, and I planted trees in them of all kinds of fruits: I made me pools of water, to water therefrom the forest where trees were reared: I got me servants and maidens, and had servants born in my house; also I had great possessions of herds and flocks above all that were before me in Jerusalem: I gathered me also silver and gold and the peculiar treasure from kings and from the provinces: I got me men singers and women singers; and the delights of the sons of men, as musical instruments and that of all sorts. So I was great, and increased more than all that were before me in Jerusalem: also my wisdom remained with me. And whatever mine eyes desired I kept not from them. I withheld not my heart from any joy. . . . Then I looked on all the works that my hands had wrought, and on the labour that I had laboured to do: and, behold, all was vanity and vexation of spirit, and there was no profit from them under the sun. And I turned myself to behold wisdom, and madness, and folly. . . . But I perceived that one event happeneth to them all. Then said I in my heart, As it happeneth to the fool, so it happeneth even to me, and why was I then more wise? Then I said in my heart, that this also is vanity. For there is no remembrance of the wise more than of the fool for ever; seeing that which now is in the days to come shall all be forgotten. And how dieth the wise man? as the fool. Therefore I hated life; because the work that is wrought under the sun is grievous unto me: for all is vanity and vexation of spirit. Yea, I hated all my labour which I had taken under the sun: seeing that I must leave it unto the man that shall be after me. . . . For what hath man of all his labour, and of the vexation of his heart, wherein he hath laboured under the sun? For all his days are sorrows, and his travail grief; yea, even in the night his heart taketh no rest. This is also vanity. Man is not blessed with security that he should eat and drink and cheer his soul from his own labour. . . . All things come alike to all: there is one event to the righteous, and to the wicked; to the good and to the evil: to the clean and to the unclean; to him that sacrificeth, and to him that sacrificeth not; as is the good, so is the sinner; and he that sweareth, as he that feareth an oath. This is an evil in all that is done under the sun, that there is one event unto all; yea, also the heart of the sons of men is full of evil, and madness is in their heart while they live, and after that they go to the dead. For him that is among the living there is hope: for a living dog is better than a dead lion. For the living know that they shall die: but the dead know not any thing, neither have they any more a reward; for the memory of them is forgotten. Also their love, and their hatred, and their envy, is now perished; neither have they any more a portion for ever in any thing that is done under the sun.'

So said Solomon, or whoever wrote those words.[1]

And this is what the Indian wisdom tells:

Sakya Muni, a young, happy prince, from whom the existence of sickness, old age, and

[1] Tolstoy's version differs slightly in a few places from our own Authorized or Revised version. I have followed his text, for in a letter to Fet, quoted on p. 11, vol. ii, of my *Life of Tolstoy*, he says that 'The Authorized English version [of Ecclesiastes] is bad.'

death had been hidden, went out to drive and saw a terrible old man, toothless and slobbering. The prince, from whom till then old age had been concealed, was amazed, and asked his driver what it was, and how that man had come to such a wretched and disgusting condition, and when he learnt that this was the common fate of all men, that the same thing inevitably awaited him, the young prince, he could not continue his drive, but gave orders to go home, that he might consider this fact. So he shut himself up alone and considered it. And he probably devised some consolation for himself, for he subsequently again went out to drive, feeling merry and happy. But this time he saw a sick man. He saw an emaciated, livid, trembling man with dim eyes. The prince, from whom sickness had been concealed, stopped and asked what this was. And when he learnt that this was sickness, to which all men are liable, and that he himself, the healthy and happy prince, might himself fall ill tomorrow, he again was in no mood to enjoy himself, but gave orders to drive home, and again sought some solace, and probably found it, for he drove out a third time for pleasure But this third time he saw another new sight: he saw men carrying something. 'What is that?' 'A dead man' 'What does *dead* mean?' asked the prince. He was told that to become dead means to become like that man. The prince approached the corpse, uncovered it, and looked at it. 'What will happen to him now?' asked the prince. He was told that the corpse would be buried in the ground. 'Why?' 'Because he will certainly not return to life, and will only produce a stench and worms.' 'And is that the fate of all men? Will the same thing happen to me? Will they bury me, and shall I cause a stench and be eaten by worms?' 'Yes.' 'Home! I shall not drive out for pleasure, and never will so drive out again!'

And Sakya Muni could find no consolation in life, and decided that life is the greatest of evils; and he devoted all the strength of his soul to free himself from it, and to free others; and to do this so that even after death, life shall not be renewed any more, but be completely destroyed at its very roots. So speaks all the wisdom of India.

These, then, are the direct replies that human wisdom gives, when it replies to life's question.

'The life of the body is an evil and a lie. Therefore the destruction of the life of the body is a blessing, and we should desire it,' says Socrates.

'Life is that which should not be—an evil; and the passage into Nothingness is the only good in life,' says Schopenhauer.

'All that is in the world—folly and wisdom and riches and poverty and mirth and grief—is vanity and emptiness. Man dies and nothing is left of him. And that is stupid,' says Solomon.

'To live in the consciousness of the inevitability of suffering, of becoming enfeebled, of old age and of death, is impossible—we must free ourselves from life, from all possible life,' says Buddha.

And what these strong minds said has been said and thought and felt by millions upon millions of people like them. And I have thought it and felt it.

So my wandering among the sciences, far from freeing me from my despair, only strengthened it. One kind of knowledge did not reply to life's question, the other kind replied directly confirming my despair, indicating not that the result at which I had arrived was the fruit of error or of a diseased state of my mind, but on the contrary, that I had thought correctly, and that my thoughts coincided with the conclusions of the most powerful of human minds.

It is no good deceiving oneself. It is all—vanity! Happy is he who has not been born: death is better than life, and one must free oneself from life.

VII

NOT finding an explanation in science, I began to seek for it in life, hoping to find it among the people around me. And I began to observe how the people around me—people like myself—lived, and what their attitude was to this question, which had brought me to despair.

And this is what I found among people who

were in the same position as myself in regard to education and manner of life.

I found that for people of my circle there were four ways out of the terrible position in which we are all placed.

The first was that of ignorance. It consists in not knowing, not understanding, that life is an evil and an absurdity. People of this sort—chiefly women, or very young or very dull people—have not yet understood that question of life which presented itself to Schopenhauer, Solomon, and Buddha. They see neither the dragon that awaits them nor the mice gnawing the shrub by which they are hanging, and they lick the drops of honey. But they lick those drops of honey only for a while: something will turn their attention to the dragon and the mice, and there will be an end to their licking. From them I had nothing to learn—one cannot cease to know what one does know.

The second way out is epicureanism. It consists, while knowing the hopelessness of life, in making use meanwhile of the advantages one has, disregarding the dragon and the mice, and licking the honey in the best way, especially if there is much of it within reach. Solomon expresses this way out thus: 'Then I commended mirth, because a man hath no better thing under the sun, than to eat, and to drink, and to be merry: and that this should accompany him in his labour the days of his life, which God giveth him under the sun.

'Therefore eat thy bread with joy and drink

thy wine with a merry heart. . . . Live joyfully with the wife whom thou lovest all the days of the life of thy vanity . . . for this is thy portion in life and in thy labours which thou takest under the sun. . . . Whatsoever thy hand findeth to do, do it with thy might, for there is no work, nor device, nor knowledge, nor wisdom, in the grave, whither thou goest.'

That is the way in which the majority of people of our circle make life possible for themselves. Their circumstances furnish them with more of welfare than of hardship, and their moral dullness makes it possible for them to forget that the advantage of their position is accidental. and that not every one can have a thousand wives and palaces like Solomon, that for every one who has a thousand wives there are a thousand without a wife, and that for each palace there are a thousand people who have to build it in the sweat of their brows; and that the accident that has to-day made me a Solomon may to-morrow make me a Solomon's slave. The dullness of these people's imagination enables them to forget the things that gave Buddha no peace—the inevitability of sickness, old age, and death, which to-day or to-morrow will destroy all these pleasures.

So think and feel the majority of people of our day and our manner of life. The fact that some of these people declare the dullness of their thoughts and imaginations to be a philosophy, which they call Positive, does not remove them, in my opinion, from the ranks of those who, to avoid seeing the question, lick the honey.

I could not imitate these people; not having their dullness of imagination, I could not artificially produce it in myself. I could not tear my eyes from the mice and the dragon, as no vital man can after he has once seen them.

The third escape is that of strength and energy. It consists, when one has understood that life is an evil and an absurdity, in destroying it. A few exceptionally strong and consistent people act so. Having understood the stupidity of the joke that has been played on them, and having understood that it is better to be dead than to be alive, and that it is best of all not to exist, they act accordingly and promptly end this stupid joke, since there are means: a rope round one's neck, water, a knife to stick into one's heart, or the trains on the railways; and the number of those of our circle who act in this way becomes greater and greater, and for the most part they act so at the best time of their life, when the strength of their mind is in full bloom, and few habits degrading man's mind have as yet been acquired.

I saw that this was the worthiest way of escape, and I wished to adopt it.

The fourth way out is that of weakness. It consists in seeing the truth of the situation, and yet clinging to life, knowing in advance that nothing can come of it. People of this kind know that death is better than life, but, not having the strength to act rationally—to end the deception quickly and kill themselves—they seem to wait for something. This is the escape of weakness, for if I know what is best, and it is within my power, why not yield to what is best? . . . I found myself in that category.

So people of my class evade the terrible contradiction in four ways. Strain my attention as I would, I saw no way except those four. One way was not to understand that life is senseless, vanity, and an evil, and that it is better not to live. I could not help knowing this, and when I once knew it, could not shut my eyes to it. The second way was to use life such as it is without thinking of the future. And I could not do that. I, like Sakya Muni, could not ride out hunting when I knew that old age, suffering, and death exist. My imagination was too vivid. Nor could I rejoice in the momentary accidents that for an instant threw pleasure to my lot. The third way was, having understood that life is evil and stupid, to end it by killing oneself. I understood that, but somehow still did not kill myself. The fourth way is to live like Solomon and Schopenhauer—knowing that life is a stupid joke played upon us, and still to go on living, washing oneself, dressing, dining, talking, and even writing books. This was to me repulsive and tormenting, but I remained in that position.

I see now that if I did not kill myself, it was due to some dim consciousness of the invalidity of my thoughts. However convincing and indubitable appeared to me the sequence of my thoughts and of those of the wise, that have brought us to the admission of the senselessness of life, there remained in me a vague doubt of the justice of my conclusion.

It was like this: I, my reason, have acknowledged that life is senseless. If there is nothing higher than reason (and there is not: nothing can prove that there is), then reason is the creator of life for me. If reason did not exist, there would be for me no life. How can reason deny life, when it is the creator of life? Or to put it the other way: were there no life, my reason would not exist; therefore reason is life's son. Life is all. Reason is its fruit, yet reason rejects life itself! I felt that there was something wrong here.

Life is a senseless evil, that is certain, said I to myself. Yet I have lived and am still living, and all mankind lived and lives. How is that? Why does it live, when it is possible not to live? Is it that only I and Schopenhauer are wise enough to understand the senselessness and evil of life?

The reasoning showing the vanity of life is not so difficult, and has long been familiar to the very simplest folk; yet they have lived and still live. How is it they all live and never think of doubting the reasonableness of life?

My knowledge, confirmed by the wisdom of the sages, has shown me that everything on earth—organic and inorganic—is all most cleverly arranged—only my own position is stupid. And those fools—the enormous masses of people—know nothing about how everything organic and inorganic in the world is arranged; but they live, and it seems to them that their life is very wisely arranged! . . .

And it struck me: 'But what if there is

something I do not yet know? Ignorance behaves just in that way. Ignorance always says just what I am saying. When it does not know something, it says that what it does not know is stupid. Indeed, it appears that there is a whole humanity that lived and lives as if it understood the meaning of its life, for without understanding it it could not live; but I say that all this life is senseless and that I cannot live.

'Nothing prevents our denying life by suicide. Well, then, kill yourself, and you won't discuss. If life displeases you, kill yourself! You live, and cannot understand the meaning of life—then finish it; and do not fool about in life, saying and writing that you do not understand it. You have come into good company, where people are contented and know what they are doing; if you find it dull and repulsive—go away!'

Indeed, what are we who are convinced of the necessity of suicide, yet do not decide to commit it, but the weakest, most inconsistent, and to put it plainly, the stupidest of men, fussing about with our own stupidity as a fool fusses about with a painted hussy? For our wisdom, however indubitable it may be, has not given us the knowledge of the meaning of our life. But all mankind, who sustain life—millions of them—do not doubt the meaning of life.

Indeed, from the most distant times of which I know anything, when life began, people have lived, knowing the argument about the vanity of life, which has shown me its senselessness, and yet they lived attributing some meaning to it.

From the time when any life began among men they had that meaning of life, and they led that life, which has descended to me. All that is in me and around me, all, corporeal and incorporeal, is the fruit of their knowledge of life. Those very instruments of thought with which I consider this life and condemn it were all devised not by me but by them. I myself was born, taught, and brought up thanks to them. They dug out the iron, taught us to cut down the forests, tamed the cows and horses, taught us to sow corn and to live together, organized our life, and taught me to think and speak. And I, their product, fed, supplied with drink, taught by them, thinking with their thoughts and words, have argued that they are an absurdity! 'There is something wrong,' said I to myself. 'I have blundered somewhere.' But where the mistake was, it was long before I could find out.

VIII

All these doubts, which I am now able to express more or less systematically, I could not then have expressed. I then only felt that however logically inevitable were my conclusions concerning the vanity of life, confirmed as they were by the greatest thinkers, there was something not right about them. Whether it was in the reasoning itself or in the statement of the question I did not know—I only felt that the conclusion was rationally convincing, but that that was insufficient. All these conclusions could not so convince me as to make me do what followed from my reasoning, that is to say, kill myself. And I should have told an untruth had I, without killing myself, said that reason had brought me to the point I had reached. Reason worked, but something else was also working which I can only call a consciousness of life. A force was working which compelled me to turn my attention to this and not to that; and it was this force which extricated me from my desperate situation and turned my mind in quite another direction. This force compelled me to turn my attention to the fact that I and a few hundred similar people are not the whole of mankind, and that I did not yet know the life of mankind.

Looking at the narrow circle of my equals, I saw only people who had not understood the question, or who had understood it and drowned it in life's intoxication, or had understood it and ended their lives, or had understood it and yet, from weakness, were living out their desperate life. And I saw no others. It seemed to me that that narrow circle of rich, learned, and leisured people to which I belonged formed the whole of humanity, and that those milliards of others who have lived and are living were cattle of some sort—not real people.

Strange, incredibly incomprehensible as it now seems to me, that I could, while reasoning about life, overlook the whole life of mankind that surrounded me on all sides; that I could to such a degree blunder so absurdly as to think that my life, and Solomon's and Schopenhauer's, is the real, normal life, and that the life of the milliards is a circumstance undeserving of attention—strange as this now is to me, I see that so it was. In the delusion of my pride of intellect, it seemed to me so indubitable that I and Solomon and Schopenhauer had stated the question so truly and exactly that nothing else was possible—so indubitable did it seem that all those milliards consisted of men who had not yet arrived at the apprehension of all the profundity of the question—that I sought for the meaning of my life without it once occurring to me to ask: 'But what meaning is, and has been, given to their lives by all the milliards of common folk who live and have lived in the world?'

I long lived in this state of lunacy, which, in fact if not in words, is particularly characteristic of us very liberal and learned people. But thanks either to the strange physical affection I have for the real labouring people, which compelled me to understand them and to see that they are not so stupid as we suppose, or thanks to the sincerity of my conviction that I could know nothing beyond the fact that the best I could do was to hang myself, at any rate I instinctively felt that if I wished to live and understand the meaning of life, I must seek this meaning not among those who have lost it and wish to kill themselves, but among those milliards of the past and the present who make life and who support the burden of their own lives and of ours also. And I considered the enormous masses of those simple, unlearned, and poor people who have lived and are living, and I saw something quite different. I saw that, with rare exceptions, all those milliards who have lived and are living do not fit into my divisions, and that I could not class them as not understanding the question, for they themselves state it, and reply to it with extraordinary clearness. Nor could I consider them epicureans, for their life consists more of privations and sufferings than of enjoyments. Still less could I consider them as irrationally dragging on a meaningless existence, for every act of their life as well as death itself is explained by them. To kill themselves they consider the greatest evil. It appeared that all mankind had a knowledge, unacknowledged and despised by me, of the meaning of life. It appeared that reasonable knowledge does not give the meaning of life, that it excludes life: while the meaning attributed to life by milliards of people, by all humanity, rests on some despised pseudo-knowledge.

Rational knowledge, presented by the learned and wise, denies the meaning of life, but the enormous masses of men, the whole of mankind, receive that meaning in irrational knowledge. And that irrational knowledge is faith, that very thing which I could not but reject. It is God, One in Three; the creation in six days; the devils and angels, and all the rest that I cannot accept as long as I retain my reason.

My position was terrible. I knew I could find nothing along the path of reasonable knowledge, except a denial of life; and there—in faith—was nothing but a denial of reason, which was yet more impossible for me than a denial of life. From rational knowledge it appeared that life is an evil, and people know this—it depends on them not to live; yet they lived and still live, and I myself live, though I have long known that life is senseless and an evil. By faith it appears that in order to understand the meaning of life I must repudiate my reason, the very thing for which alone a meaning is required.

IX

A CONTRADICTION arose from which there were two exits. Either that which I called reason was not so rational as I supposed, or that which seemed to me irrational was not so irrational as I supposed. And I began to verify the line of argument of my rational knowledge.

Verifying the line of argument of rational knowledge, I found it quite correct. The conclusion that life is nothing was inevitable; but I noticed a mistake. The mistake lay in this, that my reasoning was not in accord with the question I had put. The question was: 'Why should I live, that is to say, what real, permanent result will come out of my illusory transitory life—what meaning has my finite existence in this infinite world?' And to reply to that question I had studied life.

The solution of all the possible questions of life could evidently not satisfy me, for my question, simple as it at first appeared, included a demand for an explanation of the finite in terms of the infinite, and vice versa.

I asked: 'What is the meaning of my life, beyond time, cause, and space?' And I replied to the question: 'What is the meaning of my life within time, cause, and space?' It resulted that, after long efforts of thought, I replied: 'None.'

In my reasonings I constantly compared (nor could I do otherwise) the finite with the finite, and the infinite with the infinite; but for that reason I reached the inevitable result: force is force, matter is matter, will is will, the infinite is the infinite, nothing is nothing—and that was all that could result.

It was something like what happens in mathematics, when, thinking to solve an equation, we find we are working on an identity. The line of reasoning is correct, but results in the answer that *a* equals *a*, or *x* equals *x*, or *o* equals *o*. The same thing happened with my reasoning in relation to the question of the meaning of my life. The replies given by all science to that question only result in——identity.

And really, strictly scientific knowledge—that knowledge which begins, as Descartes's did, with complete doubt about everything—rejects all knowledge admitted on faith, and builds everything afresh on the laws of reason and experience, and cannot give any other reply to the question of life than that which I obtained: an indefinite reply. Only at first had it seemed to me that knowledge had given a positive reply

—the reply of Schopenhauer: that life has no meaning and is an evil. But on examining the matter I understood that the reply is not positive, it was only my feeling that so expressed it. Strictly expressed, as it is by the Brahmins and by Solomon and Schopenhauer, the reply is merely indefinite, or an identity: *o* equals *o*, life is nothing. So that philosophic knowledge denies nothing, but only replies that the question cannot be solved by it—that for it the solution remains indefinite.

Having understood this, I understood that it was not possible to seek in rational knowledge for a reply to my question, and that the reply given by rational knowledge is a mere indication that a reply can only be obtained by a different statement of the question, and only when the relation of the finite to the infinite is included in the question. And I understood that, however irrational and distorted might be the replies given by faith, they have this advantage, that they introduce into every answer a relation between the finite and the infinite, without which there can be no solution.

In whatever way I stated the question, that relation appeared in the answer. How am I to live?—According to the law of God. What real result will come of my life?—Eternal torment or eternal bliss. What meaning has life, that death does not destroy?—Union with the eternal God: heaven.

So that besides rational knowledge, which had seemed to me the only knowledge, I was inevitably brought to acknowledge that all live humanity has another irrational knowledge—faith which makes it possible to live. Faith still remained to me as irrational as it was before, but I could not but admit that it alone gives mankind a reply to the questions of life ; and that consequently it makes life possible. Reasonable knowledge had brought me to acknowledge that life is senseless—my life had come to a halt and I wished to destroy myself. Looking around on the whole of mankind I saw that people live and declare that they know the meaning of life. I looked at myself, I had lived as long as I knew a meaning of life. As to others so also to me faith had given a meaning to life and had made life possible.

Looking again at people of other lands, at my contemporaries and at their predecessors, I saw the same thing. Where there is life there, since man began, faith has made life possible for him, and the chief outline of that faith is everywhere and always identical.

Whatever the faith might be, and whatever answers it might give, and to whomsoever it gave them, every such answer gives to the finite existence of man an infinite meaning, a meaning not destroyed by sufferings, deprivations, or death. This means that only in faith can we find for life a meaning and a possibility. What, then, is this faith ? And I understood that faith is not merely 'the evidence of things not seen,' etc., and is not a revelation (that defines only one of the indications of faith), is not the relation of man to God (one has first to define faith, and then God, and not define faith through God); it is not only agreement with what has been told one (as faith is most usually supposed to be), but faith is a knowledge of the meaning of human life in consequence of which man does not destroy himself but lives. Faith is the strength of life. If a man lives he believes in something. If he did not believe that one must live for something, he would not live. If he does not see and recognize the illusory nature of the finite, he believes in the finite; if he understands the illusory nature of the finite, he must believe in the infinite. Without faith he cannot live.

And I recalled the whole course of my mental labour and was horrified. It was now clear to me that for man to be able to live he must either not see the infinite, or have such an explanation of the meaning of life as will connect the finite with the infinite. Such an explanation I had had; but as long as I believed in the finite I did not need the explanation, and I began to verify it by reason. And in the light of reason the whole of my former explanation flew to atoms. But a time came when I ceased to believe in the finite. And then I began to build up on rational foundations, out of what I knew, an explanation which would give a meaning to life; but nothing could I build. Together with the best human intellects I reached the result that *o* equals *o*, and was much astonished at that conclusion, though nothing else could have resulted.

What was I doing when I sought an answer in the experimental sciences? I wished to know why I live, and for this purpose studied all that is outside me. Evidently I might learn much, but nothing of what I needed.

What was I doing when I sought an answer in philosophical knowledge? I was studying the thoughts of those who had found themselves in the same position as I, lacking a reply to the question, 'Why do I live?' Evidently I could learn nothing but what I knew myself, namely that nothing can be known.

What am I?—A part of the infinite. In those few words lies the whole problem.

Is it possible that humanity has only put that question to itself since yesterday? And can no one before me have set himself that question—a question so simple, and one that springs to the tongue of every wise child?

Surely that question has been asked since man began; and naturally, for the solution of that question since man began, it has been equally insufficient to compare the finite with the finite and the infinite with the infinite, and since man began the relation of the finite to the infinite has been sought out and expressed.

All these conceptions in which the finite has been adjusted to the infinite, and a meaning is found for life: the conception of God, of will, of goodness, we submit to logical examination. And all those conceptions fail to stand reason's criticism.

Were it not so terrible, it would be ludicrous, with what pride and self-satisfaction we, like children, pull the watch to pieces, take out the spring, make a toy of it, and are then surprised that the watch does not go.

A solution of the contradiction between the finite and the infinite, and such a reply to the question of life as will make it possible to live, is necessary and precious. And that is the only solution which we find everywhere, always, and among all peoples: a solution descending from times in which we lose sight of the life of man, a solution so difficult that we can compose nothing like it—and this solution we light-heartedly destroy in order again to set the same question, which is natural to every one and to which we have no answer.

The conception of an infinite God, the divinity of the soul, the connexion of human affairs with God, the unity and existence of the soul, man's conception of moral goodness and evil—are conceptions formulated in the hidden infinity of human thought, they are those conceptions without which neither life nor I should exist; yet rejecting all that labour of the whole of humanity, I wished to remake it afresh myself and in my own manner.

I did not then think like that, but the germs of these thoughts were already in me. I understood, in the first place, that my position with Schopenhauer and Solomon, notwithstanding our wisdom, was stupid: we see that life is an evil and yet continue to live. That is evidently stupid, for if life is senseless, and I am so fond of what is reasonable, it should be destroyed, and then there would be no one to challenge it. Secondly, I understood that all one's reasonings turned in a vicious circle, like a wheel out of gear with its pinion. However much and however well we may reason, we cannot obtain a reply to the question; but *o* always equals *o*, and therefore our path is probably erroneous. Thirdly, I began to understand that in the replies given by faith is stored up the deepest human wisdom, and that I had no right to deny them on the ground of reason, and that those answers are the only ones which reply to life's question.

X

I UNDERSTOOD this, but it made matters no better for me. I was now ready to accept any faith, if only it did not demand of me a direct denial of reason—which would be a falsehood. And I studied Buddhism and Mohammedanism from books, and most of all I studied Christianity both from books and from the people around me.

Naturally I first of all turned to the Orthodox of my circle, to people who were learned: to Church theologians, monks, to theologians of the newest shade, and even to Evangelicals, who profess salvation by belief in the Redemption. And I seized on these believers and questioned them as to their beliefs and their understanding of the meaning of life.

But though I made all possible concessions, and avoided all disputes, I could not accept the faith of these people. I saw that what they gave out as their faith did not explain the meaning of life but obscured it, and that they themselves affirm their belief, not to answer that question of life which brought me to faith, but for some other aims alien to me.

I remember the painful feeling of fear of being thrown back into my former state of despair, after the hope I often and often experienced in my intercourse with these people.

The more fully they explained to me their doctrines, the more clearly did I perceive their error and realized that my hope of finding in their belief an explanation of the meaning of life was vain.

It was not that in their doctrines they mixed many unnecessary and unreasonable things with the Christian truths that had always been near to me: that was not what repelled me. I was repelled by the fact that these people's lives were like my own, with only this difference—that such a life did not correspond to the principles they expounded in their teachings. I clearly felt that they deceived themselves and that they, like myself, found no other meaning in life than to live while life lasts, taking all one's hands can seize. I saw this because if they had had a meaning which destroyed the fear of loss, suffering, and death, they would not have feared these things. But they, these believers of our circle, just like myself, living in sufficiency and superfluity, tried to increase or preserve them, feared privations, suffering, and death, and just like myself and all of us unbelievers, lived to satisfy their desires, and lived just as badly, if not worse, than the unbelievers.

No arguments could convince me of the truth of their faith. Only deeds which showed that they saw a meaning in life, which made what was so dreadful to me—poverty, sickness, and death—not dreadful to them, could convince me. And such deeds I did not see among the various believers in our circle. On the contrary, I saw such deeds done[1] by people of our circle who were the most unbelieving, but never by our so-called believers.

And I understood that the belief of these people was not the faith I sought, and that their faith is not a real faith but an epicurean consolation in life.

I understood that that faith may perhaps serve, if not for a consolation, at least for some distraction for a repentant Solomon on his death-bed, but it cannot serve for the great majority of mankind, who are called on not to amuse themselves while consuming the labour of others, but to create life.

For all humanity to be able to live, and continue to live attributing a meaning to life, they, those milliards, must have a different, a real knowledge of faith. Indeed, it was not the fact that we, with Solomon and Schopenhauer, did not kill ourselves that convinced me

[1] This passage is noteworthy as being one of the few references made by Tolstoy at this period to the revolutionary or 'Back-to-the-People' movement, in which many young men and women were risking and sacrificing home, property, and life itself, from motives which had much in common with his own perception that the upper layers of Society are parasitic, and prey on the vitals of the people who support them.

of the existence of faith, but the fact that those milliards of people have lived and are living, and have borne Solomon and us on the current of their lives.

And I began to draw near to the believers among the poor, simple, unlettered folk: pilgrims, monks, sectarians, and peasants. The faith of these common people was the same Christian faith as was professed by the pseudo-believers of our circle. Among them, too, I found a great deal of superstition mixed with the Christian truths; but the difference was that the superstitions of the believers of our circle were quite unnecessary to them, and were not in conformity with their lives, being merely a kind of epicurean diversion; but the superstitions of the believers among the labouring masses conformed so with their lives that it was impossible to imagine them to oneself without those superstitions, which were a necessary condition of their life. The whole life of believers in our circle was a contradiction of their faith, but the whole life of the working-folk believers was a confirmation of the meaning of life which their faith gave them. And I began to look well into the life and faith of these people, and the more I considered it the more I became convinced that they have a real faith, which is a necessity to them and alone gives their life a meaning and makes it possible for them to live. In contrast with what I had seen in our circle—where life without faith is possible, and where hardly one in a thousand acknowledges himself to be a believer—among them there is hardly one unbeliever in a thousand. In contrast with what I had seen in our circle, where the whole of life is passed in idleness, amusement, and dissatisfaction, I saw that the whole life of these people was passed in heavy labour, and that they were content with life. In contradistinction to the way in which people of our circle oppose fate and complain of it on account of deprivations and sufferings, these people accepted illness and sorrow without any perplexity or opposition, and with a quiet and firm conviction that all is good. In contradistinction to us, who the wiser we are the less we understand the meaning of life, and see some evil irony in the fact that we suffer and die, these folk live and suffer, and they approach death and suffering with tranquillity and in most cases gladly. In contrast to the fact that a tranquil death, a death without horror and despair, is a very rare exception in our circle, a troubled, rebellious, and unhappy death is the rarest exception among the people. And such people, lacking all that for us and for Solomon is the only good of life, and yet experiencing the greatest happiness, are a great multitude. I looked more widely around me. I considered the life of the enormous mass of the people in the past and the present. And of such people, understanding the meaning of life and able to live and to die, I saw not two or three, or tens, but hundreds, thousands, and millions. And they all—endlessly different in their manners, minds, education, and position as they were—all alike, in complete contrast to my ignorance, knew the meaning of life and death, laboured quietly, endured deprivations and sufferings, and lived and died, seeing therein not vanity but good.

And I learnt to love these people. The more I came to know their life, the life of those who are living and of others who are dead, of whom I read and heard, the more I loved them and the easier it became for me to live. So I went on for about two years, and a change took place in me which had long been preparing, and the promise of which had always been in me. It came about that the life of our circle, the rich and learned, not merely became distasteful to me, but lost all meaning in my eyes. All our actions, discussions, science and art, presented itself to me in a new light. I understood that it is all merely self-indulgence, and that to find a meaning in it is impossible; while the life of the whole labouring people, the whole of mankind who produce life, appeared to me in its true significance. I understood that *that* is life itself, and that the meaning given to that life is true: and I accepted it.

XI

AND remembering how those very beliefs had repelled me and had seemed meaningless when professed by people whose lives conflicted with them, and how these same beliefs attracted me and seemed reasonable when I saw that people lived in accord with them, I understood why I had then rejected those beliefs and found them meaningless, yet now accepted them and found them full of meaning. I understood that I had erred, and why I erred. I had erred not so much because I thought incorrectly, as because I lived badly. I understood that it was not an error in my thought that had hid truth from me, so much as my life itself in the exceptional conditions of epicurean gratification of desires in which I passed it. I understood that my question as to what my life is, and the answer, an evil, was quite correct. The only mistake was that the answer referred only to my life; but I had referred it to life in general. I asked myself what my life is, and got the reply: An evil and an absurdity. And really my life—a life of indulgence of desires—was senseless and evil, and therefore the reply, 'Life is evil and an absurdity,' referred only to my life, but not to human life in general. I understood the truth, which I afterwards found in the Gospels, 'that men loved darkness rather than the light, for their works were evil. For every one that doeth ill hateth the light, and cometh not to the light, lest his works should be reproved.' I perceived that to understand the meaning of life it is necessary first that life should not be meaningless and evil, and then reason is needed to explain it. I understood why I had so long wandered round so evident a truth, and that if one is to think and speak of the life of mankind, one must think and speak of that life, and not of the life of some of life's parasites. That truth was always as true as that two and two are four, but I had not acknowledged it, because on admitting two and two to be four, I had also to admit that I was bad; and to feel myself to be good was for me more important and necessary than for two and two to be four. I came to love good people, hated myself, and confessed the truth. Now all became clear to me.

What if an executioner passing his whole life in torturing people and cutting off their heads—or a hopeless drunkard, or a madman settled for life in a dark room which he has fouled, and imagined that he would perish if he left—what if he asked himself: 'What is life?' Evidently he could get no other reply to that question than that life is the greatest evil; and the madman's answer would be perfectly correct, but only as applied to himself. What if I am such a madman? What if all we rich and leisured people are such madmen? and I understood that we are really such madmen. I at any rate was certainly such.

And indeed a bird is so made that it must fly, collect food, and build a nest, and when I see that a bird does this, I have pleasure in its joy. A goat, a hare, and a wolf are so made that they must feed themselves, and must breed and feed their family, and when they do so, I feel firmly assured that they are happy and that their life is a reasonable one. Then what should a man do? He too should produce his living as the animals do, but with this difference, that he will perish if he does it alone; he must obtain it not for himself but for all. And when he does that, I have a firm assurance that he is happy and that his life is reasonable. But what had I done during the whole thirty years of my responsible life? Far from producing sustenance for all, I did not even produce it for myself. I lived as a parasite, and on asking myself, what is the use of my life? I got the reply: 'No use.' If the meaning of human life lies in supporting it, how could I—who for thirty years had been engaged not in supporting life but on destroying it in myself and in others—how could I obtain any other answer than that my life was senseless and an evil? . . . It was both senseless and evil.

The life of the world endures by some one's will—by the life of the whole world and by our lives some one fulfils his purpose. To hope to understand the meaning of that will one must first perform it by doing what is wanted of us. But if I will not do what is wanted of me, I shall never understand what is wanted of me, and still less what is wanted of us all and of the whole world.

If a naked, hungry beggar has been taken from the cross-roads, brought into a building belonging to a beautiful establishment, fed, supplied with drink, and obliged to move a handle up and down, evidently, before discussing why he was taken, why he should move the handle, and whether the whole establishment is reasonably arranged—the beggar should first of all move the handle. If he moves the handle, he will understand that it works a pump, that the pump draws water and that the water irrigates the garden beds; then he will be taken from the pumping station to another place where he will gather fruits and will enter into the joy of his master, and, passing from lower to higher work, will understand more and more of the arrangements of the establishment, and taking part in it will never think of asking why he is there, and will certainly not reproach the master.

So those who do his will, the simple, unlearned working folk, whom we regard as cattle, do not reproach the master; but we, the wise, eat the master's food but do not do what the master wishes, and instead of doing it sit in a circle and discuss: 'Why should that handle be moved? Isn't it stupid!' So we have decided. We have decided that the master is stupid, or does not exist, and that we are wise, only we feel that we are quite useless and that we must somehow do away with ourselves.

XII

THE consciousness of the error in reasonable knowledge helped me to free myself from the temptation of idle ratiocination. The conviction that knowledge of truth can only be found by living led me to doubt the rightness of my life; but I was saved only by the fact that I was able to tear myself from my exclusiveness and to see the real life of the plain, working people, and to understand that it alone is real life. I understood that if I wish to understand life and its meaning, I must not live the life of a parasite, but must live a real life, and—taking the meaning given to life by real humanity, and merging myself in that life—verify it.

During that time this is what happened to me. During that whole year, when I was asking myself almost every moment whether I should not end matters with a noose or a bullet—all that time, together with the course of thought and observation about which I have spoken, my heart was oppressed with a painful feeling, which I can only describe as a search for God.

I say that that search for God was not reasoning but a feeling, because that search proceeded not from the course of my thoughts—it was even directly contrary to them—but proceeded from the heart. It was a feeling of fear, orphanage, isolation in a strange land, and a hope of help from some one.

Though I was quite convinced of the impossibility of proving the existence of a Deity (Kant had shown, and I quite understood him, that it could not be proved), I yet sought for God, hoped that I should find Him, and from old habit addressed prayers to that which I sought but had not found. I went over in my mind the arguments of Kant and Schopenhauer showing the impossibility of proving the existence of a God, and I began to verify those arguments and to refute them. Cause, said I to myself, is not a category of thought such as are Time and Space. If I exist, there must be some cause for it, and a cause of causes. And that first cause of all is what men have called 'God.' And I paused on that thought, and tried with all my being to recognize the presence of that cause. And as soon as I acknowledged that there is a force in whose power I am, I at once felt that I could live. But I asked myself: What is that cause, that force? How am I to think of it? What are my relations to that which I call 'God'? And only the familiar replies occurred to me: 'He is the Creator and Preserver.' This reply did not satisfy me, and I felt I was losing within me what I needed for my life. I became terrified and began to pray to Him whom I sought, that He should help me. But the more I prayed the more apparent it became to me that He did not hear me, and that there was no one to whom to address myself. And with despair in my heart that there is no God at all, I said: 'Lord, have mercy, save me! Lord, teach me!' But no one had mercy on me, and I felt that my life was coming to a standstill.

But again and again, from various sides, I returned to the same admission that I could not have come into the world without any cause or reason or meaning; I could not be such a fledgling fallen from its nest as I felt myself to be. Or, granting that I be such, lying on my back crying in the high grass, even then I cry because I know that a mother has borne me within her, has hatched me, warmed me, fed me, and loved me. Where is she– that mother? If I have been deserted, who has deserted me? I cannot hide from myself that some one bore me, loving me. Who was that some one?

Again 'God'? He knows and sees my searching, my despair, and my struggle.

'He exists,' said I to myself. And I had only for an instant to admit that, and at once life rose within me, and I felt the possibility and joy of being. But again, from the admission of the existence of a God I went on to seek my relation with Him; and again I imagined *that* God—our Creator in Three Persons who sent His Son, the Saviour—and again *that* God, detached from the world and from me, melted like a block of ice, melted before my eyes, and again nothing remained, and again the spring of life dried up within me, and I despaired, and felt that I had nothing to do but to kill myself. And the worst of all was, that I felt I could not do it.

Not twice or three times, but tens and hundreds of times, I reached those conditions, first of joy and animation, and then of despair and consciousness of the impossibility of living.

I remember that it was in early spring: I was alone in the wood listening to its sounds. I listened and thought ever of the same thing, as I had constantly done during those last three years. I was again seeking God.

'Very well, there is no God,' said I to myself; 'there is no one who is not my imagination but a reality like my whole life. He does not exist, and no miracles can prove His existence, because the miracles would be my imagination, besides being irrational.

'But my *perception* of God, of Him whom I seek,' asked I of myself, 'where has that perception come from?' And again at this thought the glad waves of life rose within me. All that was around me came to life and received a meaning. But my joy did not last long. My mind continued its work.

'The conception of God is not God,' said I to myself. 'The conception is what takes place within me. The conception of God is something I can evoke or can refrain from evoking in myself. That is not what I seek. I seek that without which there can be no life.' And again all around me and within me began to die, and again I wished to kill myself.

But then I turned my gaze upon myself, on what went on within me, and I remembered all those cessations of life and reanimations that recurred within me hundreds of times. I remembered that I only lived at those times when I believed in God. As it was before, so it was now ; I need only be aware of God to live ; I need only forget Him, or disbelieve in Him, and I died.

What is this animation and dying ? I do not live when I lose belief in the existence of God. I should long ago have killed myself had I not had a dim hope of finding Him. I live, really live, only when I feel Him and seek Him. 'What more do you seek ?' exclaimed a voice within me. 'This is He. He is that without which one cannot live. To know God and to live is one and the same thing. God is life.'

'Live seeking God, and then you will not live without God.' And more than ever before, all within me and around me lit up, and the light did not again abandon me.

And I was saved from suicide. When and how this change occurred I could not say. As imperceptibly and gradually the force of life in me had been destroyed and I had reached the impossibility of living, a cessation of life and the necessity of suicide, so imperceptibly and gradually did that force of life return to me. And strange to say the strength of life which returned to me was not new, but quite old—the same that had borne me along in my earliest days.

I quite returned to what belonged to my earliest childhood and youth. I returned to the belief in that Will which produced me, and desires something of me. I returned to the belief that the chief and only aim of my life is to be better, i.e. to live in accord with that Will. And I returned to the belief that I can find the expression of that Will in what humanity, in the distant past hidden from me, has produced for its guidance: that is to say, I returned to a belief in God, in moral perfection, and in a tradition transmitting the meaning of life. There was only this difference, that then all this was accepted unconsciously, while now I knew that without it I could not live.

What happened to me was something of this kind: I was put into a boat (I do not remember when) and pushed off from an unknown shore, shown the direction to the opposite shore, had oars put into my unpractised hands, and was left alone. I rowed as best I could and moved forward; but the further I advanced towards the middle of the stream the more rapid grew the current bearing me away from my goal, and the more frequently did I encounter others, like myself, borne away by the stream. There were a few rowers who continued to row, there were others who had abandoned their oars; there were large boats and immense vessels full of people. Some struggled against the current, others yielded to it. And the further I went the more I forgot, seeing the progress down the current of all those who were adrift, the direction given me. In the very centre of the stream, amid the crowd of boats and vessels which were being borne down stream, I quite lost my direction and abandoned my oars. Around me, on all sides, with mirth and rejoicing, people with sails and oars were borne down the stream, assuring me and each other that no other direction was possible. And I believed them and floated with them. And I was carried far; so far that I heard the roar of the rapids in which I must be shattered, and I saw boats shattered in them. And I recollected myself. I was long unable to understand what had happened to me. I saw before me nothing but destruction, towards which I was rushing, and which I feared. I saw no safety anywhere, and did not know what to do; but, looking back, I perceived innumerable boats which unceasingly and strenuously pushed across the stream, and I remembered about the shore, the oars, and the direction, and began to pull back upwards against the stream and towards the shore.

That shore was God; that direction was tradition; the oars were the freedom given me to pull for the shore and unite with God. And so the force of life was renewed in me, and I again began to live.

XIII

I TURNED from the life of our circle, acknowledging that ours is not life, but a simulation of life – that the conditions of superfluity in which we live deprive us of the possibility of understanding life, and that in order to understand life I must understand not an exceptional life such as ours who are parasites on life, but the life of the simple labouring folk—those who make life—and the meaning which they attribute to it. The simple labouring people around me were the Russian people, and I turned to them, and to the meaning of life which they give. That meaning, if one can put it into words, was as follows: Every man has come into this world by the will of God. And God has so made man that every man can destroy his soul or save it. The aim of man in life is to save his soul, and to save his soul he must live 'godly' and to live 'godly' he must renounce all the pleasures of life, must labour, humble himself, suffer and be merciful. That meaning the people obtain from the whole teaching of faith transmitted to them by their pastors and by the traditions that live among the people. This meaning was clear to me and near to my heart. But together with this meaning of the popular faith of our non-sectarian folk, among whom I live, much was inseparably bound up that revolted me and seemed to me inexplicable: sacraments, Church services, fasts, and the adoration of relics and icons. The people cannot separate the one from the other, nor could I. And strange as much of what entered into the faith of these people was to me, I accepted everything; and attended the services, knelt morning and evening in prayer, fasted, and prepared to receive the Eucharist: and at first my reason did not resist anything. The very things that had formerly seemed to me impossible did not now evoke in me any opposition.

My relations to faith before and after were quite different. Formerly life itself seemed to me full of meaning, and faith presented itself as the arbitrary assertion of propositions to me quite unnecessary, unreasonable, and disconnected from life. I then asked myself what meaning those propositions had and, convinced that they had none, I rejected them. Now on the contrary I knew firmly that my life otherwise has, and can have, no meaning; and the articles of faith were far from presenting themselves to me as unnecessary—on the contrary I had been led by indubitable experience to the conviction that only these propositions presented by faith give life a meaning. Formerly I looked on them as on some quite unnecessary gibberish, but now, if I did not understand them, I yet knew that they had a meaning, and I said to myself that I must learn to understand them.

I argued as follows, telling myself that the knowledge of faith flows, like all humanity with its reason, from a mysterious source. That source is God, the origin both of the human body and the human reason. As my body has descended to me from God, so also has my reason and my understanding of life, and consequently the various stages of the development of that understanding of life cannot be false. All that people sincerely believe in must be true; it may be differently expressed but it cannot be a lie, and therefore if it presents itself to me as a lie, that only means that I have not understood it. Furthermore I said to myself, the essence of every faith consists in its giving life a meaning which death does not destroy. Naturally for a faith to be able to reply to the questions of a king dying in luxury, of an old slave tormented by overwork, of an unreasonable child, of a wise old man, of a half-witted old woman, of a young and happy wife, of a youth tormented by passions, of all people in the most varied conditions of life and education—if there is one reply to the one eternal question of life: 'Why do I live, and what will result from my life?' —the reply, though one in its essence, must be endlessly varied in its presentation, and the more it is one, the more true and profound it is, the more strange and deformed must it naturally appear in its attempted expression, conformably to the education and position of each person. But this argument, justifying in my eyes the queerness of much on the ritual side of religion, did not suffice to allow me in the one great affair of life—religion—to do things which seemed to me questionable. With all my soul I wished to be in a position to mingle with the people, fulfilling the ritual side of their religion; but I could not do it. I felt that I should lie to myself, and mock at what was sacred to me, were I to do so. At this point, however, our new Russian theological writers came to my rescue.

According to the explanation these theologians gave, the fundamental dogma of our faith is the infallibility of the Church. From the admission of that dogma follows inevitably the truth of all that is professed by the Church. The Church as an assembly of true believers united by love, and therefore possessed of true knowledge, became the basis of my belief. I told myself that divine truth cannot be accessible to a separate individual; it is revealed only to the whole assembly of people united by love. To attain truth one must not separate; and in order not to separate, one must love and must endure things one may not agree with.

Truth reveals itself to love, and if you do not submit to the rites of the Church, you transgress against love; and by transgressing against love you deprive yourself of the possibility of recognizing the truth. I did not then see the sophistry contained in this argument. I did not see that union in love may give the greatest love, but certainly cannot give us divine truth expressed in the definite words of the Nicene Creed. I also did not perceive that love cannot make a certain expression of truth an obligatory condition of union. I did not then see these mistakes in the argument and, thanks to it, was able to accept and perform all the rites of the Orthodox Church without understanding most of them. I then tried with all the strength of my soul to avoid all arguments and contradictions, and tried to explain as reasonably as possible the statements of the Church I encountered.

When fulfilling the rites of the Church, I humbled my reason and submitted to the tradition possessed by all humanity. I united myself with my forefathers: the father, mother, and grandparents I loved. They and all my predecessors believed and lived, and they produced me. I united myself also with the millions of the common people, whom I respected. Moreover, those actions had nothing bad in themselves ('bad' I considered the indulgence of one's desires). When rising early for Church services, I knew I was doing well, if only because I was sacrificing my bodily ease to humble my mental pride, for the sake of union with my ancestors and contemporaries, and for the sake of finding the meaning of life. It was the same with my preparations to receive Communion, and with the daily reading of prayers with genuflections, and also with the observance of all the fasts. However insignificant these sacrifices might be, I made them for the sake of something good. I fasted, prepared for Communion, and observed the fixed hours of prayer at home and in church. During Church service I attended to every word, and gave them a meaning whenever I could. In the Mass the most important words for me were: 'Let us love one another in conformity!' The further words, 'In unity we believe, in the Father, the Son, and Holy Ghost,' I passed by, because I could not understand them.

XIV

It was then so necessary for me to believe in order to live that I unconsciously concealed from myself the contradictions and obscurities of theology. But this reading of meanings into the rites had its limits. If the chief words in the prayer for the Emperor became more and more clear to me, if I found some explanation for the words 'and remembering our Sovereign Most-Holy Mother of God and all the Saints, ourselves and one another, we give our whole life to Christ our God,' if I explained to myself the frequent repetition of prayers for the Tsar and his relations by the fact that they are more exposed to temptations than other people and therefore are more in need of being prayed for—the prayers about subduing our enemies and evil under our feet (even if one tried to say that *sin* was the enemy prayed against), these and other prayers, such as the 'cherubic song' and the whole sacrament of the oblation, or 'the chosen warriors,' etc. --quite two-thirds of all the services—either remained completely incomprehensible or, when I forced an explanation into them, made me feel that I was lying, thereby quite destroying my relation to God and depriving me of all possibility of belief.

I felt the same about the celebration of the

chief holidays. To remember the Sabbath, that is to devote one day to God, was something I could understand. But the chief holiday was in commemoration of the Resurrection, the reality of which I could not picture to myself or understand. And that name of 'Resurrection' was also given to the weekly holiday.[1] And on those days the Sacrament of the Eucharist was administered, which was quite unintelligible to me. The rest of the twelve great holidays, except Christmas, commemorated miracles—the things I tried not to think about in order not to deny: the Ascension, Pentecost, Epiphany, the Feast of the Intercession of the Holy Virgin, etc. At the celebration of these holidays, feeling that importance was being attributed to the very things that to me presented a negative importance, I either devised tranquillizing explanations, or shut my eyes in order not to see what tempted me.

Most of all this happened to me when taking part in the most usual Sacraments, which are considered the most important: baptism and communion. There I encountered not incomprehensible but fully comprehensible doings: doings which seemed to me to lead into temptation, and I was in a dilemma—whether to lie, or to reject them.

Never shall I forget the painful feeling I experienced the day I received the Eucharist for the first time after many years. The service, confession, and prayers were quite intelligible and produced in me a glad conscious-

[1] In Russia Sunday is called Resurrection-day.

ness that the meaning of life was being revealed to me. The Communion itself I explained as an act performed in remembrance of Christ, and indicating a purification from sin and the full acceptance of Christ's teaching. If that explanation was artificial I did not notice its artificiality: so happy was I at humbling and abasing myself before the priest—a simple, timid country clergyman—turning all the dirt out of my soul and confessing my vices, so glad was I to merge in thought with the humility of the fathers who wrote the prayers of the office, so glad was I of union with all who have believed and now believe, that I did not notice the artificiality of my explanation. But when I approached the altar gates, and the priest made me say that I believed that what I was about to swallow was truly flesh and blood, I felt a pain in my heart: it was not merely a false note, it was a cruel demand made by some one or other who evidently had never known what faith is.

I now permit myself to say that it was a cruel demand, but I did not then think so: only it was indescribably painful to me. I was no longer in the position in which I had been in youth, when I thought all in life was clear; I had indeed come to faith because, apart from faith, I had found nothing, certainly nothing, except destruction; therefore to throw away that faith was impossible, and I submitted. And I found in my soul a feeling which helped me to endure it. This was the feeling of self-abasement and humility. I humbled myself, swallowed that flesh and blood without any blasphemous feelings, and with a wish to believe. But the blow had been struck and, knowing what awaited me, I could not go a second time.

I continued to fulfil the rites of the Church and still believed that the doctrine I was following contained the truth, when something happened to me which I now understand but which then seemed strange.

I was listening to the conversation of an illiterate peasant, a pilgrim, about God, faith, life, and salvation, when a knowledge of faith revealed itself to me. I drew near to the people, listening to their opinions on life and faith, and I understood the truth more and more. So also was it when I read the Lives of Holy Men, which became my favourite books. Putting aside the miracles, and regarding them as fables illustrating thoughts, this reading revealed to me life's meaning. There were the lives of Makarius the Great, the story of Buddha, there were the words of St. John Chrysostom, and there were the stories of the traveller in the well, the monk who found some gold, and of Peter the publican. There were stories of the martyrs, all announcing that death does not exclude life; and there were the stories of ignorant, stupid men, who knew nothing of the teaching of the Church, but who yet were saved.

But as soon as I met learned believers, or took up their books, doubt of myself, dissatisfaction, and exasperated disputation were roused within me, and I felt that the more I entered into the meaning of these men's speech, the more I went astray from truth and approached an abyss.

XV

How often I envied the peasants their illiteracy and lack of learning! Those statements in the creeds, which to me were evident absurdities, for them contained nothing false; they could accept them and could believe in the truth—in the truth I believed in. Only to me, unhappy man, was it clear that with truth falsehood was interwoven by finest threads, and that I could not accept it in that form.

So I lived for about three years. At first. when I was only slightly associated with truth as a catechumen, and was only scenting out what seemed to me clearest, these encounters struck me less. When I did not understand anything, I said, 'It is my fault, I am sinful'; but the more I became imbued with the truths I was learning, the more they became the basis of my life, the more oppressive and the more painful became these encounters, and the sharper became the line between what I do not understand because I am not able to understand it, and what cannot be understood except by lying to oneself.

In spite of my doubts and sufferings I still clung to the Orthodox Church. But questions of life arose which had to be decided; and the decision of these questions by the Church—contrary to the very bases of the belief by which I lived,—obliged me at last to renounce communion with Orthodoxy as impossible. These questions were: first the relation of the Orthodox Eastern Church to other Churches—to the Catholics and to the so-called sectarians. At that time, in consequence of my interest in religion, I came into touch with believers of various faiths: Catholics, Protestants, Old-Believers, Molokans,[1] and others. And I met among them many men of lofty morals who were truly religious. I wished to be a brother to them. And what happened? That teaching which promised to unite all in one faith and love—that very teaching, in the person of its best representatives, told me that these men were all living a lie; that what gave them their power of life was a temptation of the devil; and what we alone possess the only possible truth. And I saw that all who do not profess an identical faith with themselves are considered by the Orthodox to be heretics; just as the Catholics and others consider the Orthodox to be heretics. And I saw that the Orthodox (though they try to hide this) regard with hostility all who do not express their faith by the same external symbols and words as themselves; and this is naturally so: first, because the assertion that you are in falsehood and I am in truth, is the most cruel thing one man can say to another; and secondly, because a man loving his children and brothers cannot

[1] A sect that rejects sacraments and ritual.

help being hostile to those who wish to pervert his children and brothers to a false belief. And that hostility is increased in proportion to one's greater knowledge of theology. And to me, who considered that truth lay in union by love, it became self-evident that theology was itself destroying what it ought to produce.

This temptation is so obvious to us educated people who have lived in countries where various religions are professed, and have seen the contempt, self-assurance, and invincible contradiction with which Catholics behave to the Orthodox Greeks and to the Protestants, and the Orthodox to Catholics and Protestants, and the Protestants to the two others, and the similar attitude of Old-Believers, Pashkovites (Russian Evangelicals), Shakers, and all religions—that the very obviousness of the temptation at first perplexes us. One says to oneself: it is impossible that it is so simple and that people do not see that if two assertions are mutually contradictory, then neither of them has the sole truth which faith should possess. There is something else here, there must be some explanation. I thought there was, and sought that explanation, and read all I could on the subject, and consulted all whom I could. And no one gave me any explanation, except the one which causes the Sumsky Hussars to consider the Sumsky Hussars the best regiment in the world, and the Yellow Uhlans to consider that the best regiment in the world is the Yellow Uhlans. The ecclesiastics of all the different creeds, through their best representatives, told me nothing but that they believed themselves to have the truth, and the others to be in error, and that all they could do was to pray for them. I went to archimandrites, bishops, elders, monks of the strictest orders, and asked them; but none of them made any attempt to explain the matter to me, except one man, who explained it all, and explained it so that I never asked any one any more about it. I said that for every unbeliever turning to belief (and all our young generation are in a position to do so) the question that presents itself first is, why is truth not in Lutheranism nor in Catholicism, but in Orthodoxy? Educated in the high school, he cannot help knowing—what the peasants do not know—that the Protestants and Catholics equally affirm that their faith is the only true one. Historical evidence, twisted by each religion in its own favour, is insufficient. Is it not possible, said I, to understand the teaching in a loftier way, so that from its height the differences should disappear, as they do for one who believes truly? Can we not go further along a path like the one we are following with the Old-Believers? They emphasize the fact that they have a differently shaped cross and different alleluias and a different procession round the altar. We reply: You believe in the Nicene Creed, in the seven sacraments, and so do we. Let us hold to that, and in other matters do as you please. We have united with them by placing the essentials of faith above the unessentials. Now with the Catholics, can we not say: You believe in so and so and in so and so, which are the chief things, and as for the Filioque clause and the Pope—do as you please. Can we not say the same to the Protestants, uniting with them in what is most important?

My interlocutor agreed with my thoughts, but told me that such concessions would bring reproach on the spiritual authorities for deserting the faith of our forefathers, and this would produce a schism; and the vocation of the spiritual authorities is to safeguard in all its purity the Greco-Russian Orthodox faith inherited from our forefathers.

And I understood it all. I am seeking a faith, the power of life; and they are seeking the best way to fulfil in the eyes of men certain human obligations. And fulfilling these human affairs they fulfil them in a human way. However much they may talk of their pity for their erring brethren, and of addressing prayers for them to the throne of the Almighty—to carry out human purposes violence is necessary, and it has always been applied, and is and will be applied. If of two religions each considers itself true, and the other false, then desiring to attract others to the truth, men will preach their own doctrine. And if a false teaching is preached to the inexperienced sons of their Church—which has the truth—then that Church cannot but burn the books and remove the man who is misleading its sons. What is to be done with a sectarian—burning, in the opinion of the Orthodox, with the fire of false doctrine—who in the most important affair of life, in faith, misleads the sons of the Church? What can be done with him, except to cut off his head, or to incarcerate him? Under the Tsar Alexis Mikhaylovich, people were burned at the stake, that is to say, the severest method of punishment of the time was applied, and in our day also, the severest method of punishment is applied—detention in solitary confinement.[1]

And I turned my attention to what is done in the name of religion and was horrified, and I almost entirely abjured Orthodoxy.

The second relation of the Church to a question of life was with regard to war and executions.

At that time Russia was at war. And Russians, in the name of Christian love, began to kill their fellow men. It was impossible not to think about this, and not to see that killing is an evil repugnant to the first principles of any faith. Yet prayers were said in the churches for the success of our arms, and the teachers of the Faith acknowledged killing to be an act resulting from the Faith. And besides the murders during the war, I saw, during the disturbances which followed the war, Church dignitaries and teachers and monks of the lesser and stricter orders who approved the killing of helpless, erring youths. And I took note of all that is done by men who profess Christianity, and I was horrified.

[1] At the time this was written, capital punishment was considered to be abolished in Russia.

XVI

And I ceased to doubt, and became fully convinced that not all was true in the religion I had joined. Formerly I should have said that it was all false; but I could not say so now. The whole of the people had a certain knowledge of the truth, for otherwise they could not have lived. Moreover, that knowledge was accessible to me, for I had felt it and had lived by it. But I no longer doubted that there was also falsehood in it. And all that had previously repelled me now presented itself vividly before me. And though I saw that among the peasants there was a smaller admixture of the lies that repelled me than among the representatives of the Church, I still saw that in the people's belief also falsehood was mixed with the truth.

But where did the truth and where did the falsehood come from? Both the falsehood and the truth were contained in the so-called holy tradition and in the Scriptures. Both the falsehood and the truth had been handed down by what is called the Church.

And whether I liked or not, I was brought to the study and investigation of these writings and traditions—which till now I had been so afraid to investigate.

And I turned to the examination of that same theology which I had once rejected with such contempt as unnecessary. Formerly it seemed to me a series of unnecessary absurdities, when on all sides I was surrounded by manifestations of life which seemed to me clear and full of sense; now I should have been glad to throw away what would not enter a healthy head, but I had nowhere to turn to. On this teaching religious doctrine rests, or at least with it the only knowledge of the meaning of life that I have found is inseparably connected. However wild it may seem to my firm old mind, it was the only hope of salvation. It had to be carefully, attentively examined in order to understand it, and not even to understand it as I understand the propositions of science: I do not seek that, nor can I seek it, knowing the peculiarity of the knowledge of faith. I shall not seek the explanation of everything. I know that the explanation of everything, like the commencement of everything, must be concealed in infinity. But I wish to understand in a way which will bring me to what is inevitably inexplicable. I wish to recognize anything that is inexplicable, as being so not because the demands of my reason are wrong (they are right, and apart from them I can understand nothing), but because I recognize the limits of my intellect. I wish to understand in such a way that everything that is inexplicable shall present itself to me as being necessarily inexplicable, and not as being something I am under an arbitrary obligation to believe.

That there is truth in the teaching is to me indubitable; but it is also certain that there is falsehood in it, and I must find what is true and what is false, and must disentangle the one from the other. I am setting to work upon this task. What of falsehood I have found in the teaching, and what I have found of truth, and to what conclusions I came, will form the following parts of this work, which if it be worth it, and if any one wants it, will probably some day be printed somewhere.

1879.

The foregoing was written by me some three years ago, and will be printed.

Now, a few days ago, when revising it and returning to the line of thought and to the feelings I had when I was living through it all, I had a dream. This dream expressed in condensed form all that I had experienced and described, and I think therefore that, for those who have understood me, a description of this dream will refresh and elucidate and unify what has been set forth at such length in the foregoing pages. The dream was this :—

I saw that I was lying on a bed. I was neither comfortable nor uncomfortable : I was lying on my back. But I began to consider how, and on what, I was lying—a question which had not till then occurred to me. And observing my bed, I saw I was lying on plaited string suspenders attached to its sides : my feet were resting on one such suspender, my calves on another, and my legs felt uncomfortable. I seemed to know that those suspenders were movable, and with a movement of my foot I pushed away the furthest of them at my feet—it seemed to me that it would be more comfortable so. But I pushed it away too far and wished to reach it again with my foot, and that movement caused the next suspender under my calves to slip away also, so that my legs hung in the air. I made a movement with my whole body to adjust myself, fully convinced that I could do so at once; but the movement caused the other suspenders under me to slip and to become entangled, and I saw that matters were going quite wrong: the whole of the lower part of my body slipped and hung down, though my feet did not reach the ground. I was holding on only by the upper part of my back, and not only did it become uncomfortable but I was even frightened. And then only did I ask myself about something that had not before occurred to me. I asked myself: Where am I, and what am I lying on? and I began to look around, and first of all to look down in the direction in which my body was hanging, and whither I felt I must soon fall. I looked down and did not believe my eyes. I was not only at a height comparable to the height of the highest towers or mountains, but at a height such as I could never have imagined.

I could not even make out whether I saw anything there below, in that bottomless abyss over which I was hanging and whither I was being drawn. My heart contracted, and I experienced horror. To look thither was terrible. If I looked thither, I felt that I should at once slip from the last suspender and perish. And I did not look. But not to look was still worse, for I thought of what would happen to me directly

I fell from the last suspender. And I felt that from fear I was losing my last supports, and that my back was slowly slipping lower and lower. Another moment and I should drop off. And then it occurred to me that this cannot be real. It is a dream. Wake up! I try to arouse myself but cannot do so. What am I to do? What am I to do? I ask myself, and look upwards. Above, there is also an infinite space. I look into the immensity of sky and try to forget about the immensity below, and I really do forget it. The immensity below repels and frightens me; the immensity above attracts and strengthens me. I am still supported above the abyss by the last suspenders that have not yet slipped from under me; I know that I am hanging; but I look only upwards and my fear passes. As happens in dreams, a voice says: 'Notice this, this is it!' And I look more and more into the infinite above me and feel that I am becoming calm. I remember all that has happened, and remember how it all happened; how I moved my legs, how I hung down, how frightened I was, and how I was saved from fear by looking upwards. And I ask myself: Well, and now am I not hanging just the same? And I do not so much look round as experience with my whole body the point of support on which I am held. I see that I no longer hang as if about to fall, but am firmly held. I ask myself how I am held: I feel about, look round, and see that under me, under the middle of my body, there is one suspender, and that when I look upwards I lie on it in the position of securest balance, and that it alone gave me support before. And then, as happens in dreams, I imagined the mechanism by means of which I was held ; a very natural, intelligible, and sure means, though to one awake that mechanism has no sense. I, in my dream, was even surprised that I had not understood it sooner. It appeared that at my head there was a pillar, and the security of that slender pillar was undoubted, though there was nothing to support it. From the pillar a loop hung very ingeniously and yet simply, and if one lay with the middle of one's body in that loop and looked up, there could be no question of falling. This was all clear to me, and I was glad and tranquil. And it seemed as if someone said to me: 'See that you remember.'

And I awoke.

1882.

WHAT I BELIEVE

CONTENTS

INTRODUCTION

I LIVED in the world for fifty-five years, and after the first fourteen or fifteen of childhood I was for thirty-five years a nihilist in the real meaning of that word, that is to say not a Socialist or revolutionary as those words are generally understood, but a nihilist in the sense of an absence of any belief.

Five years ago I came to believe in Christ's teaching, and my life suddenly changed; I ceased to desire what I had previously desired, and began to desire what I formerly did not want. What had previously seemed to me good seemed evil, and what had seemed evil seemed good. It happened to me as it happens to a man who goes out on some business and on the way suddenly decides that the business is unnecessary and returns home. All that was on his right is now on his left, and all that was on his left is now on his right; his former wish to get as far as possible from home has changed into a wish to be as near as possible to it. The direction of my life and my desires became different, and good and evil changed places. This all occurred because I understood Christ's teaching otherwise than as I had formerly understood it.

I am not seeking to interpret Christ's teaching, but only to tell how I understood what is simple, plain, clear, intelligible, indubitable, and addressed to all men in it, and how what I understood changed my soul and gave me tranquillity and happiness.

I do not wish to interpret Christ's teaching, but should only wish to forbid artificial interpretations of it.

All the Christian Churches have always admitted that all men—unequal in their knowledge and minds, wise or foolish—are equals before God, and that God's truth is accessible to them all. Christ even said that it was the will of God that to the foolish should be revealed what was hidden from the wise.

Not all can be initiated into the deepest mysteries of dogmatics, homiletics, patristics, liturgics, hermeneutics, apologetics, etc., but all may and should understand what Christ said to all the millions of simple, unlearned people who have lived and are living. And it is just this which Christ said to all these simple people who had as yet no possibility of turning for explanations of his teaching to Paul, Clement, John Chrysostom, and others—it is just this that I want to tell to all men. The thief on the cross believed Jesus and was saved. Would it really have been evil or have harmed anyone had the thief not died on the cross but come down from it and told men how he learned to believe in Christ?

I, like that thief on the cross, have believed Christ's teaching and been saved. And this is no far-fetched comparison but the closest expression of the condition of spiritual despair and horror at the problem of life and death in which I lived formerly, and of the condition of peace and happiness in which I am now.

I, like the thief, knew that I had lived and was living badly, and saw that the majority of people around me lived as I did. I, like the thief, knew that I was unhappy and suffering, and that around me people suffered and were unhappy, and I saw no way of escape from that position except by death. I, like the thief to the cross, was nailed by some force to that life of suffering and evil. And as, after the meaningless sufferings and evils of life, the thief awaited the terrible darkness of death, so did I await the same thing.

In all this I was exactly like the thief, but the difference was that the thief was already dying, while I was still living. The thief might believe that his salvation lay there beyond the grave, but I could not be satisfied with that, because beside a life beyond the grave life still awaited me here. But I did not understand that life. It seemed to me terrible. And suddenly I heard the words of Christ and understood them, and life and death ceased to seem to me evil, and instead of despair I experienced happiness and the joy of life undisturbed by death.

Surely it can harm no one, if I tell how this befell me?

Moscow,
January 22, 1884.

WHAT I BELIEVE

CHAPTER I

A KEY TO THE GOSPEL TEACHING

I HAVE told why I formerly did not understand Christ's teaching, and how and why I have now understood it, in two large works: *A Criticism of Dogmatic Theology* and *A New Translation and Harmony of the Four Gospels, with Explanations*. In those works I try methodically and step by step to examine all that hides the truth from men, and verse by verse retranslate, compare, and synthesize the four Gospels.

For six years this has been my work. Every year, every month, I discover fresh and fresh elucidations and confirmations of my fundamental thought, correct errors that from haste or over-eagerness have crept into my work, and add to what has been done. My life, not much of which remains, will probably end before this work is completed.[1] But I am convinced that the work is needed, and therefore while I still have life I do what I can.

Such is my prolonged external work at

[1] This book was completed in January 1884, Tolstoy continued to live and work till November 1910.

theology and the Gospels. But my internal work, of which I wish to tell here, was different. It was not a methodical investigation of theology and of the texts of the Gospels, but an instantaneous discarding of all that hid the real meaning of the teaching and an instantaneous illumination by the light of truth. It was an occurrence such as might befall a man who, by the guidance of a wrong drawing, was vainly seeking to reconstruct something from a confused heap of small bits of marble, if he suddenly guessed from the largest piece that it was quite a different statue from what he had supposed, and having begun to reconstruct it, instead of the former incoherence of the pieces he saw a confirmation of his belief in every piece, which with all the curves of its fracture fitted into other pieces and formed one whole. That was what happened to me, and it is this that I wish to relate.

I wish to relate how I found the key to the understanding of Christ's teaching, which revealed to me the truth with a clearness and assurance that excluded all doubt.

This discovery was made by me thus. Since I first read the Gospels for myself when almost a child, what touched and affected me most of all was Christ's teaching of love, meekness, humility, self-sacrifice, and repayment of good for evil. Such always was for me the essence of Christianity—that in it which my heart loved, and for the sake of which, after passing through despair and unbelief, I accepted as true the meaning the labouring Christian folk attribute to life, and submitted myself to the faith professed by them, namely the faith of the Orthodox Church. But, having submitted to the Church, I soon noticed that I did not find in her teaching confirmation or explanation of those principles of Christianity which seemed to me most important. I noticed that that aspect of Christianity which was dear to me is not the chief thing in Church teaching. I saw that what seemed to me most important in Christ's teaching is not so recognized by the Church; she treats something else as most important. At first I did not attach importance to this peculiarity of Church teaching. 'Well, what of it?' thought I—'The Church, besides ideas of love, humility, and self-sacrifice, admits also this dogmatic, external meaning. That is foreign to me and even repels me, but there is nothing harmful in it.'

But the longer I lived in submission to the Church, the more noticeable it became that this characteristic of her teaching was not so harmless as it at first seemed to me to be. The Church repelled me by the strangeness of her dogmas and her acceptance and approval of persecutions, executions, and wars. The mutual denunciation by one another of various congregations also repelled me. But what shattered my trust in the Church was just her indifference to what seemed to me the essence of Christ's teaching, and her partiality for what seemed to me unessential.

I felt that something was wrongly put, but what was wrong I could not at all make out.

I could not make it out because the teaching of the Church not only did not deny what seemed to me the chief thing in Christ's teaching, but fully acknowledged it, acknowledging it somehow so that what was chief in Christ's teaching no longer occupied the first place. I could not reproach the Church for denying what was essential, but the Church acknowledged the essential matter in a way that did not satisfy me; she did not give me what I expected of her.

I went over from nihilism to the Church only because I was conscious of the impossibility of life without faith, without a knowledge of what is good and what is evil, apart from my animal instincts. This knowledge I thought I should find in Christianity, but Christianity as it then appeared to me was only a certain frame of mind, very indefinite, from which clear and obligatory rules of conduct were not deducible, and for such rules I turned to the Church. But the Church gave me rules that did not bring me any nearer to the state of mind dear to me, but rather removed me further from it, and I could not follow her. What was necessary and dear to me was life based on the Christian truths; the Church, however, gave me rules of life which were quite foreign to the truths I prized. The rules given by the Church about faith in dogmas, observation of the Sacraments, fasts, and prayers were to me unnecessary; and rules based upon the Christian truths were absent. Nor was that all. The Church rules weakened and sometimes plainly destroyed that Christian frame of mind which alone gave meaning to my life. What disturbed me most of all was that all human evils—the condemnation of individuals, of whole peoples, of other religions, and the executions and wars which resulted from such condemnations—were all justified by the Church. The teaching of Christ about humility, not judging, forgiveness of injuries, self-sacrifice and love, was extolled in words, but at the same time in practice the Church approved of what was incompatible with this teaching.

Was it possible that the teaching of Christ was such that these contradictions were inevitable? I could not believe it. Moreover, what always seemed to me surprising was that, as far as my knowledge of the Gospels went, those passages on which the definite Church dogmas were based were the most obscure; while those from which one derived the practical teaching were the clearest and most definite. Yet the dogmas and those Christian obligations which result from them were defined by the Church in the clearest and most precise manner, while of the practical fulfilment of the teaching mention was made in the most indefinite, foggy, mystical way. Could Christ possibly have wished this when delivering his teaching? A solution of my doubts could only be found in the Gospels. So I read and re-read them. Out of them all, the Sermon on the Mount always stood out for me as something special, and I read it more often than anything else.

Nowhere else did Christ speak with such authority—nowhere else does he give so many clear, intelligible moral rules directly appealing to the heart of every man. Nowhere did he speak to a larger crowd of the common people. If there were any clear, definite Christian rules, they ought to be expressed here. In these three chapters of Matthew I sought a solution of my perplexity. Often and often did I re-read the Sermon on the Mount and experienced the same feeling every time: a thrill of exaltation at the verses about turning the other cheek, surrendering one's cloak, reconciliation with all men, love of one's enemies, but also a dissatisfied feeling. The words of God addressed to all lacked clearness. A too impossible renunciation of everything was demanded, destroying all life as I understood it, and therefore it seemed to me that such renunciation could not be the obligatory condition of salvation; but if that were not so, then there was nothing definite and clear. I read not the Sermon on the Mount alone, but all the Gospels, as well as all the theological commentaries on them. The theological explanation that the precepts of the Sermon on the Mount are indications of the perfection towards which men should strive, but that fallen man, immersed in sin, cannot by his own strength attain this perfection, and that his safety lies in faith, prayer, and the Sacraments—such explanations did not satisfy me.

I did not agree with this because it always seemed strange to me why Christ, knowing in advance that the fulfilment of his teaching was unattainable by man's individual strength, gave such clear and admirable rules relating directly to each individual man. In reading these rules it always seemed to me that they related directly to me and demanded my personal fulfilment. Reading them, I always experienced a joyous confidence that I could immediately, from that very hour, fulfil them all, and I wished and endeavoured to do this. But as soon as I experienced difficulty in doing this, I involuntarily remembered the Church's teaching that man is weak and cannot do these things by his own strength, and I weakened.

They told me we must believe and pray.

But I felt I had little faith, and therefore could not pray. They told me one must pray God to give faith—the very faith that gives the prayer that gives the faith that gives the prayer—and so on to infinity.

But both reason and experience showed me that only *my* efforts to fulfil Christ's teaching could be effective.

And so, after many, many vain seekings and studyings of what was written in proof and disproof of the Divinity of this teaching, and after many doubts and much suffering, I again was left alone with my heart and the mysterious book. I could not give it the meaning others gave it, could not find any other meaning for it, and could not reject it. And only after disbelieving equally all the explanations of the learned critics and all the explanations of the learned theologians, and after rejecting them all (in accord with Christ's words, 'Except ye turn and become as little children, ye shall in no wise enter into the kingdom of heaven'), I suddenly understood what I had not formerly understood. I understood it not as a result of some artificial, recondite transposition, harmonization, or reinterpretation; on the contrary, everything revealed itself to me because I forgot all the interpretations. The passage which served me as key to the whole was Matt. v. 38, 39: 'Ye have heard that it was said, An eye for an eye and a tooth for a tooth: But I say unto you, Resist not him that is evil.' And suddenly, for the first time, I understood this verse simply and directly. I understood that Christ says just what he says, and what immediately happened was not that something new revealed itself, but that everything that obscured the truth fell away, and the truth arose before me in its full meaning. 'Ye have heard that it was said, An eye for an eye and a tooth for a tooth: But I say unto you, Resist not him that is evil.' These words suddenly appeared to me as something quite new, as if I had never read them before. Previously when reading that passage I had always, by some strange blindness, omitted the words, '*But I say unto you, Resist not him that is evil,*' just as if those words had not been there, or as if they had no definite meaning.

Subsequently, in my talks with many and many Christians familiar with the Gospels, I often had occasion to note the same blindness as to those words. No one remembered them; and often when speaking about that passage Christians referred to the Gospels to verify the fact that the words were really there. In the same way I had missed those words and had begun understanding the passage only from the words which follow, 'But whosoever smiteth thee on thy right cheek, turn to him the other also . . .' and so forth; and these words always appeared to me as a demand to endure sufferings and deprivations that are unnatural to man. The words touched me, and I felt that it would be admirable to act up to them; but I also felt that I should never be strong enough to fulfil them merely in order to suffer. I said to myself, 'Very well, I will turn the other cheek, and I shall be again struck. I will give what is demanded and everything will be taken from me. I shall have no life—but life was given me, so why should I be deprived of it? It cannot be that Christ demands it.' That was what I formerly said to myself, imagining that in these words Christ extolled sufferings and deprivations, and extolling them, spoke with exaggeration and therefore inexactly and obscurely. But now, when I had understood the words about not resisting him that is evil, it became plain to me that Christ was not exaggerating nor demanding any suffering for the sake of suffering, but was only, very definitely and clearly, saying what he said. He says: 'Do not resist him that is evil, and while doing this know in advance that you may meet people who, having struck you on one cheek and not met with resistance, will strike you on the other, and having taken away your coat will take your cloak also; who, having availed themselves of your work, will oblige you to do more work, and will not repay what they borrow . . . should this be so, continue nevertheless to abstain from resisting the evil man. Continue, in spite of all this, to do good to those who will beat you and insult you.' And when I understood these words as they are said, at once all that was obscure became clear, and what had seemed exaggerated became quite exact. I understood for the first time that the centre of gravity of the whole thought lies in the words, 'Resist not him that is evil,' and that what follows is only an explanation of that first proposition. I understood that Christ does not command us to present the cheek and to give up the cloak in order to suffer, but commands us not to resist him that is evil, and adds that this may involve having to suffer. It is just like a father sending his son off on a distant voyage, who does not order the son not to sleep at night and not to eat enough, and to be drenched and to freeze, but says to him, 'Go your road, and if you have to be drenched and to freeze, continue your journey nevertheless.' Christ does not say, 'Offer your cloak and suffer,' but he says, 'Resist not him that is evil, and no matter what befalls you do not resist him.' These words, 'Resist not evil,' or 'Resist not him that is evil,' understood in their direct meaning, were for me truly a key opening everything else, and it became surprising to me that I could so radically have misunderstood the clear and definite words: 'It was said, An eye for an eye and a tooth for a tooth: But I say unto you, Resist not him that is evil, and no matter what he does to you, suffer and surrender, but resist him not.' What can be clearer, more intelligible, and more indubitable than that? And I only needed to understand these words simply and directly as they were said and at once Christ's whole teaching, not only in the Sermon on the Mount but in the whole of the Gospels, everything that had been confused, became intelligible; what had been contradictory became harmonious, and, above all, what had appeared superfluous became essential. All merged into one whole, and one thing indubitably confirmed another like the pieces of a broken statue when they are replaced in their true position. In this Sermon and in the whole of the Gospels everything confirmed the same teaching of non-resistance to evil. In this Sermon, as everywhere else, Christ never represents his disciples—that is to say, the people who fulfil the law of non-resistance to evil—otherwise than as turning the cheek to the smiter, giving up the cloak, persecuted, beaten, and destitute. Everywhere Christ repeatedly says that only he can be his disciple who takes up his cross and abandons everything; that is to say, only he who is ready to endure all consequences that result from the fulfilment of the law of non-resistance to evil. To his disciples Christ says: 'Be beggars; be ready without resisting evil to accept persecution, suffering, and death.' He himself prepares for suffering and death without resisting evil, and sends Peter away because he complains of this. He himself dies forbidding resistance to evil, and without deviating from his teaching. All his first disciples fulfilled this commandment of non-resistance, and passed their lives in poverty and persecutions, never returning evil for evil.

So Christ says what he says. It is possible to affirm that it is very difficult always to obey this rule. It is possible not to agree with the statement that every man will be happy if he obeys this rule. It may be said that it is stupid, as unbelievers say that Christ was a dreamer and an idealist who enunciated impracticable rules which his disciples followed from stupidity. But it is quite impossible not to admit that Christ said very clearly and definitely just what he meant to say, namely that according to his teaching man should not resist evil, and that therefore whoever accepts his teaching must not resist evil. And yet neither believers nor unbelievers understand this simple, clear meaning of Christ's words.

CHAPTER II

THE COMMAND OF NON-RESISTANCE

WHEN I understood that the words 'resist not him that is evil' meant 'resist not him that is evil,' my former conception of the meaning of Christ's teaching was suddenly changed, and I was horrified, not at the fact that I had not understood it, but at the strange way in which I had understood the teaching up to that time. I knew, we all know, that the meaning of Christ's teaching is in love to men. To say 'turn your cheek, love your enemies' is to express the essence of Christianity. I knew this from childhood. But why did I not understand these simple words simply, but sought in them some allegorical meaning? 'Resist not him that is evil' means 'never resist him that is evil,' that is, never do violence, never do an act that cannot but be contrary to love, and if they then insult you, bear the insult and still do not inflict violence on any one else. He said it so clearly and simply that it is impossible to say it more clearly. How was it that I, believing or trying to believe that he who said it was God, declared that to fulfil this by my own strength was impossible? The Master says to me, 'Go and chop wood,' and I reply, 'I cannot do that by my own strength.' Replying so, I say one of two things, either that I do not believe what the Master says, or that I do not wish to do what he commands. Of the commandment of God which he gave us to perform, and of which he said, 'Whoso doeth this and teacheth men so shall be called great,' etc., of which he said that only those who do it shall receive life; the command which he himself fulfilled and which he expressed so clearly and simply that there can be no doubt about its meaning. It was of this command that I who had never even tried to fulfil it said, 'It is impossible to perform it by my own strength; I need supernatural aid.' God came down on earth to give salvation to men. That salvation consists in this. The Second Person of the Trinity, God the Son, suffered for people and redeemed their sins before his Father, and gave men the Church in which is preserved the grace which is administered to believers. But besides all this that same Son of God also gave people a teaching and an example of life for their salvation. How was it that I said that the rules of life expressed by him simply and clearly for all men were so difficult of accomplishment as to be even impossible without miraculous aid? He not only did not say that, but he said, 'Do it. He that does not do it will not enter into the kingdom of heaven.' And he never said that the performance was difficult. On the contrary he said, 'My yoke is easy and my burden is light.' John the Evangelist said, 'His law is not hard.' How was it that I said that what God had told us to do, that act the performance of which he had so exactly defined and of which he had said that to do it was easy, that which he himself performed as a man and which was performed by his first followers—how was it that I said that to do it was so difficult as to be even impossible without miraculous aid? If a man applied the whole strength of his mind to destroy some law that had been given, what more effective for the destruction of such a law could that man say than that the law itself was impracticable, and that the intention of the lawgiver himself concerning his law was that it was impracticable and that to fulfil it needed miraculous aid? And that is just what I thought concerning the law of non-resistance to evil; and I began to remember how this strange thought entered my head—that the law of Christ was divine but that its fulfilment was impossible—and reconsidering my past I understood that that thought was never conveyed to me in its complete nakedness (it would have repelled me), but that I, without noticing it, had sucked it in with my mother's milk from my very first childhood, and the whole of my subsequent life had only confirmed in me this strange delusion.

From childhood I was taught that Christ was God and that his teaching was divine, but at the same time I was taught to respect those institutions which secured by violence my safety from evil men. I was taught to respect these institutions by the priests. I was taught to resist the evil man, and it was inculcated that it is degrading and shameful to submit to the evil man and to endure him. They taught me to judge and to execute; afterwards they taught me to go to war—that is to say to resist the evil man by murder, and the army of which I was a member was called the 'Christ-loving Army,' and its activities were sanctified by the blessings of the Church. Moreover, from childhood and until I was a man I was taught to respect what directly contradicted the law of Christ; to resist an injurer, to revenge myself by violence for a personal, family, or national insult. All this was not merely not condemned, but it was instilled into me that all this was excellent and not contrary to the law of Christ.

All my circumstances, my tranquillity, the safety of myself and my family and my property were all based on the law repudiated by Christ, on the law of a tooth for a tooth. The doctors of the Church taught that Christ's teaching was divine, but its performance impossible on account of human frailty, and only Christ's blessing can assist its performance. The worldly teachers and the whole construction of our life plainly admitted the impracticability and fantastic nature of Christ's teaching, and by words and deeds taught what was opposed to it. The admission of the impracticability of God's teaching had gradually to such a degree impregnated me and had become so familiar, and it coincided to such a degree with my desires, that I had never before noticed the contradiction with which I was faced. I did not see that it is impossible at one and the same time to confess Christ as God, the basis of whose teaching is non-resistance to him that is evil, and consciously and calmly to work for the establishment of property, law-courts, government, and military forces, to establish a life contrary to the teaching of Christ, and to pray to that same Christ that the law of non-resistance to him that is evil and of forgiveness should be fulfilled among us. That which is so clear had not yet occurred to me: that it would be much simpler to arrange and organize life according to the law of Christ and then to pray that there should be law-courts, executions, and wars if they are so necessary for our welfare.[1]

[1] Many philosophies are logically sound and irrefutable once one grants them the premises from which they start. The chandelier is often solid and brilliant, the only question is whether the hook which attaches it to the ceiling is sufficiently firm to support it. So it is with Tolstoy's philosophy of Christian anarchy. Once accept his thesis that Jesus, by saying 'resist not him that is evil,' intended to forbid any use of physical force to prevent any one from doing whatever evil he likes, and that he was divinely and absolutely right in laying down that principle, and there is no logical escape from the ultimate conclusion that any Government using force, all compulsory law, all police, and all protection of life or property is immoral.

It is therefore important to examine the context, intention, and scope of the passage referred to, and to ask whether, had Jesus wished to give it the extension and application Tolstoy gives it, he would not have done so explicitly, not leaving such tremendous conclusions to be deduced from such brief remarks. 'Sweet reasonableness' would hardly have been predicated of Christ's teaching had he allowed his repudiation of 'an eye for an eye' to carry him to such an extreme in the contrary direction.

And I understood how my mistake had arisen. It had arisen from obedience to Christ in words and denial of him in deeds.

The command of non-resistance to him that is evil is one that makes a complete whole of all the teaching, but this only if it is not a mere saying, but an obligatory rule—a law to be fulfilled.

It is really a key which opens everything, but only when it is pushed into the lock. The treatment of this statement as a mere saying impossible of fulfilment without supernatural aid is the destruction of the whole teaching, and what but an impossibility can any teaching appear to men from which the unifying, fundamental thesis has been removed? To an unbeliever it even appears simply stupid and cannot appear otherwise.

To put an engine in position, to heat the boiler, to set it in motion, but not to attach the connecting belt, was what was done with the teaching of Christ when people began to teach that you can be a Christian without fulfilling the law of non-resistance to him that is evil.

I was recently reading the Fifth Chapter of Matthew with a Jewish Rabbi. At almost every sentence the Rabbi said, 'That is in the Jewish Canon. That is in the Talmud,' and he pointed out to me in the Old Testament and the Talmud *dicta* very similar to the *dicta* of the Sermon on the Mount. But when we came to the verse about non-resistance to him that is evil he did not say, 'And that is in the Talmud,' but only ironically asked me:

'Do the Christians fulfil that? Do they turn the other cheek?' I had no reply, especially as I knew that at that very time Christians were not only not turning the other cheek, but were striking cheeks the Jews had turned. But I was interested to know whether there was anything similar in the Old Testament or in the Talmud, and I asked him about this. He replied. 'No, it is not there. But tell me whether the Christians fulfil this law.' By this question he showed me that the presence of this rule in the Christian law, which not only is not performed by any one, but which Christians themselves admit to be impracticable, is an admission of the irrationality and superfluity of the Christian law. And I had no reply to give him.

Now having understood the meaning of this teaching, I see clearly the strange internal contradiction with which I was faced. Having admitted Christ to be God and his law to be divine, and having at the same time arranged my life in contradiction to the teaching, what was left me but to admit that the teaching was impracticable? In words I admitted the teaching of Christ to be holy, in practice I professed a quite unchristian teaching and admitted and submitted to unchristian institutions which surrounded me on all sides.

The whole of the Old Testament says that the misfortunes of the Jewish people were the effect of their believing in false gods and not in the true God. Samuel, in his First Book, chapters viii. and xii., told the people that to all their former disobedience they had added a new one. Instead of God who had been their King they had chosen a man-king, whom they thought would save them. Do not believe in 'vain things,' says Samuel to the people (xii. 21). It cannot help you or save you because it is 'vain'—empty. That you may not perish together with your king, cling to the one God.

And it was faith in that 'vain thing,' in empty idols, that hid the truth from me. On the path to it, hiding its light from me, stood those 'vain things' which I had not strength to reject.

I was walking the other day towards the Borovitski Gates of the Moscow Kremlin. At the gates sat an old crippled beggar, wrapped round the ears with some rag. I took out my purse to give him something.[1] Just then, coming down from the Kremlin, ran a manly, ruddy young fellow, a grenadier in his regimental sheepskin coat. The beggar, on seeing the soldier, jumped up in dismay, and ran limping down towards the Alexandrov Gardens. The grenadier started to catch him, but, without overtaking him, stopped and began abusing the

[1] Tolstoy always gave away small change to beggars he met, in accord with the usual practice of religious folk in a country which had no State poor-relief organization, and also in accord with the injunction 'Give to him that asketh of thee!' He sometimes admitted that his gift might do harm and that the man might go and drink it; but he argued that the goodwill on the giver's part indicated by the gift was more important than the possible ill effects to the recipient.

beggar for not obeying the prohibition to sit at the gateway. I awaited the grenadier at the gate. When he came up to me I asked him if he could read.

'I can, what about it?' 'Have you read the Gospels?' 'I have.' 'And have you read, "For I was an hungered, and ye gave me no meat"?' And I quoted that passage. He knew it and listened to it, and I saw that he was uneasy. Two passers-by stopped to listen. It was plain that the grenadier was hurt to feel that he, fulfilling his duty excellently and driving beggars away from the place they had to be driven from, suddenly appeared to be in the wrong. He was agitated, and was evidently seeking a rejoinder. Suddenly in his clever black eyes a light gleamed, and he turned sideways to me as though to walk away. 'And have you read the Military Code?' asked he. I said I had not read it. 'Then don't talk,' said the grenadier, tossing his head triumphantly, and adjusting his coat he proceeded confidently to his post. This was the only man I ever met in all my life who quite logically decided the eternal question with which our social state, being what it is, faced me and faces every man who calls himself a Christian.

CHAPTER III

THE LAW OF GOD AND THE LAW OF MAN

It is wrongly said that the Christian teaching relates only to personal salvation and not to public, political questions. That is merely audacious and barefaced assertion, which is most obviously false and collapses as soon as it is seriously considered. Very well, I will not resist the evil doer, I will turn my cheek as a private individual, say I to myself; but if an enemy comes, or the people are oppressed, and I am called on to take part in the struggle against the evil men, and to go and kill them, then it is imperative for me to decide wherein lies the service of God, and wherein the service of 'the vain thing.' Am I to go to the war or not? I am a peasant, and am chosen to serve as a village elder, a judge, or a juryman, and I am told to take an oath, to judge and to inflict punishment. What am I to do? Again I have to choose between the law of God and the law of man. Or I am a monk, living in a monastery, and some peasants have taken our hay and I am sent to participate in the struggle against the evil men, and to take legal proceedings against the peasants. Again I have to choose. No one can escape from the question. I speak not merely of our class, whose activity consists almost entirely in resisting evil men: in the army, in the courts of justice, or in civil offices —there is not a single private person, however humble, who has not to choose between serving God by obeying His command, or serving the 'vain thing'—state institutions. My private life is interwoven with the general life of the state, which demands of me an unchristian activity directly contrary to the law of Christ. Now with universal military service and the liability of all to serve on a jury, this dilemma is sharply presented to us all in a very striking manner. Every man must take the weapons of murder—a sword and a bayonet, and must either kill, or at least load the rifle and sharpen the sword, that is prepare to kill. Every citizen must appear at the law-courts and participate in trial and punishment, that is to say must repudiate Christ's law about not resisting him that is evil, and must do it not merely in words but in deeds.

The grenadier's question—The Gospel or the military code? The law of God or man's law? —now presents itself to humanity as it did in the days of Samuel. It presented itself to Christ himself, and to his disciples. It stands before those who now wish to be Christians in deed, and it stood before me.

The law of Christ, and his teachings of love, humility, and self-repudiation had previously always touched my heart and attracted me. But from all sides, both in history and around me at the present day and in my own life, I saw a contrary law, repugnant to my heart and conscience and reason, but harmonizing with my animal instincts. I felt if I accepted the law of Christ I should be isolated and it would go ill with me, I should be one of the persecuted and suffering, as Christ predicted. While if I accepted man's law, every one would approve of it, and I should be at peace, secure, and have at my service all manner of theological subtleties to set my conscience at rest. I should laugh and be merry as Christ said. I felt this, and therefore did not penetrate into the meaning of Christ's law, but tried to understand it so that it should not prevent my living my accustomed animal life. But to understand it so was impossible, and therefore I did not understand it at all.

In this non-comprehension I reached a state of perplexity which now astonishes me, and as an example of that perplexity I will give my former understanding of the words, 'Judge not, that ye be not judged' (Matt. vii. 1), 'Judge not and ye shall not be judged: condemn not, and ye shall not be condemned' (Luke vi. 37). The institution of law-courts in which I took part, and which defended the safety of my property, appeared to me so indubitably sacred and accordant with the law of God that it never occurred to me that these sayings could mean anything but that one must not speak ill of one's neighbour. It never entered my head that in those words Christ could have spoken of the law-courts, of the Zemstvo, of the Criminal Court, of the

District Courts and magistrates, and of all the Senates and departments. Only when I understood the words about not resisting him that is evil in the direct sense, only then did the question occur to me of Christ's attitude to all those courts and departments. And seeing that he must have disapproved of them, I asked myself: Does it not mean that one must not merely refrain from condemning one's neighbour verbally, but must not judge him in the courts—must not condemn one's neighbour by means of our law-courts?

In Luke vi. 37–49, these words are spoken immediately after the teaching of non-resistance to evil and of returning good for evil. Following the words, 'Be merciful as your Father in heaven is merciful,' come the words, 'Judge not, and ye shall not be judged: condemn not, and ye shall not be condemned.' Does not this mean that besides not blaming one's neighbour one must not set up law-courts, nor judge one's neighbour in them? said I. And I only had to formulate that question, and my heart and my common sense at once replied affirmatively.

I know how this understanding of the words startles one at first. It startled me too. To show how far I was from such an understanding of the words I will confess to a shameful stupidity. When I had already become a believer, and read the Gospels as a divine book, I used, as a joke, to say to my friends, on meeting any of them who were public prosecutors or judges: 'And you go on judging, though it is written, "Judge not that ye be not judged."'

So sure was I that those words could mean nothing more than a prohibition of evil-speaking, that I did not understand the terrible mockery of holy things my words contained. I had gone so far that, being convinced that these plain words did not mean what they do mean, I used them jokingly in their true sense.

I will recount in detail how all my doubts—whether these words could be understood except as meaning that Christ totally forbids the human institution of any law-court, and that he could mean nothing else by those words—were destroyed.

The first thing that struck me, when I understood the law of non-resistance to the evil man in its direct meaning, was that man's courts of law are not in accord with it, but are directly opposed to it and to the meaning of the whole teaching, and that Christ therefore, if he thought of the law-courts, must have condemned them.

Christ says: 'Resist not him that is evil.' The purpose of the courts is to resist the evil man. Christ tells us to return good for evil. The courts repay evil for evil.[1] Christ tells

[1] Tolstoy here, and subsequently, begs the question whether it may not benefit a man to be forcibly restrained from pursuing an evil course. Confusion arises from the simultaneous discussion of the actual words attributed to Jesus and the general question of what really is true and sensible about man's relation to his fellow men. Tolstoy argued, in another place, that Christ's word should only be accepted as authoritative because they are true and reasonable. After that it is arguing in a circle to say that they are true and reasonable because uttered by Christ.

us not to distinguish good people from bad. The courts are entirely concerned in making the distinction. Christ says, forgive all men. Forgive not once, not seven times, but endlessly. Love your enemies and do good to them that hate you. The courts do not forgive, but punish. They deal out not good but evil to those they call the enemies of society. So it appeared evident that Christ must have condemned the courts. But, thought I, perhaps Christ had nothing to do with the law-courts and was not thinking of them. But I saw that this could not be: from the day of his birth and until his death Christ came in conflict with the courts of Herod, of the Sanhedrin, and of the high priests. And I noticed that Christ often spoke directly of the courts as of an evil. He warned his disciples that they would be judged; and he told them how to bear themselves in the courts. Of himself he said that he would be condemned; and he himself set an example of how one should treat man's courts of law. Therefore Christ thought of these human courts, which condemned him and his disciples and which have condemned and are condemning millions of people. Christ saw this evil and plainly indicated it. At the execution of the sentence of the court on the woman taken in adultery he plainly repudiated the court and showed that man must not judge, because he is himself guilty. And he expressed that same thought several times, saying that with dirt in one's own eye one cannot see the dirt in another's eye and that the blind must not lead the blind. He even explains what results from such a blunder. The pupil becomes like his master.

But perhaps having said this about the judgement on the woman taken in adultery and having put forth parables about the foundations of the house, referring to the general weakness of mankind, he nevertheless does not forbid appeals to human courts of law for the purpose of obtaining protection from evil men. But I saw that this is quite inadmissible.

In the Sermon on the Mount, addressing everybody, he says: 'And if any man will sue thee at law and take away thy coat, let him have thy cloak also.' Therefore he forbids any one to go to law. But perhaps Christ speaks only of each man's personal relation to the courts, and does not condemn the process of law itself, but allows in Christian society of people who judge others in institutions established for that purpose? But neither can this be supposed. Christ, in the prayer he gave, bids all men without exception to forgive others that they may be forgiven their own sins. And he repeats the thought often. Therefore every man when he prays and before bringing his gift to the altar should forgive every one. How can a man, who by the faith he professes must always forgive all men, judge and condemn any one in the law-courts? It follows that, according to Christ's teaching, there can be no such things as Christian courts which inflict punishment.

But perhaps the context shows that in this passage Christ, when he says, 'Judge not, that ye be not judged,' was not thinking of human courts of justice? But this again is not so; on the contrary, it is clear from the context that when he said, 'Judge not,' Christ was speaking precisely of the institution of law-courts. In Matthew and Luke, before saying, 'Judge not,' he says: Resist not him that is evil, endure evil, do good to all men. And before that, in Matthew, he repeats the words of the Hebrew criminal code, 'An eye for an eye, and a tooth for a tooth.' And after this reference to the criminal law, he says: But ye shall not do so; resist not him that is evil; and then he adds, 'Judge not.' Therefore Christ speaks precisely of human criminal law, and repudiates it by the words, 'Judge not.'

Moreover, in Luke, he not only says, 'Judge not,' but 'Judge not . . . and condemn not.' That word 'condemn,' which has so similar a meaning, was not added for nothing. The addition can have had only one aim—to elucidate the sense in which the word 'judge' is used.

If he had meant to say, do not judge *your neighbour*, he would have added that word 'neighbour,' but he adds the word which is translated 'do not condemn,' and then adds, 'that ye be not condemned; forgive all men and you will be forgiven.'

But perhaps, all the same, Christ was not thinking of the law-courts when he said this, and I may be attributing my own thought to his words which had a different meaning.

So I asked myself how Christ's first disciples, the Apostles, regarded man's law-courts. Did they acknowledge them, or approve of them?

In chap. iv. 11, the Apostle James says: 'Speak not evil one of another, brethren, for he that speaketh evil of his brother, and judgeth his brother, speaketh evil of the law, and judgeth the law: but if thou judge the law, thou art not a doer of the law, but a judge. One only is the law-giver, and judge, even he who is able to save or to destroy: Who art thou that judgeth another?'

The word translated 'speak evil of' is καταλάλεω. Without referring to the dictionary one can see that this word must mean indict. And so it does, as any one may convince himself by a reference to the dictionary. It is translated, "Who speaks evil of his brother, speaks evil of the law.' One involuntarily asks, Why? However much I may speak evil of my brother, I do not speak evil of the law; but if I indict and bring my brother before the court of law, I evidently thereby condemn the law of Christ: that is to say, I consider the law of Christ insufficient and indict and condemn his law. Then it is clear that I do not fulfil his law, but constitute myself its judge. The judge, says Christ, is he who can save. But how shall I, who am not able to save, be a judge, and inflict punishments?

The whole passage speaks of human law-courts and repudiates them. The whole of the Epistle is full of that thought. In the Epistle of James (ii. 1–13) it is said: (1) ['My brethren, let the faith of our Lord Jesus Christ be held without respect of persons.] (2) For if there come unto your assembly a man with a gold ring, in fine clothing, and there come in also a poor man in vile clothing; (3) And ye have regard to him that weareth the fine clothing, and say unto him, Sit thou here in a good place; and say to the poor, Stand thou there, or sit here under my footstool: (4) Are ye not then partial in yourselves, and are become judges of evil thoughts? (5) Hearken, my beloved brethren, Hath not God chosen the poor of this world, rich in faith and heirs of the kingdom which he hath promised to them that love him? (6) But ye have despised the poor. Do not rich men oppress you and themselves drag you before the judgement seats? Do not they blaspheme that worthy name by the which ye are called? (8) If ye fulfil the royal law according to the scripture, Thou shalt love thy neighbour as thyself (Lev. xix. 18), ye do well. (9) But if ye have respect to persons, ye commit sin, and are convicted of the law as transgressors. (10) For whosoever shall keep the whole law, and yet offend in one point, he is guilty of all. (11) For he who said, Do not commit adultery, said also, Do not kill. Now if thou commit no adultery, yet if thou kill, thou art become a transgressor of the law (Deut. xxii. 22; Lev. xviii. 17–25). (12) So speak ye, and so do, as they that shall be judged by the law of liberty. (13) For he shall have judgement without mercy that hath showed no mercy; and mercy rejoiceth against judgement.' The last words have often been translated: 'Mercy is proclaimed in the courts,' and were so translated to imply that there may be Christian courts of law, but that they must be merciful.

James exhorts the brethren not to make distinctions between people. If you make distinctions, you διεκρίθητε, are divided in your minds, like the judges with evil intentions in the courts. You have judged the poor to be worse. But on the contrary it is the rich man who is worse. He both oppresses you and drags you before the courts. If you live according to the law of love of your neighbour, according to the law of charity (which, in distinction from the other law, James calls the 'law of the Lord'), you do well. But if you regard persons, and make distinctions between man and man, you are offenders against the law of mercy. And, having probably in mind the example of the woman taken in adultery whom they brought before Christ that she might be stoned, or the sin of adultery in general, James says that he who executes the adulterers will be guilty of murder and will infringe the external law. For the same external law forbids both adultery and murder. He says: '*Behave like men who are judged by the law of liberty*. For there is no mercy for him who has no mercy, and *therefore mercy destroys the courts.*'

How could that be said more clearly and

definitely? All discrimination between people is forbidden, every judgement that this man is good and that man evil, directly indicates that the human courts are undoubtedly bad, and proves that the court itself is criminal, as it executes people for offences, and therefore itself infringes God's law of charity.

I read the Epistles of St. Paul, who himself suffered from the courts, and in the very first chapter of the Epistle to the Romans I found a reprimand which he addresses to the Romans for their various sins and errors, and among the rest for their courts (v. 32): 'Who knowing the judgement of God, that they which commit such things are worthy of death, not only do the same, but have pleasure in them that do them.' Chap. ii. 1: '*Therefore thou art without excuse, O man, whosoever thou art, who judgest; for wherein thou judgest another, thou condemnest thyself; for thou that judgest dost practise the same things.* (2) And we are sure that the judgement of God is according to truth against them which commit such things. (3) And thinkest thou this, O man, that judgest them which do such things, and doest the same, that thou shalt escape the judgement of God? (4) Or despisest thou the riches of his goodness and forbearance and longsuffering; not knowing that the goodness of God leadeth thee to repentance?'

The Apostle Paul says that they, knowing the righteous law of God, themselves do wrong and teach others to do the same, and therefore the man who judges cannot be justified.

Such is the attitude to the law-courts which I found in the Epistles of the Apostles ; and in their lives as we all know man's courts appeared an evil and a temptation which had to be endured with firmness and with submission to the will of God.

By reconstructing in one's imagination the position of the first Christians among the heathen, one can easily understand that the Christians, who were persecuted in man's law-courts, could not prohibit law-courts. Only incidentally could they allude to that evil, condemning its foundations, as they did.

I consulted the Fathers of the Church of the first centuries, and saw that they always define the difference between their teaching and that of all others by the fact that they never put compulsion on any one in any way and never went to law with any one (see Athenagoras and Origen), did not execute, but only endured, the torments to which they were condemned by man's courts. All the martyrs, by their deeds, made the same profession. I saw that all the Christians, till the time of Constantine, regarded the law-courts not otherwise than as an evil which had to be patiently endured, and that the thought could never enter the head of any Christian of those days that Christians could take part in prosecutions. I saw that the words of Christ, '*Judge not that ye be not judged,*' were understood by his first disciples as I now understand them in their direct meaning : 'Do not prosecute in the courts, and do not participate in them.'

Everything indubitably confirmed my conviction that the words 'Judge not and condemn not' mean, do not judge in the courts; yet the explanation that it means, do not malign your neighbour, is so generally accepted, and so boldly and confidently do the courts flourish in all Christian countries, supported even by the Church, that I long doubted the correctness of my interpretation. If everybody could explain the matter in this way and organize Christian courts, then probably they had some ground for so doing, and there is something I do not understand, said I to myself. There must be grounds on which the words are understood to mean 'to malign,' and there must be grounds for instituting Christian courts.

And I examined the explanations of the ecclesiastical theologians. In all these interpretations, from the fifth century onward, I found that the words were taken in the sense of condemnation of one's neighbour, that is, maligning. And as the words are taken only to mean condemning one's neighbour in words, the question arises—how can one refrain from condemning? Evil must be condemned! Therefore all the interpretations revolve round the question, what one may and what one may not condemn. It is said (St. Chrysostom and Theophilus) that for the servants of the Church it must not be understood as a prohibition to judge, for the Apostles themselves judged. It is said that probably Christ referred to the Jews who condemned their neighbours for small sins and themselves committed great ones.

But nowhere is a word said of the institution of courts of law and of the relation in which the courts stand to this condemnation of judging. Does Christ forbid them, or allow them?

To that particular question no reply is given, as though it were quite obvious that as soon as a Christian occupied a judge's seat, he might not merely condemn his neighbour, but have him executed.

I consulted the Greek, the Catholic, and the Protestant writers, and the writers of the Tübingen school and of the historical school. All of them, even the most free-thinking, understood those words as a condemnation of evil-speaking. But why the words, contrary to the whole teaching of Christ, are understood so narrowly that the courts are not included in the prohibition of judging; why it is supposed that Christ, forbidding as an evil deed a condemnation of one's neighbour that involuntarily slips from one's tongue, does not consider as evil and does not forbid a similar condemnation uttered deliberately and associated with the infliction of violence on the person condemned is not explained, nor is there the slightest hint that it is possible for 'condemnation' to mean the judging which takes place in the law-court and from which millions of people suffer. More than that, in dealing with these words, 'Judge not and condemn not,' reference to that most cruel habit of legal condemnation is carefully avoided, and even fenced off. The theologian-interpreters remark that Christian law-courts must exist and do not conflict with the law of Christ.

Noticing this, I began to doubt the good faith of these interpretations, and referred to the translation of the words 'judge' and 'condemn'—the very matter with which I ought to have begun.

In the original these words are κρίνω and καταδικάζω. The incorrect translation of the word καταδικάζω in the Epistle of James, where it is translated by the words 'speak evil of,' confirmed my suspicion of the incorrectness of the translations.

I looked how the words κρίνω and καταδικάζω are translated in the Gospels in different languages, and I saw that the word which in the Vulgate is translated *condemnare*, is translated in a similar way in French, while in Slavonic it is 'condemn,' and Luther translates it *Verdammen*, to curse.

The contrast of these translations strengthened my doubts, and I asked myself: What does and what can the Greek word κρίνω, employed in both the Gospels, mean, and also the word καταδικάζω, used by Luke the Evangelist, who, in the opinion of the experts, wrote rather good Greek? How would a man translate those words who knew nothing of the Gospel teaching and the existing interpretations of it, but had before him merely that saying?

I consulted the general dictionary and found that the word κρίνω has many different meanings, and among them very commonly the meaning of sentencing in the law-court, even executing, but that it never has the meaning of evil-speaking. I consulted the New Testament dictionary and found that the word is often used in the New Testament in the sense of to sentence in court. It is sometimes used in the sense of differentiation, but never in the sense of evil-speaking. And so I see that the word κρίνω may be translated variously, but that a translation which makes it mean 'speak evil' is the most far-fetched and unexpected of all.

Then I inquired about the word καταδικάζω coupled to κρίνω, the word of many meanings —evidently on purpose to define the sense in which the writer was using that word. In the general dictionary I found that *the word never has any other meaning than to condemn in court to punishment or execution.* I looked in the New Testament dictionary, and found that the word is used in the Epistle of James v. 6, 'Ye have condemned and killed the just'; the word 'condemned' is this same word καταδικάζω, used in reference to Christ, who was condemned. *And in no other way is this word ever used in the whole of the New Testament, or in any Greek dialect.*

What does this all mean? What absurdity have I arrived at? I, and every one in our society, if we have ever considered the fate of mankind, have been horrified at the sufferings and the evil introduced into man's life by man's criminal law—an evil both for the judged and for those who judge: from the executions of

Genghiz Khan to the executions of the French Revolution and those of our day.

No one with a heart can have escaped an impression of horror and doubt in goodness at even hearing, not to say seeing, the execution[1] of men by other men: the floggings to death with rods,[2] guillotines, and scaffolds.

In the Gospels, each word of which we consider holy, it is directly and clearly said: You have had a criminal law—'An eye for an eye,'—but I give you a new law, 'Resist not him that is evil.' Obey this law, all of you: do not inflict evil for evil, but do good always and to all men, forgive all men.

Further, it is clearly said: '*Do not go to law.*' And, that doubt about the meaning of the words may be impossible, it is added, '*Do not condemn to punishment in the courts.*'

My heart says clearly and distinctly: do not execute. Science says, do not execute; the more you execute the more evil will there be; Reason says, do not execute, evil cannot be cut off by evil. The word of God, in which I believe, says the same. And I, reading the whole teaching, and reading the words: '*Judge not that ye be not judged, condemn not that ye be not condemned, forgive and ye shall be forgiven,*' admit that this is the word of God, say that it means that I must not go about talking scandal

[1] See *Confession*, p. 14.

[2] A method of punishment frequently practised in the army under Nicholas I. The sentence was so many thousand strokes, and the prisoner had to run the gauntlet between ranks of soldiers, the result often being death from collapse.

and maligning people, and continue to consider the law-court to be a Christian institution, and to consider myself both a judge[1] and a Christian. And I was horrified at the grossness of the deception in which I was involved.

1 Tolstoy was an Arbiter of the Peace for about a year in 1862, after the emancipation of the serfs, his duties being to adjust differences between the landed proprietors and the newly emancipated serfs.

CHAPTER IV

MISUNDERSTANDING OF CHRIST'S TEACHING

I NOW understand what Christ meant when he uttered the words: 'It was said to you: an eye for an eye, and a tooth for a tooth. But I say unto you: resist not him that is evil, but bear with him.' Christ said: It has been instilled into you, and you are accustomed to think that it is good and reasonable to resist evil by force and to tear out an eye for an eye, to institute criminal courts, police, an army, and to defend yourselves from foes; but I say, Do not use violence, do not take part in violence, do no harm to any one,[1] not even to those whom you call 'enemies.'

I now understand that Christ, in the position he takes up of non-resistance to the evil man, is speaking not only of what will result directly for each man from non-resistance to him that

[1] Tolstoy intended no sophistry, but there is unconscious sophistry in the suggestion that the purpose of the Criminal Courts is to injure certain people. He leaves unnoticed the benefit those Courts confer by making it plain what we must not do to one another. One of the greatest benefits conferred by law is that it supplies a degree of definiteness to human relations, which renders co-operation possible even among people whose opinions differ. It diminishes the amount of strife and friction that would otherwise exist.

is evil but, in contradiction to the principle under which mankind lived in his time, under the law of Moses and under the Roman law, and now lives under various legal codes, he sets up the principle of non-resistance to the evil man, which principle according to his teaching should be the basis of man's social life, and should free mankind from an evil they inflict on themselves. He says: You think that your laws correct evil—they only increase it. There is but one way to end evil—by rendering good for evil to all men without distinction. For thousands of years you have tried your principle; now try my contrary one.'

I have recently spoken to people of most divergent opinions about this law of Christ's—non-resistance to the evil man. It did occur, though rarely, that I met some who agreed with me. But, strange to say, two kinds of people never, even in principle, tolerated a straightforward understanding of the law, but always warmly defended the justice of resistance to the evil-doer. These are people who belong to the two extreme poles: patriotic Conservative Christians, who consider their Church to be the only true one, and Revolutionary Atheists. Neither these nor those wish to abandon the right to resist by violence what they consider evil. And the wisest and most learned of them are quite unwilling to see the simple and obvious truth that if one admits that one man may use violence to oppose what he considers evil, another may do the same to resist what he, in turn, considers evil.

A correspondence lately passed through my hands between an Orthodox Slavophil and a Christian-Revolutionary, which was instructive in this respect. The one advocated the violence of war on behalf of our oppressed brother-Slavs; the other, a revolutionary violence on behalf of our oppressed brethren, the Russian peasants. Both demanded violence, and both relied on the teaching of Christ.

People in general understand Christ's teaching in very various ways, but not in the direct, simple meaning which inevitably flows from his words.

We have arranged our whole life on the very foundations he denies. We do not wish to understand his teaching in its simple, direct meaning, and we assure ourselves and others either that we do not acknowledge his teaching or that it is unsuited to us. The so-called believers believe that Christ is God, the Second Person of the Trinity, who descended to earth to show us how to live, and they arrange most elaborate ceremonies necessary for the administration of the sacraments, for erecting churches, for sending out missionaries, for ordaining priests, for the direction of their flocks, for amending the creeds, but one little thing they forget—namely, to do what he told us to do. The unbelievers try to arrange their lives in all sorts of ways, only not according to the law of Christ, having decided in advance that that law will not do. But no one wishes to try doing as he bids us. Moreover, before even trying to do it, both the believers and the non-believers decide in advance that it is impossible.

He says simply and clearly: the law of resistance by violence to him that is evil, which you have made the basis of your lives, is false and unnatural; and he gives another basis—non-resistance—which in his opinion can alone deliver mankind from evil. He says: You think your laws of violence correct evil; they only increase it. You have tried for thousands of years to destroy evil by evil, but instead of destroying it you have increased it. Do what I do, and you will know whether it is true.

He not only says this but in his whole life, and by his death, he carries out his teaching of non-resistance to the evil man.

Believers hear all this, they read it in their churches, they say the words are divine and that he who spoke them was God, but they say: It is all very well, but it is impossible with our arrangement of life—it would upset the whole way of life to which we are accustomed and which we like. Therefore we believe all this only as being an ideal towards which humanity must strive—an ideal to be attained by prayer and by faith in the sacraments and the redemption, and in the resurrection from the dead. Others, the unbelievers, the free-thinking investigators of Christ's teaching—Strauss, Renan, and others—who follow the historic method, having thoroughly imbibed the Church's explanation that Christ's teaching has no direct reference to life but is a visionary doctrine consoling to feeble-minded people, say most seriously that Christ's teaching was only fit to be preached to the savage inhabitants of the wilds of Galilee; but that for us, with our culture, it appears merely a sweet dream—'du charmant docteur,' as Renan says. In their opinion Christ could not rise high enough to understand all the wisdom of our civilization and culture. Had he stood on the height of education on which these learned people stand he would not have talked such charming rubbish about the birds of the air, about turning one's cheek, and about not being troubled for to-morrow. These learned historians judge of Christianity by the Christianity they see in our society. The Christianity of our society and day regards our present life as true and sacred, with its organizations, prisons, solitary confinements, *Ciros*,[1] factories, newspapers, brothels and parliaments, and from the teaching of Christ it selects only what does not infringe that life.[2] But, as Christ's teaching is the negation of all that life, nothing is accepted of it except mere words. The learned historians see

[1] The translator finds himself in a difficulty when he has to devise an equivalent for the most improper type of Moscow restaurant.

[2] This passage is an excellent example of Tolstoy's power of sarcasm. The scorn he pours both on those who wish Christianity to be a mere epicurean consolation, and on those who, while criticizing Christianity, see it through the eyes of the others, is effective; but one should note how, urged by his moral and intellectual indignation against these people, he slips in a juxtaposition of brothels and parliaments, which is the first word of an argument later pushed to far-reaching and very questionable conclusions.

this, and, as they are under no necessity to hide it, as it is hidden by the pseudo-believers, this version of Christ's teaching deprived of all substance is subjected to profound criticism and very rightly repudiated. The deduction is clear that there never was anything in Christianity except dreamy ideals.

It would seem as though, before judging Christ's teaching, one should understand what it consists of, and to decide whether his teaching is reasonable or not one should first of all admit that he said what he said; but that is just what is not done either by the Church or by the free-thinking expositors. And we know very well why they do not do it.

We know very well that Christ's teaching always included and includes the denial of all those human illusions, those 'vain things,' empty idols, which we, by calling them Church, State, culture, science, art and civilization, think we can separate from the ranks of delusions. But it is just against them that Christ speaks, without excluding any 'empty idols.'

Not Christ only, but all the Hebrew prophets, John the Baptist, and all the world's true sages, have spoken of that same State, culture, and civilization, as an evil, ruinous to mankind.

Suppose a builder says to a man, 'Your house is bad, it must be entirely rebuilt,' and then gives details as to what beams should be cut, and how it should be done and where they should be stored. The man does not listen to the words about the house being bad and being rebuilt, but with a pretence of respect listens to the builder's further instructions and arrangements in the house. Obviously, all the advice given by the builder will appear inapplicable, and any disrespectful person will say plainly that his advice is stupid. This is what happens with regard to Christ's teaching.

Not finding a better comparison, I made use of the above. And then I remembered that Christ, when preaching his doctrine, used that same comparison. He said: I will destroy your temple and in three days will build a new one. For that he was crucified; and it is for that very thing that his teaching is now crucified.

The least one can demand of people who judge any doctrine is that they should judge of it in the sense in which the teacher himself understood it. And he understood his teaching not as a distant ideal for humanity, obedience to which is impossible, nor as a mystical poetic fantasy wherewith he captivated the simple-minded inhabitants of Galilee. He understood his teaching as a real thing, and a thing which would save mankind. And he did not dream on the cross, but died for his teaching, and many others are dying and will yet die. Of such a teaching one cannot say that it is a dream!

Every true doctrine is a dream to those in error. We have come to this, that there are many people (of whom I was one) who say that this teaching is visionary because it is not natural to man. It is not in accord, they say, with man's nature to turn the other cheek when one cheek is struck; it is not natural to give what is one's own to another; it is unnatural to work for others instead of for oneself. It is natural to man, they say, to defend his safety, and the safety of his family and his property: in other words, it is natural for man to struggle for his own existence. The learned jurists prove scientifically that man's most sacred duty is to defend his rights, that is—to struggle.

But it is sufficient to free oneself for a moment from the thought that the order which exists and has been arranged by men is the best and is sacrosanct, for the objection that Christ's teaching is not accordant with man's nature to turn against the objector. Who will deny that to murder or torture, I will not say a man, but to torture a dog or kill a hen or calf is contrary and distressing to man's nature? (I know people who live by tilling the land, and who have given up eating meat merely because they had themselves to kill their own animals.) Yet the whole structure of our lives is such that each man's personal advantage is only obtained by inflicting suffering on others, which is contrary to human nature. The whole order of our life, the whole complex mechanism of our institutions, designed for the infliction of violence, witness to the extent to which violence is contrary to human nature. Not a single judge would decide to strangle with a rope the man he condemns to death from the bench. Not a single magistrate would make up his mind himself to take a peasant from his weeping family and shut him up in prison. None of our generals or soldiers, were it not for discipline, oaths of allegiance, and declarations of war, would, I will not say kill hundreds of Turks and Germans, and destroy their villages, but would even decide to wound a single man. All this is only done thanks to a very complex state and social machinery the purpose of which is so to distribute the responsibility for the evil deeds that are done that no one should feel the unnaturalness of those deeds. Some men write the laws ; others apply them ; a third set drill men and habituate them to discipline, that is to say, to senseless and implicit obedience ; a fourth set—the people who are disciplined—commit all sorts of deeds of violence, even killing people, without knowing why or wherefore. But a man need only, even for a moment, free himself mentally from this net of worldly organization in which he is involved to understand what is really unnatural to him.

As soon as we cease to affirm that the customary evil we employ is an immutable divine truth it becomes obvious which of the two is natural and accordant to man : violence, or the law of Christ. Is it to know that my tranquillity and safety and that of my family, and all my pleasures, are purchased by the destitution, corruption, and misery of millions ; by hangings every year, by hundreds of thousands of suffering prisoners, by millions torn from their homes and stupefied by discipline—soldiers, policemen, and gendarmes who, armed with pistols against hungry people, safeguard my amusements; to purchase every sweet morsel I put into my mouth or into the mouths of my children, with the sufferings to humanity that are unavoidable for the procuring of these morsels? Or to know that, be the morsel what it may, it is mine only when no one else needs it and when no one has to suffer on account of it?[1]

It is only necessary once to understand that this is so, and that every pleasure of mine, every moment of tranquillity under our organization of life, is purchased by the deprivations and sufferings of thousands who are restrained by violence; one need but once understand that fact, to understand what is natural to man's entire nature—that is to say, not merely to his animal nature, but to his reasonable and animal nature. One need but understand the law of Christ in its full meaning, with all its consequences, in order to understand that Christ's teaching is not contrary to man's nature, but that it really consists in rejecting what is unnatural to man's nature, namely,

[1] This passage, which occurs here incidentally, forms the keynote of some of Tolstoy's later economic treatises. He says, and means, that no one has a right to keep anything any one else wishes to take. A man who wishes to get needful work efficiently done and requires accustomed tools for the purpose, will not find himself able to agree with the thesis. One consideration clashes with another, and in the experience of life we have to deal with comparative values more often than with absolute and abstract principles.

the visionary human doctrine of resistance to evil which now makes life unhappy.

Christ's doctrine of non-resistance to him that is evil is a dream! But that the life of men, in whose souls pity and love for one another is implanted, has been passed, and is now being passed, by some in organizing executions at the stake, knouts, and breakings on the wheel, lashes, the splitting of nostrils, tortures, handcuffs, penal servitude, gallows, shootings, solitary confinements, prisons for women and children, in arranging the slaughter of tens of thousands in wars, in organizing periodic revolutions and Pugachev [1] revolts, and the life of others in carrying out all these horrors, and the life of a third set in evading these sufferings and avenging themselves for them—is this not a dreadful dream?

One has but to understand Christ's teaching to understand that the world, not that which God gave for man's delight, but the world men have devised for their own destruction, is a dream, and a very wild and terrible dream—the raving of a maniac from which one need but awake in order never to return to that terrible nightmare.

God descended to earth; the Son of God—one of the Persons of the Trinity—became flesh and redeemed Adam's sin; this God, we were taught to think, must have said something secret, mystical, difficult to understand, and only to be understood by the aid of faith and

[1] Pugachev was the Cossack leader of a very serious peasant revolt in the time of Catherine II.

the sacraments; and suddenly it appears that the word of God is so simple, so clear, so reasonable. God says simply: Do not do evil to one another—and there will be no evil. Is it possible that God's revelation is so simple? Can it be that God only said that? It seems to us that we all knew that: it is so simple.

Elijah, the prophet, fleeing from men, hid in a cave, and it was revealed to him that God would appear to him at the entrance to the cave. A storm arose that broke the trees. Elijah thought this was God, and looked; but God was not there. Then came thunder; the thunder and lightning were terrible. Elijah went out to look whether God was not there; but God was not there either. Then there came an earthquake; fire arose from the earth, the rocks were rent. and the mountains quaked. Elijah looked, but God was still not there. Then a light, quiet breeze arose, bringing the refreshing scent of the fields. Elijah looked—and God was there! Such, too, are these simple words of God: 'Resist not him that is evil.'

They are very simple, but in them is expressed the law of God and man, one and eternal. The law is to such an extent eternal that if there is in history a movement forward towards the elimination of evil, it is thanks only to those men who have so understood Christ's teaching, and have endured evil and not resisted it by violence. Progress towards the welfare of mankind is made not by the persecutors but by the persecuted. As fire does not extinguish fire, so evil cannot extinguish evil. Only goodness, meeting evil and not infected by it, conquers evil. That this is so is in man's spiritual world an immutable law comparable to the law of Galileo, but even *more immutable*, clearer and more complete. People may deviate from it and hide it from others, but nevertheless the progress of humanity towards what is good can only be accomplished by that path. Every step forward is made solely in the path of non-resistance to evil. And in the face of all possible temptations and threats, the disciples of Christ may with more assurance than Galileo, declare: 'And yet, not by violence, but by goodness alone can you destroy evil.' If that advance is slow, this is thanks solely to the fact that the clearness, simplicity, reasonableness, inevitability and necessity of Christ's teaching is hidden from the majority of men in the most cunning and dangerous way, hidden under a different doctrine falsely called his.

CHAPTER V

JESUS AND THE MOSAIC LAW

EVERYTHING confirmed the fact that the meaning of Christ's teaching that had disclosed itself to me was true. But it was long before I could accustom myself to the strange idea that after Christ's law had been professed by millions of people for 1800 years, and after thousands of men had devoted their lives to the study of that law, it had now been my fate to rediscover it as a novelty. But, strange as it might be, such was the case; Christ's teaching of non-resistance to evil arose before me as a total novelty of which I had not had the slightest conception. And I asked myself: How could this come about? I must have had some false conception of the meaning of the teaching to cause me so to misunderstand it. And such a false conception really existed.

When approaching the Gospel doctrine, I was not in the position of one who, never having heard anything of Christ's teaching, suddenly hears it for the first time; but I already possessed a whole ready-made theory of how I ought to understand it. Christ did not appear to me as a prophet who was revealing a divine law; but as one who completed and explained a divine law already known to me and indubitable. I already possessed a complete, definite, and very complex teaching about God, the creation of the world and of man, and about His commandments given to man through Moses.

In the Gospels I encountered the words, 'Ye have heard that it was said, An eye for an eye, and a tooth for a tooth; but I say unto you, Resist not him that is evil.' The words, 'an eye for an eye, and a tooth for a tooth,' were the law of Moses. The words, 'Resist not evil, or him that is evil,' were the new law, which repealed the first.

Had I approached Christ's teaching without that theological theory imbibed with my mother's milk, I should have understood the simple meaning of his words. I should have understood that Christ denies the old law, and gives a new law of his own. But it had been instilled into me that Christ did not deny the law of Moses, but on the contrary confirmed it all to the last jot and tittle and completed it. Verses 17 and 18 of Matt. v., in which this is affirmed, had always, when I read the Gospels, struck me as obscure, and had evoked doubts. From what I then knew of the Old Testament, especially the last books of Moses, in which such minute, meaningless, and often cruel, rules are laid down, each preceded by the words: 'And the Lord said unto Moses,' it seemed to me strange that Christ could confirm the whole of that law, and incomprehensible why he did so. But I then left the question undecided: I accepted unverified the interpretation instilled into me from childhood, that both these laws are productions of the Holy Ghost, that they agree, and that Christ confirms the law of Moses, supplements it, and completes it.

How that completion was effected, how the contradictions are solved which strike one's eye in the Gospels themselves, both in these verses and in the words, 'But I say unto you,' I never clearly explained to myself. But now, having recognized the simple and direct meaning of Christ's teaching, I understood that these two laws are contradictory, and that there can be no talk of their agreement, or of completing the one by the other, but that we must accept one or the other, and that the common explanation of verses 17 and 18 in Matt. v. (which had formerly struck me by their obscurity) must be incorrect.

And on re-reading those verses (the ones which had always seemed to me so obscure) I was amazed by the simple and clear meaning in them, which suddenly revealed itself to me.

That meaning revealed itself to me not because I devised or transposed anything, but simply because I rejected the artificial interpretation which has been attached to that passage.

Christ says (Matt. v. 17–19): 'Think not that I came to destroy the law or the teaching of the prophets; I came not to destroy, but to fulfil. For verily I say unto you, Till heaven and earth pass away, one jot or one tittle shall in no wise pass away from the law till all things be accomplished.'

And verse 20 adds: 'Except your righteousness shall exceed the righteousness of the scribes and Pharisees, ye shall in no wise enter into the kingdom of heaven.'

Christ says: I have not come to destroy the eternal law, for the fulfilment of which your Scriptures and prophecies were written, but I have come to teach you to fulfil the eternal law; and I speak not of that law of yours which your scribes and Pharisees call the Law of God, but of that eternal law which is less changeable than the heavens and the earth.

I express the thought in fresh words merely to tear the meaning away from the customary false interpretation. Were it not for that false interpretation it would be impossible to express this thought better or more exactly than it is expressed in those verses.

The interpretation that Christ does not deny the law is based on the fact that to the word 'law' in this passage—thanks to the comparison made with the iota (jot) of the written law—is attributed the meaning of the 'written law' instead of the 'eternal law'—though this is quite gratuitous, and in contradiction to the meaning of the words. But Christ is not speaking of the written law. If he had spoken of the written law he would have used the customary expression, the law *and* the prophets, as he always does when speaking of the written law. But he employs a different expression: the law *or* the prophets. If he were speaking of the written law he would also in the next verse, which supplies a continuation of the thought, have used the words 'the law *and* the prophets,' and not the word 'the law' without addition, as actually stands in that verse. More than that, however, Christ uses the same expression in the Gospel of Luke in a connection which makes its meaning indubitable. In Luke xvi. 15, 16 Christ says to the Pharisees who assumed righteousness in the written law: 'Ye are they that justify yourselves in the sight of men; but God knoweth your hearts: for that which is exalted among men is an abomination in the sight of God. *The law and the prophets* were until John: from that time the Gospel of the Kingdom of God is preached, and every one entereth into it [by his own efforts].' [1]

And then in the following verse, 17, he says: 'But it is easier for heaven and earth to pass away, than for one tittle of the law to fail.' By the words, '*the law and the prophets* were until John,' Christ repeals the written law. By the words, 'It is easier for heaven and earth to pass away than for one tittle of the law to fail,' he confirms the eternal law. In the first words he says, 'the law and the prophets'—that is to say the written law; in the second he says simply '*the law*,' therefore the law eternal. Consequently it is clear that here the eternal law is contrasted with the written law,[2] and

[1] Where Tolstoy's translation diverges in meaning from our Revised and Authorized Versions, his words are enclosed in square brackets.

[2] More than that, as though to prevent any possible doubt as to which law he is speaking of, he immediately, in this connexion, gives an example—a very striking example—of a contradiction of the law of Moses with the eternal law of which no atom can fail; giving

that just the same contrast is made in the context in Matthew, where the eternal law is defined by the words, *the law or the prophets.*

The history of verses 17 and 18 in their variations is remarkable. In most of the texts there is only the word 'law' without the addition of 'prophets.' In these versions there can be no suggestion that it means the written law. In other copies, in Tischendorf's, and in the canonical version, there is the addition of 'prophets,' not with the conjunction 'and,' but with the conjunction 'or'—*the law or the prophets*—which also excludes the meaning of the written law and gives the meaning of the eternal law.

In some of the texts not accepted by the Church the addition of 'prophets' with the conjunction 'and,' and not 'or,' finds place—and in these same versions, when the word 'law' is repeated 'and the prophets' is also repeated. So that the meaning of the whole utterance in these versions is given as though Christ spoke only of the written law.

These variations supply the history of the interpretation of that passage. The only clear rendering of the passage is that Christ here, as in Luke, is speaking of the eternal law. But among the copyists of the Gospel manuscripts were some who wished to assert the obligatori-

the sharpest contradiction to the Mosaic law that occurs in the Gospels, he says (Luke xvi. 18): 'Every one that putteth away his wife and marrieth another, committeth adultery.' That is to say that, whereas in the written law divorce is allowed, in the eternal law it is a sin.—L. T.

ness of the written law of Moses, and these scribes added to the word 'law' the additional words 'and the prophets,' and changed the meaning.

Other Christians, who did not acknowledge the books of Moses, either excluded the addition or changed the word 'and,' *καί*, to the word 'or,' *ἤ*. And with this word 'or' the passage entered into the canonical version. But despite the clearness and certainty of the meaning of the text in that form in which it had entered the canon, the canonical interpreters continued to interpret it in the spirit that had prompted the alternative which had not been accepted in the text. The passage was submitted to innumerable explanations which were the further removed from its plain meaning in proportion as the interpreter agreed less with the real, direct, simple meaning of Christ's teaching; and most of the interpreters retain the apocryphal sense—the very one rejected by the text.

Fully to convince oneself that in these verses Christ is speaking only of the eternal law, it is worth while to examine the meaning of the word which served the pseudo-interpreters as an excuse. In Russian the word *zakon* (law), in Greek *νόμος*, and in Hebrew *torah*, all have two main meanings: one is the law itself (that which is right) without reference to its expression; the other conception is that of the written expression of what certain people consider to be the law. These two different meanings exist in all languages.

In Greek, in the Epistles of Paul, this distinction is sometimes marked by the use of the article. Without an article, Paul uses this word chiefly in the meaning of the 'written law,' but with the article in the meaning of the 'eternal law of God.'

Among the ancient Hebrews, in the prophets, as Isaiah, the word 'law,' *torah*, is always used in the meaning of the one eternal revelation and teaching of God independent of verbal expression. And this same word 'law,' *torah*. in Ezra for the first time, and in the latest period in Talmudic times, began to be used to mean the five written books of Moses, over which the general title of *Torah* was inscribed, as we use the word Bible, but with this difference, that we have a word to distinguish the conception of the Bible from that of the law of God, while in Hebrew one and the same word was used for both conceptions.

And therefore Christ, using the word 'law,' *torah*, employs it now to confirm it, when he uses it, in the meaning given it by Isaiah and the other prophets, of the law of God which is eternal, and now to reject it when he means by it the five books of the law. But for the sake of distinction when (rejecting it) he uses this word in the meaning of the written law, he always adds the words 'and the prophets,' or prefixes the word 'your' to the word 'law.' When he says, 'Whatsoever ye would that men should do unto you, even so do ye also unto them, for this is the law and the prophets.' he is speaking of the written law. He says that the whole of the written law can be compressed into this one expression of the eternal law, and by these words he annuls the written law.

When he says (Luke xvi. 16), 'The law and the prophets were until John,' he is speaking of the written law, and by these words denies its authority.

When he says (John vii. 19), '*Did not Moses give you the law*, and yet none of you doeth the law?' or (John viii. 17), 'In *your* law it is written,' or (John xv. 25), 'The word that is written in *their* law,' he is speaking of the written law: the law he denied, the law which condemned him to death. (John xix. 7) 'The Jews answered Pilate, We have a law, *and by that law he ought to die*.' Evidently that law of the Jews, on the basis of which they executed him, is not the law Christ taught. But when Christ says, 'I came not to destroy the law, but to teach you to fulfil it, for nothing can change in the law, but all must be fulfilled,' he is speaking not of the written law but of the divine eternal law, and is confirming it.

But let us suppose that all these are merely formal proofs; let us suppose that I have carefully selected contexts and variations and have carefully hidden everything opposed to my interpretation; let us suppose that the Church's interpretation is very clear and convincing, and that Christ really did not infringe the law of Moses but left it in full strength. Suppose that to be so. But then, what did Christ teach?

According to the Church's explanations he

taught that he, the Second Person of the Trinity, the Son of God the Father, came to the earth and by his death redeemed Adam's sin. But every one who has read the Gospels knows that in them Christ says nothing, or speaks very vaguely, about that. But assuming that we do not know how to read, and that the above assertions really are made there: at any rate, Christ's indication that he is the Second Person of the Trinity and redeems the sins of humanity occupies the smallest and most obscure portion of the Gospels. What, then, does all the rest of Christ's teaching consist of? It is impossible to deny, and Christians have always acknowledged, that the chief content of Christ's message is the teaching of life: how men should live with one another.

Having admitted that Christ taught a new way of life, one has to picture to oneself some definite kind of people among whom he taught.

Let us imagine to ourselves Russians, or Englishmen, or Chinese, or Indians, or even savages on an island, and we shall see that every people always has its rules of life, its law of life, and that therefore if a teacher teaches a new law of life he thereby destroys the former law: without destroying it he cannot teach. So it would be in England, in China, and among ourselves. The teacher will inevitably destroy our laws, which we consider precious and almost holy; but among us it might occur that the preacher, teaching us a new way of life, will only destroy our civil law, our State law, or our customs, but will not touch the laws we consider divine—though it is hard to imagine this. But among the Jewish people who then had only one code of law—entirely divine and embracing the whole of life to its minutest details—among such a people what could a preacher teach who declared in advance that the whole law of the people among whom he was preaching was valid? But let us say that this, too, is not a proof. Let those who interpret the words of Christ to mean that he confirmed the whole law of Moses explain this to themselves: Who it was that, throughout his active career, Christ exposed? Against whom did he revolt, calling them Pharisees, lawyers, and scribes? Who was it that rejected Christ's teaching? Whose High Priest had him crucified? If Christ acknowledged the law of Moses, where were those true adherents of that law who approved of him for doing so? Can it be that there was not one such?

The Pharisees, we are told, were a sect. The Jews do not say so! They say: The Pharisees were the faithful adherents of the law. But let us grant that they were a sect. The Sadducees were also a sect. Where, then, were the people who were not a sect, but true believers?

In the Gospel of John they all—Christ's enemies—are called simply the Jews. And they did not agree with Christ's teaching and were opposed to him simply because they were Jews. But in the Gospels not only the Pharisees and Sadducees are represented as Christ's enemies: among his enemies the lawyers are also mentioned, the very men who conserved the law of Moses; the Scribes, the very men who read the law; the Elders, the very ones who were always considered the representatives of national wisdom.

Christ said: 'I came not to call the righteous, but sinners to repentance'—to a change of life, *μετανοία*. Where and who, then, were these righteous? Was Nicodemus the only one? But even Nicodemus is represented to us as a kindly but erring man. We are so accustomed to the very strange explanation that the Pharisees and some wicked Jews crucified Christ, that the simple question never enters our heads: Where were those who were not Pharisees and not wicked, but real Jews who kept the law? One has only to put that question and it all becomes plain. Christ—whether he was God or man—brought his teaching into the world among a people who kept a law which regulated the whole of their lives and was called the law of God. What relation could Christ have to that law?

Every prophet—every teacher of a faith, revealing the law of God to men—inevitably encounters among men something people believe to be the law of God, and so he cannot avoid making use of the word law in a double sense; for it means what people falsely consider to be the law of God, 'your law,' and it also means the true, eternal law of God. But besides being unable to avoid a double use of that word, the preacher usually does not wish to avoid it, but intentionally unites the two meanings: indicating that the law, which, taken in its entirety is false, and which is professed by those whom he is addressing, does contain certain eternal truths. And every preacher will take those laws which are fundamentally true as the basis of his sermon. That is what Christ did among the Jews, among whom both laws were called by the one word *torah*. Christ, in reference to the law of Moses—and to a yet greater extent in reference to the prophets, especially Isaiah. whose words he constantly quoted—acknowledged that in the Hebrew law and prophets there are eternal and divine truths coincident with the eternal law, and these—such as the saying, 'Love God and thy neighbour'—he takes as the basis of his teaching. Christ often expresses this thought. (Luke x. 26) He says, 'What is written in the law ? how readest thou ?' In the law also there are eternal truths to be found, if you only know how to read it. And he points out more than once that the commandment in their law relating to the love of God and of one's neighbour is a commandment of the eternal law. In Matt. xiii. 52, Christ, after all the parables by which he explained to his Apostles the meaning of his teaching, finally, as referring to all that had preceded, said : 'Therefore every scribe [that is every literate person, who has learned the truth] is like unto a householder, which bringeth forth out of his treasure [indiscriminately, both together] things new and old.'

St. Irenaeus, and following him the whole Church, understood these words in that way;

but quite arbitrarily, and to the infringement of the meaning of the whole speech, attached to them also the implication that all that was old was sacred. The plain meaning is that he who seeks what is good takes not only what is new but what is old, and that it must not be rejected simply because it is old. By these words Christ says that he does not deny those things in the old law which are eternal. But when he is spoken to of the whole law or its forms, he says that one must not pour new wine into old bottles. Christ could not confirm the whole law, but neither could he reject the whole law and the prophets—that law in which is said, 'Love thy neighbour as thyself,' and those prophets whose words he often used to express his own thoughts. And lo and behold, instead of this simple, clear understanding of these words, which as they were spoken and in the way they confirm the whole of Christ's teaching are very simple, a misty explanation is substituted introducing a contradiction where none existed, and thereby destroying the meaning of the teaching and reducing it to verbiage, and practically re-establishing the teaching of Moses in all its savage cruelty.

According to all the Church's interpretations, especially since the fifth century, Christ did not infringe the written law, but confirmed it. But how did he confirm it? How can the law of Christ be united with the law of Moses? To that no reply is given. In the interpretations a play of words is made use of, and it is said that Christ fulfilled *the law of Moses* in that in him the prophecies were fulfilled, and that Christ, *through us*, by man's faith in him, fulfils the law. The only question essential to every believer (as to how to unite two contradictory laws governing human life) is left without even an attempt to meet it. And the contradiction between the verse in which it is said that Christ does not destroy the law and the verses which say, 'Ye have heard that it was said . . . but I say unto you . . . ,' and again between the whole spirit of the teaching of Moses and that of Christ, remains in full force.

Any one interested in this question should look at the Church's interpretations of this passage, from St. John Chrysostom to our times. Only by reading these long dissertations will he be clearly convinced that here no solution of the contradiction is offered, but that a contradiction is artificially introduced where none existed.

The impossible attempts to unite the ununiteable clearly indicated that this union is not the result of a mistake, but has a clear and definite aim—it was needed. And it is even obvious why it was needed.

This is what St. John Chrysostom says, replying to those who rejected the Mosaic law (*Homilies on the Gospel of Matthew*. Part 1. Homily xvi. Pusey's Library of the Fathers, pp. 236–7) :—

'In the next place, they criticize the Law in the Old Covenant, which bids us put out *an eye for an eye, and a tooth for a tooth*, and straightway they insult and say: "Why, how can he be good who speaks so?" What then do we say in answer to this? That it is the highest kind of philanthropy. For He made this law, not that we might strike out one another's eyes, but that fear of suffering by others might restrain us from doing any such thing to them. As therefore He threatened the Ninevites with overthrow, not that He might destroy them (for had that been His will, He ought to have been silent), but that He might by fear make them better, and so quiet His wrath: so also hath He appointed a punishment for those who wantonly assail the eyes of others, that if good principles dispose them not to refrain from such cruelty, fear may restrain them from injuring their neighbour's sight.

'And if this be cruelty, it is cruelty also for the murderer to be restrained, and the adulterer checked. But these are the sayings of senseless men, and of those that are mad to the extreme of madness. For I, so far from saying that this comes of cruelty, should say, that the contrary to this would be unlawful, according to men's reckoning. And whereas thou sayest, "Because He commanded to pluck out *an eye for an eye*, therefore He is cruel"; I say that if He had not given this commandment then He would have seemed, in the judgement of most men, to be that which thou sayest He is.'

St. John Chrysostom definitely accepts the law of a tooth for a tooth as divine, and *what opposes the taking of a tooth for a tooth* (that is to say, Christ's teaching of non-resistance) as unlawful (pp. 237–8). 'For let us suppose that this law has been done away,' says St. John Chrysostom, 'and that no one feared the punishment ensuing thereupon, but that licence had been given to all the wicked to follow their own dispositions in all security, to adulterers, and to murderers, to perjured persons and to parricides; would not all things have been turned upside down? Would not cities, market-places and houses, sea and land, and the whole world, have been filled with unnumbered pollutions and murders? Every one sees it. For when there are laws, and fear, and threats, our evil dispositions are hardly checked; were even this security taken away, what is there to prevent men's choosing vice? and what degree of mischief would not then come revelling upon the whole of human life? The rather, since cruelty lies not only in allowing the bad to do what they will, but in another thing too quite as much; to overlook, and leave uncared for, him who hath done no wrong, but who is without cause or reason suffering ill. For tell me: were any one to gather together wicked men from all quarters, and arm them with swords, and bid them go about the whole city, and massacre all that came in their way, could there be anything more like a wild beast than he? And what if some other should bind, and confine with the utmost strictness, those whom that man had armed, and should snatch from out those lawless hands them who were on the point of being butchered, could anything be greater humanity than this?'

St. John Chrysostom does not say by what standard one would be guided in determining who are evil. What if he were himself evil, and imprisoned the good?[1]

'Now then, I bid thee transfer these examples to the Law likewise, for He that commands to pluck out *an eye for an eye*, hath laid the fear as a kind of strong chain upon the souls of the bad, and so resembles him, who detains those assassins in prison; whereas he who appoints no punishment for them, doth all but arm them by such security, and acts the part of that other, who was putting the swords in their hands, and letting them loose over the whole city.'

If St. John Chrysostom acknowledged the law of Christ, he should explain who will pluck out the eyes and the teeth and cast others into prison. If he who forbids us to do so, that is to say if God Himself, plucked them out, there would be no contradiction, but it is men who have to do it; and these men the Son of God has commanded that it should not be done. God said, pluck out teeth, and His

[1] Here Tolstoy introduces an argument which occurs repeatedly in his works. He diverts the argument as to whether a man of good will, who desires to preserve the peace, is morally justified in forcibly restraining a murderer, by a reference to the difficulty of judging the facts of each case rightly. The moral issue is perplexed by the introduction of a simultaneous consideration of the fact that man is intellectually fallible.

Son said, do not pluck them out. One or the other has to be acknowledged; and St. John Chrysostom, and following him the Church in general, acknowledges the command of God the Father, that is to say of Moses, and rejects the command of the Son, that is of Christ, whose teaching he is supposed to profess. Christ rejects the law of Moses and gives his own. For a man believing in Christ there is no contradiction. Disregarding the law of Moses, he believes in the law of Christ and fulfils it. For one believing in the law of Moses there is also no contradiction. The Jews consider the words of Christ vain, and believe in the law of Moses. There is a contradiction only for those who wish to live by the law of Moses, but assure themselves and others that they believe the law of Christ—for those whom Christ calls hypocrites, the offspring of vipers.

Instead of acknowledging one of the two, the law of Moses or of Christ, they acknowledge both to be divinely true.

But when the question touches life itself, the law of Christ is simply denied and the law of Moses acknowledged.

In this false interpretation, if one examines its meaning, lies a terrible drama of the struggle of evil and darkness with goodness and light.

Among the Jewish people, confused by innumerable external rules laid on them by the Levites as divine laws and each stamped with the words 'The Lord said unto Moses,' Christ appeared. He found not only the relations of man to God, his sacrifices, holidays and fasts, but all the relations of man to man—the national, civil, and family relations—and all the details of private life—circumcisions, the washings of man's person, and of his cups and his dress—all defined to the last detail, and all acknowledged as the command of God, the law of God. What can, I will not say Christ—God, but a prophet or an ordinary teacher, teach to such a people without infringing this law, which defines everything down to the smallest details? Christ, like all the prophets, selects from among the things the people considered to be the law of God that which was really the law of God. He takes the foundations, and rejects all the rest, and unites his own revelation of the eternal law with these foundations. There is no need to destroy everything, but inevitably the law, which was considered equally obligatory in all its parts, is broken. Christ does this; and he is accused of breaking what was considered to be the law of God, and for this he is executed. But his teaching remains among his disciples and passes into another circle and into other centuries. But in this other circle, and these other centuries, the new teaching is again overgrown by similar accretions, interpretations, and explanations—again mean human inventions replace the divine revelation. Instead of 'And the Lord said unto Moses,' we are told[1]: 'It seemed good to the Holy Ghost and to us,' and again the letter hides the spirit. And, most surprising of all, the teaching of Christ becomes involved with all that

[1] By the Councils of the Church. The expression first occurs in Acts xv. 28.

torah (in the meaning of the written law) which he could not but reject. That *torah* is acknowledged to be the production of the revelation of his Spirit of truth, of the Holy Ghost, and he is himself caught in the meshes of his own revelation, and his whole teaching is reduced to nothing.

So that is why, after 1,800 years, so strange a thing befell me, as to have to discover the meaning of Christ's teaching as though it were something new.

I did not have to discover it, but I had to do what has been done and is being done by all who seek God and His law: to disentangle the eternal law of God from among all the other things people have called by that name.

CHAPTER VI

THE FIVE COMMANDMENTS

AND so, when I understood Christ's law to be the law of Christ, and not the law of Moses and Christ, and understood the statement of that law, which directly disavows the law of Moses, the Gospels as a whole, instead of their former obscurity, disunion, and contradictoriness, disclosed themselves as one indivisible whole, and amid them the essence of the whole teaching became clear, expressed in the five simple, clear commandments of Christ, accessible to everyone (Matt. v. 21–48), but about which I had till then known nothing. Throughout the Gospels Christ's commandments and their fulfilment are spoken of.

All the theologians speak of Christ's commandments, but what those commandments were I formerly did not know. It seemed to me that the commands of Christ consisted in this : to love God, and my neighbour as myself. But I did not see that this could not be Christ's commandment, because it is a commandment of 'them of old time' (Deut. and Lev.). The words (Matt. v. 19) 'Whosoever shall break one of these least *commandments*, and shall teach men so, shall be called least in the kingdom of heaven,' I attributed to the laws of Moses. And the fact that the new commandments of Christ are clearly and definitely expressed in verses 21–48 of Matt. v. never entered my head. I did not see that where Christ says, 'It was said to you; but I say unto you,' new and definite commands of Christ are given, namely, according to the number of references to the ancient law (and counting two references to adultery as one). five new, clear, and definite commandments of Christ.

About the Beatitudes and their number I had heard, and had met with enumerations and explanations in Scripture lessons, but of Christ's commands I had never heard anything. To my surprise I had to discover them.

This is how I did so. In Matt. v. 21–26, it is said: 'Ye have heard that it was said by them of old time, Thou shalt not kill [Exod. xx. 13], and whosoever shall kill shall be in danger of the judgement. But I say unto you, that whosoever is angry with his brother without a cause shall be in danger of the judgement: and whosoever shall say to his brother, Raca, shall be in danger of the council; and whosoever shall say, Thou fool, shall be in danger of hell fire. If therefore thou art offering thy gift at the altar, and there rememberest that thy brother hath aught against thee; leave there thy gift before the altar and go thy way, first be reconciled to thy brother, and then come and offer thy gift. Agree with thine adversary quickly, whiles thou art in the way with him; lest haply the adversary deliver thee to the judge and the judge deliver thee to the officer, and thou be cast into prison. Verily I say unto thee, Thou shalt by no means come out thence, till thou hast paid the uttermost farthing.'

When I understood the commandment of non-resistance to him that is evil it seemed to me that these verses about anger ought to have as clear a meaning, and one as applicable to life as the commandment about resisting him that is evil. The meaning I had formerly attributed to those words was that every one should always avoid anger against others and should never use words of abuse, but should live at peace with all men without exception; but there were words in the text which excluded that meaning. It was said: Do not be angry 'without a cause,' so that no unconditional injunction to be peaceable is found in the words. Those words 'without a cause' perplexed me: and to solve my doubts I consulted the interpretations of the theologians, and to my amazement I found that the interpretations of the Fathers of the Church are chiefly directed to explaining when anger is excusable and when it is not excusable. All the Church interpretations lay particular stress on the meaning of the words *without a cause*, and explain the passage in the sense that one must not insult innocent people, and one must not employ words of abuse, but that anger is not always unjustifiable; in confirmation of which view they quote the anger of saints and Apostles.

I could not but admit that, though it contradicts the whole sense of the Gospels, this explanation that anger, as they say, is not forbidden by the word of God, follows from and finds support in the words *without a cause*—which occur in verse 22. These words change the meaning of the whole utterance.

Be not angry *without a cause.* Christ bids us forgive all, forgive endlessly. He himself forgives, and forbids Peter to be angry with Malchus when Peter, not without cause it would seem, defended his Master who was being led to crucifixion. And this same Christ, for the instruction of all men, says: Do not be angry *without a cause*, and thereby sanctions anger with a cause—anger which is deserved. Christ preaches peace to all the plain folk, and suddenly, as though explaining that this does not refer to all cases, but that there are cases when one may be angry with one's brother, he inserts the words *without a cause.* In the interpretations it is explained that there is timely anger. But who, asked I, is to be judge of when anger is timely? I have never seen angry people who considered their anger untimely. They all consider their anger just and useful. Those words destroy the whole meaning of the verse. But the words stood in Holy Writ, and I could not cancel them. Yet those words were as though to the saying, *Love thy neighbour* were added, *Love thy good neighbour*, or, *Love the neighbour whom thou approvest of.*

The whole meaning of the passage was destroyed for me by the words *without a cause.* The verses that said that before praying one must be reconciled to those who are angry with one, which without the words 'without a cause' would have had a plain and obligatory meaning, also acquired this conditional meaning.

It seemed to me that Christ should have forbidden all anger, all ill-will, and, for its elimination, bidden every one, before he brings his sacrifice—that is to say, before entering into communion with God—to remember whether there is not some one who is angry with him. And if there is any one who rightfully or wrongfully is angry with you, you must first go and be reconciled, and only then bring your offering or your prayer. So it seemed to me; but according to the commentaries the passage must be understood conditionally.

In all the commentaries it is explained that one must try to be at peace with all, but if that is impossible, owing to the depravity of those who are at strife with you, you must be at peace in your soul, in your thoughts, and then the enmity of the others against you need not prevent your praying. Besides this, the words that declare that whoso says 'Raca' and 'Thou fool' is terribly guilty always seemed to me strange and obscure. If one is forbidden to scold, why are such weak, almost unabusive words selected as examples? And also why is so terrible a threat directed against him who lets fall such a weak word of abuse as 'Raca,' which means 'a nobody'? This too is obscure.

I felt that there was a misunderstanding similar to that which occurred with reference to the words, 'judge not.' I felt that, as in that interpretation so in this, what is simple, important, definite, and practicable is all changed into what is obscure and indefinite. I felt that Christ could not understand the words, 'Go, be reconciled to thine adversary,' in the way they are explained to us, as meaning, 'Be reconciled in your thoughts.' What does being reconciled in one's thoughts mean? It seemed to me that Christ was demanding what he elsewhere expressed in the words of the prophets: 'I will have mercy and not sacrifice'—that is to say, love to man. And therefore, if you wish to please God, before praying at morning and evening, at matins and evensong, remember whether any one is angry with you and go and arrange matters so that he may not be angry with you, and, after that, pray if you please. And then we are told that this is only 'in thought.' I felt that the whole interpretation which destroyed for me the direct and clear meaning of the passage was based on the words 'without a cause.' If they were struck out, the meaning would be clear; but against my interpretation all the expositors were ranged, as well as the canonical Gospel, with the words, 'without a cause.' If I yield on this point I may as well yield on others at my fancy; and other people may do the same. The whole matter lay in those words. If they were not there, all would be clear. And I tried to find some philological explanation of the words which would not infringe the whole meaning. I looked up the Greek word interpreted 'without a cause' in the dictionaries; and I saw that this word, in Greek εἰκῆ, means 'without purpose,' 'inconsiderately.' I tried to give it a meaning which would not infringe the sense of the passage, but evidently the addition of that word has the meaning which is given it. I consulted other dictionaries, but the meaning given of the word was the same. I consulted the context, and found that the word is employed only once in the Gospel, namely, in this passage. In the Epistles it is employed several times. In the First Epistle to the Corinthians, xv. 2, it is used just in this sense. Therefore it is impossible to explain it otherwise, and one has to admit that Christ said: *Do not be angry unnecessarily!* I must confess that for me to admit that Christ could in this passage use such obscure words, which can be understood so that nothing remains of their meaning, was tantamount to rejecting the whole Gospel. There remained one last hope: Is the word found in all the manuscripts? I looked up the manuscripts. I referred to Greisbach, who shows all the variations—that is to say, he shows in what manuscripts and by what Fathers of the Church an expression is used. I looked, and was at once thrown into an ecstasy by observing that to this passage there are remarks—there are variations. I went on and found that the variations all refer to the word εἰκῆ, 'without a cause.' Most of the manuscripts of the Gospel and the quotations of the passage in the Fathers of the Church do not contain the word at all! Therefore most of them understood the matter as I do. I then referred to Tischendorf—to the oldest text—and the word was not there at all! I looked at Luther's translations, where I might have got at the matter most quickly, and the word was not there either.

The very word which infringes the whole meaning of Christ's teaching was added to the Gospels in the fifth century, and is not to be found in the best manuscripts.

Someone inserted the word, and there were others who approved of it and wrote commentaries upon it.

Christ could not, and did not, utter that dreadful word; and the first, simple, direct meaning of the whole passage, which occurred to me and occurs to every one, is the true meaning.

But, more than this, I had only to understand that Christ's words always forbid all anger against any one whatever, for the injunction not to say to any one, 'Raca,' or 'Thou fool,' which had formerly perplexed me, to receive another meaning than that Christ forbids the use of abusive words. The strange, untranslated Hebrew word, *Raca*, supplied me with the clue. *Raca* means trampled on, destroyed, non-existing; and the word *rak*, a very usual word, has the sense of exclusion, *only not*. *Raca* means a man who should not be accounted a man. In the plural the word *rekim* is used in the Book of Judges (ix. 4) where it means 'lost persons.' And that is the word Christ bids us not to use of any man. As he bids us not use another word, *fool*, so also he bids us not use *raca*, which professes to free us from our human obligations to our neighbour. We get angry and do evil to men, and to justify ourselves we say that he with whom we are angry is a lost or insane man. And just those two words Christ bids us not to use of men or to men. Christ bids us not be angry with any one, and not justify our anger by declaring a man to be lost or insane.

And so, instead of a cloudy, indefinite expression admitting of arbitrary interpretation, in Matt. v. 21–28, I found Christ's first clear and definite commandment: Live at peace with all men, and never consider your anger against any man justified. Do not consider any one nor call any one lost or a fool (v. 22). And not only must you not consider your anger against another justifiable, but you must not consider another's anger against yourself causeless; and therefore if any one is angry with you, though he be in the wrong, yet before saying your prayers go and remove his hostile feeling (v. 23, 24). Try in advance to destroy any enmity between yourself and others that it may not flame up and destroy you (v. 25, 26).

After the first commandment, with equal clearness the second revealed itself to me. It also begins with a reference to the ancient law. In Matt. v. 27–30 it is said: 'You have heard that it was said by them of old time, Thou shalt not commit adultery [Ex. xx. 14]. But I say unto you, that whosoever looketh on a woman to lust after her hath committed adultery with her already in his heart. And if thy right eye causeth thee to stumble, pluck it out, and cast it from thee[1]; for it is profitable for thee that one of thy members should perish, and not thy whole body be cast into hell. But if thy right hand causeth thee to stumble, cut it off and cast it from thee: for it is profitable for thee that one of thy members should perish, and not thy whole body go into hell.'

Matt. v. 31–2: 'It was said also, Whosoever shall put away his wife, let him give her a writing of divorcement [Deut. xxiv. 1]. But I say unto you, every one that putteth away his wife [besides the sin of adultery, gives her cause to commit adultery], and whosoever shall marry her that is put away committeth adultery.'[2]

The meaning of these words appeared to me to be this: a man should not admit even the thought that he can have connexion with any woman but the one with whom he first has sexual relations,[3] and must never change

[1] Tolstoy sometimes carries his adherence to the letter of Christ's saying to an extreme, but in the case of this text it will be noticed that he does not agree with those Russian sectarians who rely on the surgical operation of castration as a desirable corrective of sexual desire.

[2] It will be noticed that Tolstoy's translation of this passage, in the words inserted in square brackets, differs from our Authorized or Revised Versions and helps to make sense of the passage.

[3] Note that this view was alluded to in *Anna Karenina* (vol. i, chap. xxiv, p. 98, World's Classics edition), where the incident was borrowed from the actual life of Tolstoy's brother, Dmitry, who took a woman he had found in a brothel to live with him, and regarded her as a wife to whom he was bound for life.

her for another, as was permitted by the Mosaic law.

As in the First Commandment against anger we are advised to extinguish anger at its commencement, advice that is illustrated by the comparison with a man brought before a court of justice, so here Christ says that adultery arises from the fact that women and men regard each other as objects of desire. That this may not be so, it is necessary to remove all that might arouse lust. One must avoid all that evokes lust, and, having once united oneself with a woman, must under no circumstances abandon her, for the abandonment of wives causes depravity. The abandoned wives tempt other men, and spread depravity abroad in the world.

The wisdom of this commandment impressed me. It removes all the evil that flows from sexual relations. Men and women, knowing indulgence in sexual relations to lead to strife, should avoid all that evokes desire; and, knowing it to be the law of man's nature to live in couples, should unite with one another in couples and never under any circumstances infringe these alliances; so that the whole evil of strife caused by sexual relations is removed by the fact that there are no solitary men or women left deprived of married life.[1]

[1] Tolstoy delighted in absolute laws, and was eager to attribute perfection and finality to those he formulated. But this law, of which he fully approved when he wrote this book in 1884, no longer satisfied him when in 1889 he wrote the *Kreutzer Sonata,* and in the *Afterword* thereto declared that marriage for a

But the words which had always surprised me when reading the Sermon on the Mount, *except for the sin of adultery*, understood in the sense that a man may divorce his wife if she has committed adultery, now struck me yet more forcibly.

In addition to the fact that there is something undignified in the way of expressing this thought, putting this strange exception to the general rule (which is introduced like a note to a paragraph of a code of laws) beside profoundly important truths, the exception itself contradicts the fundamental thought.

I turned to the commentators, and they all (St. John Chrysostom and the others), and even the learned theological critics such as Reuss, admitted that these words meant that Christ sanctions divorce in case of a wife's adultery, and that in Matt. xix. in Christ's remarks forbidding divorce, the words 'except for fornication' mean the same thing. I read and re-read chapter v. 32, and it seemed to me that it could not mean an approval of divorce. To verify this I referred to the contexts, and found in the Gospels of Matt. xix., Mark x., and Luke xvi. and in the First Epistle of Paul to the Corinthians, an explanation of the teaching

Christian must always be 'a fall, a sin.' The explanation of his change of view lay in the fact that his wife disagreed with his wish to renounce his property, and he found that his physical affection for her made it hard for him to adhere to his principles. Marriage was therefore an obstacle to right life, and as such it seemed to him, should be shunned by a Christian.

of marriage inviolability without any exceptions.[1]

In Luke xvi. 18 is said: 'Every one that putteth away his wife, and marrieth another, committeth adultery: and he that marrieth one that is put away from a husband committeth adultery.'

In Mark x. 5–12 it is also said, without any exception: 'For your hardness of heart Moses wrote this commandment. But from the beginning of the creation, male and female made he them. For this cause shall a man leave his father and mother, and cleave unto his wife; and the twain shall become one flesh: so that they are no more twain, but one flesh. What therefore God hath joined together let no man put asunder. And in the house his disciples asked him again of this matter. And he said unto them, Whosoever shall put away his wife, and marry another, committeth adultery against her. And if she herself shall put away her husband, and be married to another, she committeth adultery.' The same is repeated in Matt. xix. 4–9.

In the First Epistle of Paul to the Corinthians, vii. 1–12, the idea of forestalling depravity by each husband and wife, when once they have united, not abandoning one another, but

[1] At a time when Parliament has to deal with the marriage laws, it is in place to remember that Tolstoy wrote solely of what he considered to be Christian duty, entirely apart from legal enactment or Church ceremony of any kind. He disapproved of legal interference with the right of man or woman to form or rescind unions with one another.

satisfying one another in sexual relations, is developed. It is also plainly said that neither of them must on any account desert the other to have relations with some one else.

By Mark, Luke, and Paul's Epistle divorce is not sanctioned. The sense of the explanation that a husband and a wife are one flesh, united by God—an explanation repeated in two of the Gospels—does not sanction divorce. By Christ's whole teaching which bids us forgive all, and makes no exception in the case of an unfaithful wife, divorce is not sanctioned. The meaning of the whole passage, which explains that the dismissal of a wife is the cause of depravity, gives it no sanction.

On what is the interpretation based which sanctions divorce from an adulterous wife? Only on the words in Matt. v. 32, which seemed to me so strange. They are interpreted by every one to mean that Christ sanctions divorce if a wife commits adultery, and these same words are repeated in many of the copies of the Gospels and by many Fathers of the Church instead of the words *except for fornication* (Matt. xix. 5-9).

Again I began to consider these words, but it was long before I could understand them. I saw that there must be a mistake in translation and interpretation, but where the mistake lay I was long unable to discover. The mistake was evident. Contrasting his commandment with the law of Moses, under which any man, as is there said, who hates his wife, can dismiss her and give her a writing of divorcement, Christ says: '*But I say unto you, that every one that putteth away his wife, saving for the cause of fornication* [or, *besides the cause of fornication*], *causeth her to commit adultery.*' These words present no antithesis to the Mosaic law, nor even any decision as to whether one may, or may not, divorce. It is only said that putting away a wife gives her occasions to commit adultery.

And then suddenly an exception is made in the case of a wife guilty of adultery. This exception concerning a wife guilty of adultery, when the matter in hand related to the husband, would in any case be strange and unexpected, and occurring where it does it is simply stupid, for it destroys even such doubtful meaning as the verse otherwise had. It is said that putting away a wife occasions her to commit adultery, and it then allows you to put away a wife guilty of adultery; as though a wife guilty of adultery will then no longer commit adultery.

But, more than that, when I examined this passage more carefully I noticed that it does not even make sense grammatically. It is said that *every one that putteth away his wife, saving for the cause of fornication, causeth her to commit adultery*, and the sentence ends! It refers to a man, and says that if he puts away his wife he gives her occasion to commit adultery. Why is it said, *saving for the cause of the wife's adultery*? If it were said that a man, divorcing his wife for any cause except her commission of adultery, commits adultery, then the sentence would be correct. As it is, to the grammatical subject, *every one that putteth away*, there is no predicate except *causeth*. How can that predicate relate to the words *saving for the cause of fornication*? It is impossible to 'cause, saving for the wife's fornication'! Even if with the words 'saving for the cause of fornication' were included the words 'the wife's,' or 'her' (which is not done), even then those words could not relate to the predicate 'causeth.' These words, in the accepted interpretation, are related to the predicate, *putteth away*, but *putteth away* is not the chief predicate: the chief predicate is *causeth*. Why is 'except for the cause of fornication' wanted? With adultery or without it a husband who puts away his wife equally *causeth*. The expression reads as though some one were to say: 'Whoso depriveth his son of food, except for [or besides] the sin of cruelty, causeth him to be cruel.' Such an expression evidently cannot imply that the father may deprive his son of food if the son is cruel. If it has any meaning it can only be that the father who deprives his son of food, besides the sin of being cruel himself, causes the son too to be cruel. So the Gospel expression would have a meaning if, instead of the words *the sin of fornication*, it read 'the sin of voluptuousness, dissoluteness,[1] or any-

[1] Tolstoy's indictment of the received translation of various passages in the Gospels has had considerable circulation, and by many readers is accepted as authoritative. As yet, so far as the present translator knows, no prominent Churchman has either admitted any of the alleged errors, or produced any

thing of that kind, expressing not an action but a quality.

And I asked myself: Is it not simply said that he who puts away his wife, besides being himself guilty of dissoluteness (since people divorce one wife in order to take another), causes his wife also to commit adultery? If the word 'fornication' in the text is expressed by a word that may also mean dissoluteness, the meaning is clear.

What has so often happened in such cases occurred again this time. The text confirmed my supposition, so that no further doubt about it was possible.

The first things that caught my eye on looking at the Greek text was that the word πορνεία is translated by the same word 'fornication' that is used to translate the word

reasoned rejoinder to Tolstoy's assertions. A pronouncement on these matters from some recognized and impartial authority of admitted competence would therefore be valuable as a help towards clearing up questions which are as important as they are doubtful.

The only contribution the present translator can make to the matter is to record the fact that, some fifteen years after *What I Believe* was written, he asked Tolstoy whether he still held to the interpretations he had advanced when dealing with the Gospels. Tolstoy replied that he had ceased to attach special importance to precise words attributed to Jesus, and admitted that, in his anxiety to counteract the bias he detected in the 'Orthodox' translation, he had sometimes overstrained the sense too much in a contrary direction, as one engaged on demagnetizing a watch may sometimes expose it to too strong an opposite influence; but he thought his Greek reliable.

μοιχᾶσθαι, which is quite a different word. But perhaps these words are synonymous, or are used in the Gospels alternatively? I looked up all the dictionaries, both the general dictionary and the Gospel dictionary, and I saw that the word πορνεία, which corresponds to the Hebrew *zono*, and to the Latin *fornicatio*, the German *Hurerei*, French *libertinage*, and the English 'incontinence,' has a most definite meaning, and never, in any dictionary, has meant or can mean the act of fornication, *adultère*, *Ehebruch*, as it is translated. It means a sinful condition or quality, and never an action, and should not be translated by 'fornication.' Moreover, I see that the word 'adultery,' and 'to commit adultery,' is everywhere in the Gospels, and even in these verses, represented by the word μοιχεύω. And I only had to correct this evidently intentional error in translation for the meaning given by the commentators on this passage and on the passage in chap. xix. to become quite impossible, and for it to become indubitable that πορνεία relates to the husband.

The translation any one knowing Greek would make is this: παρεκτός—besides, λόγου—the *sin*, πορνείας—of dissoluteness, ποιεῖ—he causes, αὐτήν—her, μοιχᾶσθαι—to commit adultery; and the result is, word for word: 'he who puts away his wife, besides the sin of dissoluteness, causes her to commit adultery.'

The same sense is found in ch. xix. One need but correct the erroneous translation of the word πορνεία, and replace the word 'fornication' by the word 'dissoluteness,' for it to become plain that the words: εἰ μὴ ἐπὶ πορνεία cannot refer to the wife. And as the words παρεκτὸς λόγου πορνείας can only mean 'besides the husband's sin of dissoluteness,' so the words εἰ μὴ ἐπὶ πορνεία in ch. xix. can only refer to the husband's dissoluteness. The words are—εἰ μὴ ἐπὶ πορνεία, word for word: 'if not from dissoluteness.' And this meaning appears: that Christ, replying in this passage to the belief of the Pharisees, who supposed that if a man left his wife, not to live dissolutely but in order to marry another woman, he was not committing adultery—Christ says that the leaving of one's wife, i.e. the cessation of marital relations with her, even if not occasioned by dissoluteness, but done for the sake of marriage-union with another, is also adultery. And a plain meaning results which accords with the whole teaching, with the context, with the grammar, and with logic.

And this clear and simple meaning, flowing from the words themselves and from the whole teaching, I had to discover with the greatest difficulty. Indeed, read the verse in German or in French, where it is plainly said *pour cause d'infidélité*, and, *à moins que cela ne soit pour cause d'infidélité*, and can you guess that it means something quite different? The word παρεκτός, which in all the dictionaries means *excepté*, *ausgenommen*, *besides*, is translated by a whole *sentence*—*à moins que cela ne soit*; the word πορνείας is translated *infidélité*,

Ehebruch, fornication. And on this intentional perversion of the text rests an interpretation which infringes the moral, religious, grammatical, and logical sense of Christ's words.

Again I was confirmed in the terrible but joyful truth that the meaning of Christ's teaching is plain and simple and its statements are important, but that interpretations of it, based on a wish to justify existing evil, have so obscured it that it has to be rediscovered with difficulty. It became plain to me that if the Gospels had been discovered half burnt or obliterated it would have been easier to recover their meaning than it is now, when dishonest interpretations have been applied to them with the direct purpose of perverting and hiding the meaning of the teaching. In this case it was still plainer than in the former that some private aim of justifying the divorce of some Ivan the Terrible had been the reason for obscuring the whole doctrine of marriage.

As soon as one rejects the commentaries, in place of what was obscure and indefinite the definite and clear second commandment of Christ reveals itself.

Do not make the desire for sexual relations into an amusement; let every man, if he is not a eunuch—that is, if he needs sexual relations—have a wife, and each wife a husband, and let the husband have only *one* wife and the wife only *one* husband, and under no pretext infringe the sexual union of one with the other.

Immediately after the second commandment

comes again a reference to the ancient law, and the third commandment is set forth (Matt. v. 33–7): 'Again, ye have heard that it hath been said by them of old time, Thou shalt not forswear thyself, but shalt perform unto the Lord thine oaths [Lev. xix. 12; Deut. xxiii. 21]: but I say unto you, Swear not at all; neither by heaven, for it is God's throne: nor by the earth; for it is his footstool: neither by Jerusalem; for it is the city of the great King. Neither shalt thou swear by thy head, because thou canst not make one hair white or black. But your speech shall be, Yea, yea; Nay, nay: for whatsoever is more than these is of the evil one.'

This passage, when I had read it before, had always perplexed me. It did so, not (as did the passage about divorce) by its obscurity, nor by contradicting other passages (as did the sanction of anger with a cause), nor by the difficulty of fulfilling it (as with the passage about offering the other cheek); on the contrary, it perplexed me by its clearness, simplicity, and ease. Side by side with rules, the profundity and importance of which terrified and touched me, one suddenly found such an unnecessary, empty, easy rule, which was of no consequence to me or to others. As it was, I swore neither by Jerusalem, nor by God, nor by anything else, and it cost me no effort to abstain: besides which, it seemed to me that whether I swore or not could have no importance to any one. And wishing to find an explanation of this rule, which perplexed me by its ease, I turned to the interpreters; and this time the interpreters really helped me.

They all see in these words a confirmation of the third commandment of Moses—not to swear by the name of God. They explain these words to mean that Christ, like Moses, forbids us to pronounce God's name in vain. But besides this, the interpreters also explain that this law of Christ's—not to swear—is not always obligatory and does not relate at all to an oath of loyalty which each citizen gives to those who hold authority[1]; and texts are selected from Holy Writ, not to confirm the direct meaning of Christ's injunction, but to prove that it may and should be disobeyed.

It is said that Christ himself confirmed an oath in a court of law when in reply to the High Priest's words, 'I adjure thee by the living God,' he replied, 'Thou hast said.' It is said that the apostle Paul called God to witness the truth of his words, which is evidently the same as an oath; it is said that oaths were enjoined by the law of Moses, and that God did not abolish these oaths; it is said that it is only vain, pharisaical, hypocritical oaths that are abolished.

And on understanding the meaning and aim

[1] A reason Tolstoy ignores for forbidding oaths is, that as the belief (common in primitive times) that men can stake their lives or possessions on the veracity of their assertions and that the deity will enforce the penalties should the oath be a false one, fades away, the use of such oaths becomes incompatible with intellectual integrity, and therefore fails to accomplish its object and even conflicts with it.

of these explanations, I understood that Christ's injunction concerning oaths is not at all so insignificant, easy, and unimportant as it had seemed to me when, among the oaths prohibited by Christ, I had not included oaths demanded by the State.

And I asked myself: Is it not said here that the oath is also forbidden for which the Church commentators are so anxious to make an exception? Is not the oath here forbidden, that very oath without which the separation of men into nations is impossible, and without which a military class is impossible? Soldiers are those who do all the violence, and they call themselves 'the sworn.'[1] Were I to ask the Grenadier how he solves the contradiction between the Gospels and the military code he would tell me that he has been sworn in: that is to say, has taken an oath on the Gospels. Such replies have always been given me by military men. So necessary is an oath for the organization of the terrible evil which is produced by violence and war, that in France, where Christianity is officially rejected, the oath is nevertheless retained. Indeed if Christ had not said 'Swear not at all,' he ought to have said it. He came to destroy evil, and, had he not abolished the oath, this enormous evil would have remained in the world. Perhaps it will be said that in the time of Christ that evil was not noticeable. But this is untrue:

[1] In Russian literally 'the oath.' The equivalent English expressions, 'volunteers' or 'conscripts,' do not carry the same significance, though in England they also take an oath of allegiance.

Epictetus and Seneca spoke about not taking an oath to any one ; in the laws of Manu that rule is found. Why should I say that Christ did not see this evil ? And especially when he said this so directly, clearly, and even minutely.

He said : *Swear not at all*. That expression is as simple, clear, and indubitable as the words 'Judge not and condemn not,' and as little susceptible of misinterpretation, especially as it is added, in conclusion, that anything demanded of you beyond *yes* and *no* comes from the source of evil.

Really, if Christ's teaching is that one should always obey the will of God, how can a man swear to obey the will of man ? The will of God may not coincide with the will of man. Indeed, in this very passage Christ says that very thing. He says, Swear not by thy head, for not only thy head, but every hair of it, is in God's power. The same is said in the Epistle of James.

At the end of his Epistle, in conclusion, the Apostle James says (ch. v. 12) : *But above all things, my brethren, swear not, neither by the heaven, nor by the earth, nor by any other oath : but let your yea be yea, and your nay, nay ; that ye fall not under judgement*. The Apostle says plainly why one should not swear : the oath by itself appears innocent, but from it people fall under judgement, and therefore *swear not at all*. How could what is said both by Christ and by the Apostle be said more plainly ?

But I had been so entangled that I long asked myself in astonishment : Can it be that it means what it does mean ? How is it that we are all made to swear on the Gospels? It is impossible!

But I had already read the commentators and had seen how this impossibility was accomplished.

As with the explanations of the words, Judge not, do not be angry with anybody, do not break the bond of husband and wife, so also here. We have established our ways of life, we like them, and wish to consider them sacred. Then comes Christ, whom we consider to be God, but we do not wish to abandon our ways of life. What are we to do? Where possible, slip in the words *without a cause*, and reduce the rule against anger to nothing; where possible, like the most unscrupulous of unjust judges, interpret the meaning of the articles of the law so as to make it mean the very reverse, and that instead of a command never to divorce one's wife it should mean that one may divorce her. And where, as in the case of the words *Judge not, and condemn not, and swear not at all*, it is quite impossible to misinterpret, act boldly and directly contrary to the teaching, affirming that we are obeying it. Indeed the chief obstacle to understanding that the Gospels forbid every vow, and especially every oath of allegiance, is that pseudo-Christian teachers with extraordinary effrontery oblige men, on the Gospels themselves, to swear by the Gospels—that is to say, oblige them to do what is contrary to the Gospels.

How can it occur to a man who is obliged to swear on a cross, or on the Gospels, that the cross is sacred because on it he was crucified who forbade us to swear, and that when taking an oath one perhaps kisses, as what is sacred, the very place[1] in the book where it clearly and definitely says: *Swear not at all.*

But this effrontery no longer disconcerted me. I saw clearly that in Matt. v., verses 33 to 37, a definite and practicable third commandment is clearly expressed: Never take an oath to any one, anywhere, about anything. Every oath is extorted for evil ends. Following this third commandment comes a fourth reference and a fourth commandment (Matt. v. 38–42; Luke vi. 29, 30): 'Ye have heard that it was said, An eye for an eye, and a tooth for a tooth: but I say unto you, Resist not him that is evil: but whosoever smiteth thee on thy right cheek, turn to him the other also. And if any man would go to law with thee, and take away thy coat, let him have thy cloak also. And whosoever shall compel thee to go one mile, go with him twain.[2] Give to him that asketh thee, and from him that would borrow of thee turn not thou away.'

I have already spoken of the direct and definite meaning of these words, and of the

[1] In Russian Courts the oath was administered on the open Gospels.

[2] If Christ wished to lay down that it is wrong ever to use physical force to prevent any man from doing what he wishes to do (and that is the rule Tolstoy deduces) it is curious that Christ gives here an illustration of going two miles with a man who demands that you accompany him one; for, with reference to the second mile, there is clearly no reference to the use of physical force, any more than in the following example of lending to him who asks.

fact that we have no right to give them an allegorical interpretation. The commentaries on these words, from St. John Chrysostom's till to-day, are truly amazing. These words please everybody, and in references to them they make all kinds of profound conjectures, excepting one only, namely, that the words have their plain meaning. The Church commentators, not at all embarrassed by the authority of him whom they call God, most calmly restrict the meaning of his words. They say: 'It is, of course, understood that all these commandments about enduring wrongs, about renouncing revenge, are in fact directed against the Jewish spirit of relentlessness, and do not prohibit either public measures for restricting evil and *punishing evil-doers*, or the private, personal exertions and efforts of each individual to maintain the inviolability of his rights, to correct wrong-doers, and to deprive ill-intentioned men of the possibility of harming others; for otherwise the spiritual laws of the Saviour would themselves, in the Jewish way, become mere words, and might serve to promote the success of evil and the suppression of virtue. A Christian's love should be like God's love; but the divine love refrains from limiting and punishing evil only so long as it remains within limits more or less innocuous to God's glory and to the safety of one's neighbours; in the contrary case evil should be limited and punished, a duty which is specially incumbent on the Government.' (The *Annotated Gospel* of the Archimandrite Michael, which is all based on the commentaries of the Fathers of the Church). The learned and freethinking Christians are also not embarrassed by the meaning of Christ's words, and correct him. They say that this is a very lofty saying, but one lacking in any possible application to life; for an application to life of the law of non-resistance to evil destroys the whole order of life, which we have so admirably arranged: so say Renan, Strauss, and all the freethinking commentators.

But one need only take the words of Christ as we take those of the first man we meet and who speaks to us—that is to say, assume that he means what he says, to do away with the necessity for any profound conjectures. Christ says: I consider that your method of securing your life is stupid and bad. I propose to you quite another method, as follows. And he speaks the words given in Matthew v. 38–42. It would seem that, before correcting those words, one should understand them. But that is just what no one wishes to do, having decided in advance that the order of our life which is infringed by those words is a sacred law of humanity.

I did not consider our life either good or sacred, and therefore understood that commandment sooner than other people. And when I had understood the words as they are spoken, I was amazed by their truth, exactitude and clarity. Christ says: 'You wish to destroy evil by evil. That is unreasonable. That there should be no evil, do none.' And then he enumerates the cases in which we are accustomed to do evil, and says that in these cases it should not be done.

This fourth commandment of Christ was the first I understood, and it was the one which disclosed to me the meaning of all the others. This fourth, simple, clear, practicable commandment says: Never resist the evil-doer by force, do not meet violence with violence. If they beat you, endure it; if they take your possessions, yield them up; if they compel you to work, work, and if they wish to take from you what you consider to be yours—give it up.

And following that fourth commandment comes a fifth reference to the old law, and the fifth commandment (Matt. v. 43–8): 'Ye have heard that it was said, Thou *shalt love thy neighbour, and hate thine enemy* [Lev. xix. 17, 18]: but I say unto you, Love your enemies, bless them that curse you, do good to them that hate you, and pray for them which despitefully use you, and persecute you: that ye may be sons of your Father which is in heaven: for he maketh his sun to rise on the evil and the good, and sendeth rain on the just and the unjust. For if ye love them that love you, what reward have ye? do not even the publicans the same? And if ye salute your brethren only, what do ye more than others? do not even the *Gentiles* the same? Ye therefore shall be perfect, as your heavenly Father is perfect.'

Those verses formerly seemed to me to be

an explanation, completion, and enforcement —I would even say an exaggeration—of the precept about not resisting the evil-doer. But, having found a simple, applicable, and definite meaning in each passage that began with a reference to the ancient law, I anticipated that the same would be the case here. After each quotation a law was announced, and each verse of the commandment had a meaning and could not be omitted, and so it should be here also. The concluding words, repeated by Luke, that God does not make distinctions between people, but sends His blessings upon all, and that you therefore should be like God, not making distinctions between people, and should not do as the Gentiles do, but should love all men and do good to all alike—those words were clear, and they appeared to me to be like a confirmation and explanation of some definite rule; but what that rule was it was long before I could discern.

To love one's enemies. That seemed impossible. It was one of those beautiful phrases which can only be regarded as indications of an unattainable moral ideal. It was either too much, or nothing at all. One could abstain from injuring an enemy, but to love him was impossible. Christ could not prescribe an impossibility. Besides that, the very first words, the reference to the ancient law, 'Ye have heard that it was said: *Thou shalt hate thine enemy*, were questionable. In previous passages Christ quotes the actual, precise words of the Mosaic law; but here he uses words which had never been uttered. He appears to misrepresent the law.

As in the case of my former perplexities, the commentaries on the Gospels explained nothing to me. They all admit that the words, 'Thou shalt hate thine enemy,' do not occur in the Mosaic law, but no explanation of this incorrect citation is given. They speak of the difficulty of loving enemies and bad people; and in most cases they correct Christ's words, and say it is impossible to love one's enemies, but possible not to wish them evil or to do them harm; incidentally it is suggested that one may and should expose, that is to say oppose, one's enemies; mention is made of various degrees of attainability of this virtue; so that the ultimate deduction to be made from the Church commentaries is that Christ, for some unknown reason, made an incorrect citation of the Mosaic law and uttered many beautiful, but really empty and inapplicable, words.

It seemed to me that this was unsatisfactory. There should be some clear and definite meaning here, as in the first four commandments. And, to understand this meaning, I first of all tried to understand the meaning of the incorrect citation from the law: *hate your enemies.* It is not for nothing that Christ, before each of his injunctions, quoted the words of the law: 'Thou shalt not kill, shalt not commit adultery,' &c., and contrasted those words with his own doctrine. Without understanding what was alluded to in the words he cites from the old law one cannot understand what he enjoined. In the commentaries it is plainly said, what cannot but be admitted, that he cites words which are not found in the law; but it is not explained why he did so, nor what this incorrect citation means. It seemed to me that one had first to explain what Christ may have meant when he cited those words which do not occur in the law. And I asked myself: What can the words mean which Christ has incorrectly quoted from the Mosaic law? In all his former citations of the law only one precept of the ancient law is quoted, as: 'Thou shalt not kill; Thou shalt not commit adultery; Thou shalt not forswear thyself; A tooth for a tooth.' And in connexion with that single precept, Christ's corresponding doctrine is announced. Here, however, two precepts are cited, and contrasted one with the other; 'Ye have heard that it was said, Thou shalt love thy neighbour, and hate thine enemy,' so that evidently the basis of the new law should deal with the difference between the two injunctions of the ancient law in reference to neighbours and enemies. And to understand more clearly wherein that difference lay, I asked myself: What do the words 'neighbour' and 'enemy' mean in Gospel language? And, on consulting the dictionaries and concordances of the Bible, I convinced myself that 'neighbour,' when used by a Jew, always meant, and only meant, a Jew. That meaning of 'neighbour' is found also in the Gospel parable of the Good Samaritan. According to the view of the Jewish lawyer, who asked

'Who is my neighbour?' a Samaritan could not be a neighbour. A similar definition of 'neighbour' is given in Acts vii. 27. 'Neighbour,' in the language of the Gospels, means fellow-countryman, a man of one's own people. Therefore, surmising that the contrast Christ is setting up in this passage by citing the words of the law, 'Ye have heard that it was said, Thou shalt love thy neighbour and hate thine enemy,' lies in the contrast of fellow-countrymen with foreigners, I asked myself what was an 'enemy' in the Jewish conception, and I found confirmation of my conjecture. The word 'enemy' is used in the Gospels almost always in the sense, not of a personal foe, but of a public, national enemy (Luke i. 71-74; Matt. xxii. 44; Mark xii. 36; Luke xx. 43, &c.). The singular number used for the word 'enemy' in these verses, in the phrase 'hate thine enemy,' indicated to me that the national enemy is referred to. The singular number refers to the collective whole of the enemy people. In the Old Testament the conception of a hostile people is always expressed in the singular.

And, as soon as I understood this, the difficulty was immediately removed as to why and how Christ, after previously always quoting the precise words of the law, could here cite words which had never been uttered. I had only to understand the word 'enemy' in the sense of national enemy, and 'neighbour' in the sense of compatriot, for that difficulty to disappear. Christ speaks of how, in the Mosaic law, the Jews were told to treat their national enemy.

All those passages, scattered through different books of the Bible, in which they are bidden to oppress, slay, and exterminate other tribes, Christ sums up in the one expression, to 'hate' —to harm—the enemy. And he says: Ye have heard that it was said that you should love your own people and hate your nation's enemy; but I say to you that you should love all men without discrimination of the race to which they belong. And as soon as I understood the words in this way, the other and chief difficulty was disposed of, as to how one should understand the words, 'love your enemies.' It is impossible to love one's personal enemies. But one can love a hostile people in the same way that one does one's own. And it became plain to me that Christ is speaking of the fact that every one is taught to consider the people of his own race as his 'neighbours,' and to consider other nations as 'enemies,' but that he bids us not to do so. He says: The law of Moses makes a distinction between Jews and Gentiles, the national enemy, but I say unto you, that you should not make that distinction. And, in fact, both in Matthew and Luke, following this commandment, he says that before God all men are equal; the sun rises and the rain falls for them all. God does not distinguish between the peoples, but does good to all alike; so should men also do to all without distinction of nationality, and not as the Gentiles, who divide themselves into different nations.

So that, once again, from different sides a plain, important, clear, and applicable meaning of Christ's words confirmed itself for me. Again, instead of misty expressions of vague philosophy, a clear, definite, important, and practicable rule discloses itself: not to make distinctions between one's own and other nations, and not to do all the things that flow from making such distinctions; not to bear enmity to foreign nations; not to make war nor to take part in warfare; not to arm oneself for war, but to behave to all men, of whatever race they may be, as we behave to our own people.

This was all so clear and simple that I was astonished I had not understood it immediately.

The cause of my not having understood it was the same as the cause of my not having promptly understood the prohibition of law-courts and of oaths. It was very difficult to understand that those courts—which are opened with a religious ceremony, and blessed by those who consider themselves the guardians of Christ's teaching—that those same courts are incompatible with a confession of Christ, being directly opposed to him. Yet more difficult was it to guess that the very oath administered to all men by the guardians of the law of Christ is directly prohibited by that law; but to guess that what in our life is considered not merely necessary and natural, but most excellent and brave—the love of one's fatherland, its defence, its exaltation, resistance to its enemies, and so forth—are not merely offences against the law of Christ but a plain repudiation of it—to guess that this is so, was very difficult. Our life has so diverged from the teaching of Christ that that very divergence has become the chief hindrance to our understanding his teaching. We have so disregarded and forgotten all he said about our way of life—his injunction not merely not to kill, but not even to hate any man; not to defend ourselves but to turn the other cheek and to love our enemies—that now, being accustomed to call people who devote their lives to killing, the Christ-loving army,[1] being accustomed to hear prayers addressed to Christ for victory over our enemies, to pride ourselves on slaying, and having made of the sword a holy symbol of murder (until a man without a sword, without a dagger, is a man to be held in contempt)—it now seems to us that Christ did not forbid war, and that if he had forbidden it he would have said so more explicitly.

We forget that Christ could not imagine people believing in his teaching of humility, love, and universal brotherhood, quietly and deliberately organizing the murder of their brother men.

Christ could not imagine that, and therefore could not forbid Christians to go to war, any more than a father, when giving his son instructions to live honestly, to wrong no one, and to give to others, could bid him abstain from highway robbery. No one of the apostles or disciples of Christ during the first centuries of Christianity could imagine that it was necessary to forbid Christians to commit the murders that

[1] Or, if that Russian expression sounds strange in English, we might call it 'a Christian army.'

are called war. This, for instance, is what Origen says in his reply to Celsus (*The Writings of Origen: Origen contra Celsum*, Lib. viii. c. 73. Ante-Nicene Christian Library, vol. xviii.).

He says: 'And in the next place Celsus urges us to help the King with all our might, and to labour with him in the maintenance of justice, to fight for him; and, if he requires it, to fight under him, or lead an army along with him. To this our answer is, that we do, when occasion requires, give help to Kings, and that, so to say, a divine help, "putting on the whole armour of God." And this we do in obedience to the injunction of the Apostle, "I exhort, therefore, that first of all, supplications, prayers, intercessions, giving of thanks, be made for all men; for Kings and all that are in authority," and the more any one excels in piety, the more effective help does he render to Kings, even more than is given by soldiers, who go forth to fight and slay as many of the enemy as they can. And to those enemies of our faith who require us to bear arms for the commonwealth, and to slay men, we reply: "Do not those who are priests at certain shrines, and those who attend on certain gods, as you account them, keep their hands free from blood that they may with hands unstained and free from human blood offer the appointed sacrifices to your gods?"'

And, finishing this chapter with an explanation that Christians are of more use by their peaceful life than are soldiers, Origen says: 'And none fight better for the King than we do.

We do not indeed fight under him, although he require it.'

Such was the attitude of the Christians of the first centuries towards war, and so did their teachers speak when addressing those powerful in the world ; and they spoke so when hundreds and thousands of martyrs were perishing for professing the Christian faith.

And now ? Now no question is asked as to whether a Christian can take part in war. All young men, educated in the teaching of the Church which is called Christian, when the time comes each autumn, present themselves at the Army Office and, with the assistance of Church pastors, violate the law of Christ. Only recently one peasant turned up who on Gospel grounds refused military service. The teachers of the Church expounded to him his error ; but, as the peasant believed not them but Christ, he was put into prison and kept there till he renounced Christ. And all this is done 1,800 years after a quite clear and definite commandment was announced to Christians by our God : Do not consider the people of other nations to be enemies, but account all men as brothers, and treat them as you treat people of your own nation : and therefore, not only do not kill those whom you call your enemies, but love them and do good to them.

And having so understood these very simple, definite commands of Christ, not subjected to any interpretation, I asked myself : How would it be if the Christian world believed in these commandments, not in the sense that they must be sung or read for the propitiation of God, but that they must be obeyed for the welfare of man? How would it be if people believed in the duty of keeping these commandments as firmly as they believe, for instance, that one must say one's prayers every day, go to Church every Sunday, avoid flesh food on Fridays, and fast every Lent? How would it be if people believed these commandments even as much as they believe in the demands made by the Church? And I pictured to myself the whole of Christendom living and educating the young according to these commandments. I pictured to myself that it was inculcated to us all and to our children from childhood upwards, by word and by example, not as now, that a man must maintain his dignity and preserve his rights against others (which can only be done by humiliating and offending others), but it was inculcated that no man has any rights, or can be superior or inferior to another; and that he only is inferior to all and most ignoble who desires to set himself above others; that there is no more humiliating condition for a man than that of being angry with another; and that my conviction that someone is insignificant or mad cannot justify my anger against him, or my strife with him. Instead of all the arrangements of our life, from the shop-windows to the theatres, novels, and women's dresses, which excite sexual desire, I imagined to myself that it was suggested to us and to our children, by word and deed, that to amuse oneself with voluptuous books, theatres and balls is the basest kind of amusement, and that every act which has for its aim to *adorn or show off* the body is the very basest and most shameful of acts. Instead of the organization of our life, in which it is considered necessary and good that a young man should be dissolute until he marries, and instead of a way of life that separates married couples being considered most natural; instead of the legalization of a class of women set apart for the service of depravity; instead of the admission of, and the sanctification of, divorce,—instead of all this, I imagined to myself that it was instilled into us by word and deed that the condition of a man who has reached the age for sexual relations and has not renounced them, but yet remains single and unmarried, is an abnormity and a shame, and that a man's desertion of her with whom he has come together and the exchanging of her for another, is not only an unnatural action, like incest, but is a cruel, inhuman action. Instead of our whole life being founded on violence, instead of each of us being punished or punishing from childhood to advanced old age, I imagined to myself that it was instilled into us all by word and deed that revenge is a most degrading animal feeling, and that violence is not merely a shameful thing but one which deprives a man of true happiness, and that the only happiness of life is such as need not be defended by violence, and that the highest respect is deserved, not by him who takes or retains what is his from others, but by him who gives up the most and serves others most. Instead of it being considered admirable and right that each man should be sworn in, and should surrender all that he holds most valuable—that is to say, his whole life—to the will of he knows not whom, I imagined that it was instilled into all, that man's reasonable will is that highest sanctuary which he may yield to no one else, and that to bind oneself by oath to any one, and about anything, is a repudiation of one's rational being and a defilement of that highest sanctuary. I pictured to myself that, instead of these national enmities which are instilled into us under the guise of love of one's country, and instead of those applauded slaughters called war, which from childhood are represented to us as the most heroic deeds—I imagined that we were imbued with horror at, and contempt for, all those activities, political, diplomatic, and military, which promote the separation of peoples; and that it was suggested to us that the recognition of any kingdoms, exclusive laws, frontiers, or territories is an indication of most savage ignorance; and that to go to war—that is to say, to kill people, people personally unknown to us, without any grounds—is the most horrible villany, to which only a lost and perverted man, degraded to the level of a beast, can descend. I pictured to myself that all men believed this, and I asked: What would be the result?

Formerly I had asked myself what would result from putting Christ's teaching, as I then understood it, into practice, and had involuntarily replied: Nothing. We shall all pray, receive the blessings of the sacraments, believe in the redemption and in salvation for ourselves and for the whole world through Christ, and nevertheless that salvation will come about, not from what we do, but because the end of the world will arrive. Christ will come in his own time, in glory, to judge the living and the dead and establish the kingdom of God, independently of our life. Now Christ's teaching, as it had revealed itself to me, had another meaning, and the establishment of the kingdom of God on earth depended on us also. The fulfilment of Christ's teaching, expressed in the five commandments, would establish the kingdom of God. The kingdom of God on earth is the peace of all men one with another. Peace among men is the highest blessing attainable by man on earth. So did the kingdom of God present itself to all the Hebrew prophets. And so has it presented itself, and does present itself, to the heart of every man. All the prophecies promise peace to mankind.

The whole of Christ's teaching consists in giving the kingdom of God, that is peace, to man. In the Sermon on the Mount, in the talk with Nicodemus, in his charge to his disciples, and in all his sermons, Christ speaks only of the things that divide men and hinder them from being at peace and entering the kingdom of God. All the parables are but a description of what the kingdom of God is, and an explanation that only by loving one's brother-men and being at peace with them can one enter it. John the Baptist, Christ's forerunner, said that the kingdom of God was drawing near, and that Jesus Christ would give it to the world.

Christ says that he brought peace on earth (John xiv. 27): 'Peace I leave with you; my peace I give unto you: not as the world giveth, give I unto you. Let not your heart be troubled, neither let it be fearful.'

And those five commandments of his really give man this peace. All five commandments have but that one aim—peace among men. Men need only trust Christ's teaching, and obey it, and there will be peace on earth; and not such a peace as men devise, temporary, accidental, and partial, but a general peace, inviolable and eternal.

The first commandment says: Be at peace with all men; do not allow yourself to consider any man insignificant or senseless (Matt. v. 22). If peace be infringed, employ all your strength to restore it. The service of God is the abolition of enmity (Matt. v. 23, 24). Be reconciled after the least difference, in order not to lose the true life. In this commandment everything is said; but Christ foresees the snares of the world which disturb peace among men, and he gives the second commandment, against the snare of sexual relations, which disturb peace. Do not regard the beauty of the flesh as an amusement; avoid this snare in advance (verses 28–30); let a man take one wife, and a woman one husband, and on no account abandon one another (32). Another snare is the oath, which leads men into sin. Know in advance that this is evil, and take no vows (34–37). The third snare is revenge, calling itself human justice. Do not avenge yourself, and do not excuse yourself on the ground that you are wronged; bear with wrongs, and do not return evil for evil (38-42). The fourth snare is the difference of nationalities—the enmity of tribes and states. Know that all men are brothers, sons of one God; and do not infringe peace with any one for the sake of national aims (43-48). If people do not fulfil any one of those commandments, peace will be disturbed. If people fulfil all these commandments, the kingdom of peace will have come on earth. The commandments exclude all evil from the life of man.

With the fulfilment of these commandments the life of men will be such as every human heart seeks and desires. All men will be brothers, and everyone will be at peace with others, enjoying all the blessings of the world during the term of life appointed him by God. Men will beat their swords into ploughshares, and their spears into pruning-hooks. Then the kingdom of God will have come: that kingdom of peace promised by all the prophets, which drew nigh in the days of John the Baptist, and which Christ foretold and proclaimed in the words of Isaiah: 'The Spirit of the Lord is upon me, because he anointed me to preach good tidings to the poor; he hath sent me to bind up the broken-hearted, to proclaim liberty to the captives, and recovery of sight to the blind, to set at liberty them that are bruised; to proclaim the acceptable year of the Lord' (Luke iv. 18, 19; Isaiah lxi. 1, 2).

The commandments of peace, given by Christ, are simple and clear; they foresee all causes of strife and, by averting it, they throw open the kingdom of God on earth. Therefore Christ is actually the Messiah. He has fulfilled that which was promised. It is we who do not carry out what all men have always desired, though it is that for which we have prayed and still pray.

CHAPTER VII

CHRIST'S TEACHING—FALSE DOCTRINE—MAN IS A SON OF GOD

Why do people not act as Christ told them to, and in the way that gives them the greatest bliss attainable by man, such as they have ever longed for and still long for? From all sides I hear one and the same reply, differently expressed: 'The teaching of Christ is very good, and it is true that were it fulfilled the kingdom of God would be established on earth; but it is difficult, and therefore impracticable.'

Christ's teaching of how men should live is divinely true, and gives men blessedness; but it is hard for them to obey it. We so often repeat this, and hear it, that the contradiction contained in the words no longer strikes us.

It is accordant with human nature to seek for what is best, and every teaching for the guidance of man's life is a teaching of what is best. If men are shown what is best for them, how can they say that they desire to do what is best, but cannot? Man's rational activity, since mankind existed, has been directed to finding out what is best among the contradictions that fill the individual life and the life of humanity in general.

Men fight for land, for things they desire, and then divide everything up and call it property; they consider that though this is difficult to institute, yet it is better so, and they hold on to property; men fight for wives and abandon children, and then conclude that it is better that each man should have his own family; and, though it is very difficult to provide for a family, people retain property and family and much else. And as soon as people considered that it was better so, then, however difficult it might be, they did it. What then do we mean when we say, The teaching of Christ is admirable, life according to Christ's teaching is better than the life we live, but we cannot live in the better way because it is difficult?

If one understands difficult to mean that it is difficult to sacrifice the momentary satisfaction of desire for the sake of a great good, then why do we not say that it is difficult to plough in order to obtain grain for bread, or to plant apple-trees in order to get apples? That it is necessary to overcome difficulties to gain a great advantage is known to every being endowed with the rudiments of reason. And yet we say that Christ's teaching is admirable, but impracticable, because it is difficult. Difficult because, following it, we must deny ourselves something we had till then. It is as if we had never heard that it is sometimes better to endure and forgo than to suffer nothing and always satisfy our lusts.

Man may be an animal, and no one need reproach him for that; but a man cannot argue that he wishes to be merely an animal. As soon as he argues he acknowledges that he is a rational being, and, admitting that, he cannot but acknowledge what is reasonable and unreasonable. Reason enforces nothing; it only sheds light.

In the dark I hurt my hand and my knee seeking the door. A man enters with a light, and I see the door. I need then, when I see the door, no longer knock myself against the wall, and still less is it reasonably possible to assert that I see the door and consider it better to pass through the door, but that it is difficult to do so, and I therefore wish to continue to knock my knee against the wall.

In this extraordinary argument that the Christian teaching is desirable for and beneficial to the world, but that men are weak, men are bad, and continue to do worse though they wish to do better, and that they can therefore not do better, there is an obvious misunderstanding.

It is evidently not a mere error in argument, but something else. There must here be some false perception. Only a false opinion that that is which is not, and that that is not which is, could bring people to such a strange denial of the practicability of that which they admit gives them blessedness. The false perception which has led to this is what is called the dogmatic Christian faith—the very thing that all who profess the Christian faith according to the Church learn from childhood in the various Orthodox, Catholic, and Protestant Catechisms.

That faith, as defined by believers, is 'the giving substance to things hoped for' (this is said by Paul, and repeated in all the theological works and catechisms, as the best definition of faith). And it is this acknowledgement of the unreal as real that has led people to the strange assertion that Christ's teaching is good for men, but does not suit men.

The teaching of this faith, in its exact expression, is as follows: A personal God, ever existing, One in Three Persons, suddenly decided to create a world of spirits. The good God created this world of spirits for their good; but it happened that one of the spirits became bad of himself and therefore unhappy. Much time passed, and God created another world, a material world, and in it man, also for man's own benefit. God created man blessed, immortal, and sinless. The blessedness of man consisted in enjoying the good of life without labour; his immortality consisted in this, that he should always so live; his sinlessness consisted in his not knowing evil.

This man was tempted in paradise by that spirit of the first creation who had made himself bad, and from that time man fell, and bore similar fallen children; and from that time people began to work, bear sickness, suffer, die, and struggle physically and spiritually; that is to say, this imaginary man became real, such as we know him, and such alone as we have any right or reason to imagine him to be. Man's condition, labouring, suffering, choosing good, and avoiding evil, and dying—that condition which exists, and other than which we cannot imagine—according to the teaching of this faith, is not man's real position, but an unnatural, accidental, and temporary position.

Although this condition continued for everybody, as this teaching tells us, from the banishment of Adam from paradise—that is to say, from the commencement of the world, till the birth of Christ, and continues in just the same way for everybody since then, yet believers have to suppose this to be only an accidental, temporary condition. According to this teaching, the Son of God, being himself God, the Second Person of the Trinity, was sent by God to earth in human form to save men from that condition which was for them accidental and temporary, and to free them from all the curses which that same God had put upon them for Adam's sin, and in order to reinstate them in their former natural condition of blessedness—that is to say, in freedom from disease and in immortality, sinlessness, and idleness. The Second Person of the Trinity, Christ, by the fact that people executed him, according to this teaching, redeemed Adam's sin and terminated man's unnatural condition, which had lasted since the beginning of the world. And since then a man who believes in Christ has again become such as he was in paradise—that is to say, immortal, free from disease, sinless, and idle.

On that part of the accomplishment of the redemption in consequence of which, since Christ, the earth has everywhere brought forth its fruits without labour, by which sickness has ceased, and children have been born without pain to their mothers—the teaching does not much insist; for, however much they may believe, it is difficult to instil into people who find it hard to toil and painful to suffer a perception that it is not hard to work nor painful to suffer. But that part of the teaching according to which death and sin are annulled is most strongly insisted on.

It is stated that the dead continue to live. And as the dead are quite unable to affirm that they have died or that they are alive, just as a stone cannot affirm that it can or cannot speak, the absence of a denial is accepted as a proof; and it is asserted that those who have died have not died. With yet greater solemnity and confidence is it asserted that, since Christ came, man, by faith in him, is freed from sin—that is to say, that since Christ's time a man need no longer shed the light of reason on his path through life, and choose what is best. He only need believe that Christ has redeemed him from sin, and then he is always sinless—that is to say, completely good. According to this teaching people should imagine that reason in them is powerless, and that therefore they are sinless—that is to say, cannot make a mistake.

A true believer should imagine that, since the time of Christ, the earth yields her produce without labour, children are born painlessly, there are no diseases, no death, and no sins—that is to say, no mistakes—in other words, that that which is, is not, and that which is not, is.

That is what is said by strictly logical theological theory.

That teaching, taken by itself, seems harmless. But divergence from the truth never is harmless, but produces consequences that are the more important, the more important is the subject misrepresented. In this case the subject of the falsehood is the whole life of humanity.

What in this teaching is called true life is personal, blissful, sinless, and eternal—that is to say, life such as no one has ever known and such as does not exist. Life as it exists, such as alone we know, the life we live and all humanity has lived and is living, is according to this teaching a fallen, bad life, merely a simulacrum of the good life proper to us.

The struggle between the inclination towards an animal life and a rational life, which lies in the soul of each man and forms the essence of each life, is completely set aside by this teaching. That struggle is relegated to an event which happened to Adam in paradise at the time of the creation. And the question whether I should eat or should not eat those apples which tempt me does not exist for us, according to this teaching. The question was decided once and for all by Adam in paradise in a negative sense. Adam sinned for me—that is to say, he made a mistake, and all men, all of us, fell irreparably, and all our attempts to live rationally are useless and even irreligious.

I am incorrigibly bad, and ought to know it. And my salvation does not depend on the fact that I can enlighten my life by reason and, recognizing good and evil, can choose the better path. No; Adam has once and for all done for me what was bad, and Christ has, once and for all, corrected that evil done by Adam, and therefore I, as a spectator, should grieve for the fall of Adam and rejoice in the redemption by Christ.

All the love of goodness and truth which lies in the soul of man, all his efforts, by reason, to shed light on life's phenomena, all man's spiritual life, is not merely unimportant, according to this teaching, but is a snare or an arrogance.

Life such as we have on earth, with all its joys and beauties, with all its struggles of reason against darkness—the life of all who have lived before me, and my whole life with its inner strivings and victories of reason, is not a true life, but a fallen, hopelessly perverted life; while the true, sinless life, is in faith—that is in imagination, that is to say, in insanity.

Let a man, setting aside the habit he has retained from childhood of accepting all this, try to look simply and straight at this teaching; let him transform himself mentally into a new man, educated outside the range of this teaching, and let him imagine what it would appear like to such a man. Surely, it is utter insanity.[1]

[1] Tolstoy's statement of Church doctrines is not one that Churchmen will readily accept, but it should be borne in mind that he had primarily in view the

And, strange and terrible as it was to think so, I could not but admit that it is so; for this alone explained to me the amazing, contradictory, senseless objection which I hear from all sides as to the practicability of Christ's teaching: *It is good, and would bring happiness to men, but men cannot fulfil it.*

Only the representation as existent of that which does not exist, and as non-existent of that which does exist, could lead to this astonishing contradiction. And such a false representation I found in the pseudo-Christian faith, which has been preached for 1,500 years.[1]

But the objection to Christ's teaching (that it is good, but impracticable) is made not only by believers but also by unbelievers, by people who do not believe, or think they do not believe, in the dogma of the fall and redemption. The objection to Christ's teaching on the score of its impracticability is made also by scientists, philosophers, and in general by people who are educated and consider themselves quite free from any superstition, and who do not believe, or think they do not believe, in anything; and who therefore consider themselves free from the superstitions of the fall and the redemption. And so at first it seemed to me. I too thought that these learned people

Russo-Greek Church at a particularly somnolent and subservient period, and also the fact that in the early 'eighties, when he was writing this book, religious opinions were still current to which the assent of no educated man is likely to be demanded to-day.

[1] Tolstoy counts from the First General Council of Christians at Nicæa, under Constantine, in A.D. 325.

had other grounds for their denial of the practicability of Christ's teaching. But, on penetrating deeper into the reason of their denial, I became convinced that the non-believers have the same false perception, that our life is not what it is, but is what they imagine it to be; and that this conception rests on the same basis as the believers' conception. Those who consider themselves unbelievers do not, it is true, believe in God, nor in Christ, nor in Adam; but in the fundamental, false conception of man's right to a blissful life, on which everything rests, they believe as firmly, or even more firmly, than the theologians.

However much privileged science and philosophy may boast themselves, asserting that they are the guides and directors of man's mind—they are not the directors but the servants. A ready-made outlook on life is always supplied to science by religion; and science only works along the paths indicated to it by religion. Religion shows man the meaning of life, and science and philosophy apply this meaning to various sides of life. And therefore, if religion gives a false meaning to life, science, educated to that religious outlook, will apply that false perception to the various phases of human life. And that is what has happened with our European-Christian science and philosophy.

Church teaching has presented the fundamental meaning of human life as being this, that man has a right to a blissful life, and that this bliss is not obtainable by man's exertion but by something outside himself; and this idea underlies all our science and philosophy.

Religion, science, and public opinion, all with one voice declare that the life we lead is bad; but that the teaching which shows how we ourselves can become better, and thereby make life better, is impracticable.

The teaching of Christ, aiming at improving human life by man's own reasonable efforts, is impracticable, says religion, because Adam fell and the world is in an evil state.

That teaching is impracticable because man's life is regulated by certain laws which are independent of man's will, says our philosophy. Philosophy and all science only repeat in other words just what religion announces by the dogma of original sin and redemption.

In the doctrine of redemption there are two fundamental propositions on which everything depends: (1) Real human life is a blissful life, but life in the world here is a bad life, irreparable by any effort of man; and (2) Redemption from this life lies in faith.

These two propositions have come to underlie the outlook on life both of believers and of unbelievers in our pseudo-Christian society. From the second proposition arose the Church, with her institutions. From the first come our public opinion and our philosophic and political theories.

All the philosophic and political theories that justify the existing order, Hegelianism and its children, are founded on that basis. Pessimism, demanding of life what life cannot give, and therefore repudiating life, also arose from it. Materialism, with its wonderful and enthusiastic assertion that man is a process and nothing else, is the lawful child of this doctrine which acknowledges life here to be a fallen life. Spiritualism, with its scientific followers, is the best proof that the scientific and philosophic outlook is not free, but based on the religious doctrine that a blissful eternal life is natural to man.

This perversion of the meaning of life has perverted the whole rational activity of man. The dogma of man's fall and redemption has hidden from men the most important and legitimate realm of human activity, and has shut out of the realm of human knowledge the knowledge of what man should do that he may become happier and better. Science and philosophy, imagining that they are counteracting pseudo-Christianity, and priding themselves thereon, are only serving it. Science and philosophy deal with anything you please, only not with the question how man can himself become better and lead a better life. What is called ethics--moral teaching--has quite disappeared from our pseudo-Christian society.

Neither believers nor unbelievers ask themselves how they should live, and how use the reason that has been given us; but they ask: Why is our human life not such as we have imagined it should be, and when will it become what we desire?

Only as a result of that false teaching, absorbed into the flesh and blood of our generation, could such an astonishing thing occur as that man—as though he had spat out the apple of knowledge of good and evil, which tradition says he ate in paradise, and had forgotten that the progress of mankind lies only in solving the contradictions between our rational and our animal natures - should set to work to use his reason in discovering the historic laws of his animal nature and of that alone.

Except the philosophic teaching of our pseudo-Christian world, the religions and philosophic teachings of all the nations known to us—Judaism, Confucianism, Buddhism, Brahminism, and the philosophy of the Greeks—all aim at arranging human life, and explaining to people how each one should strive to be better, and to lead a better life. All Confucianism consists in personal perfecting of oneself; Judaism, in the personal following of each law of God; Buddhism, in the teaching of how each man can save himself from the evil of life. Socrates taught the personal perfecting of oneself in the name of reason, and the Stoics acknowledged rational freedom as the only basis of a true life.

Man's whole rational activity could not but consist, and has always consisted, in one thing—in illuminating by reason the striving towards what is good. Free-will, says our philosophy, is an illusion; and it prides itself much on the boldness of this assertion. But free-will is not merely an illusion; it is a phrase devoid of meaning. It is a phrase invented by the theologians and criminalists, and to refute that phrase is to tilt at windmills; but reason

—that which illumines our life and obliges us to alter our actions—is not an illusion and cannot be denied. To follow wisdom for the attainment of what is good—in that has always consisted the doctrine of the true teachers of humanity, and in that lies the whole teaching of Christ, and that, being reason, can in no way be rejected by reason.

The teaching of Christ is the teaching of the son of man that is present in us all—that is to say, it is the teaching of the strife common to all men after what is good, and of the reason, shared by all, which illuminates that striving. (To prove that 'the son of man' means 'son of man' is quite superfluous. To understand by 'son of man' something else instead of what the words mean, one would have to show that Christ, to indicate what he meant to say, intentionally used words which have quite another meaning. But even if, as the Church wishes to make out, 'son of man' means son of God, even then 'son of man' also essentially means man, for Christ calls all men the sons of God.)

Christ's teaching of the son of man—son of God—which forms the basis of all the Gospels, is expressed most clearly in his talk with Nicodemus. Each man, says he, besides consciousness of his personal life in the flesh, which proceeds from a male parent in the womb of his physical mother, cannot but be conscious of his birth from above (John iii. 5, 6, 7). That which man is conscious of in himself as free is that which is born of the eternal—that which we call God (vv. 11, 14). That which is born of God (the son of God in man) we should exalt in ourselves in order to attain true life (vv. 14, 17). The son of man is the son of God 'of a like nature' (not 'only begotten'). He who exalts in himself that son of God above all else, he who believes that life dwells only in that, will not be in discord with life. Discord with life results only because people do not believe in the light within themselves (vv. 18–21). (That light of which it is said in John's Gospel that in it is life, and the life was the light of man.)

Christ taught us to exalt the son of man, who is the son of God and the light of men, above all else. He says: When you exalt [honour, raise up] the son of man, you will know that I speak nothing of myself (John xii. 32, 44, 49). The Jews did not understand his teaching, and asked: 'Who is this son of man, that must be lifted up?' (John xii. 34) And to this question he replies (v. 35): 'Yet a little while is the light in you.[1] Walk while ye have the light, that darkness overtake you not; he that walketh in the darkness knoweth not whither he goeth.' To the question, what

[1] In all the Church's translations an intentionally false rendering is given: instead of the words 'in you,' wherever those words occur the rendering is given 'with you.'—L. T.

The English Authorized Version gives 'with you,' but our Revised Version, published in 1881, gives 'among you,' and in a footnote adds the translation 'in you'; so that the meaning Tolstoy considers correct is not entirely inaccessible to English readers of the Gospel.

is meant by 'lift up the son of man,' Christ replies: Live in the light that is in man.

The son of man, according to Christ's reply, is that light in which men ought to walk while they have light within them.

Luke xi. 35: 'Look therefore whether the light that is in thee be not darkness.'

Matt. vi. 23: 'If the light that is in thee be darkness, how great is the darkness!' says he, teaching the multitude.

Before and after Christ men have said the same thing: that a divine light dwells in man, which has descended from heaven, and that that light is *reason*, and that one must serve it only, and by its aid seek for what is good. This was said by the teachers among the Brahmans and by the Hebrew prophets, and by Confucius, and Socrates, and Marcus Aurelius, and Epictetus, and by all the true sages—not the compilers of philosophic theories, but those who sought truth for their own welfare and for that of all men.[1]

[1] Marcus Aurelius says: 'Honour that which is more powerful than anything on earth, which rules and guides all men. Honour also that which is most powerful within thyself. The latter is like the former, because it uses what is within thee to guide thy life.'

Epictetus says: 'God sowed His seed not only in my father and grandfather, but in all that live on the earth, especially in those that reason, for they alone enter into relation with God, through the reason by which they are united with Him.'

In the book of Confucius it is said: 'The law of great science consists in developing and establishing the principle of the light of reason, which we have received from heaven.' That proposition is repeated several times, and serves as the basis of Confucius's teaching.—L. T.

But suddenly, according to the dogma of redemption, we admit that it is quite unnecessary to speak or think about this light within us. We must think, say the believers, about the nature of each separate person of the Trinity; what sacraments must, or must not, be performed; because the salvation of man comes not from our efforts, but from the Trinity and the correct observance of the sacraments. We must think, say the non-believers, of the laws which regulate the movements of infinitely small atoms of matter in infinite space and infinite time; but of what man's reason demands for his good there is no need to think, because the betterment of man's condition does not depend on him, but on general laws which we discover.

I am convinced that a few centuries hence the so-called 'scientific' activity of our belauded recent centuries of European humanity will furnish an inextinguishable fund of mirth and pity to future generations. For some centuries the learned men of a small western part of the great continent were in a condition of epidemic madness, imagining that eternal blissful life belonged to them, and they occupied themselves with every kind of investigation as to how, and according to what laws, this life would come to them; but they themselves did nothing, and never thought of doing anything, to make their life better. And what will seem yet more pathetic to the future historian is that he will find that these people had had a teacher who clearly and definitely indicated to them what they should do to live more happily, and that the words of this teacher were explained by some to mean that he would come on the clouds to arrange everything, and by others that this teacher's words were excellent but impracticable, because man's life was not such as they wished it to be and therefore it was not worth while to concern themselves with it, but man's reason had to be directed to the investigation of the laws of life, without regard to what is good for man.

The Church says: Christ's teaching is impracticable because life here is but an imitation of true life; it cannot be good, it is all evil. The best way to live such a life is to despise it and live by faith—that is, by imagining a future, blissful, eternal life, and to live here as one is living, and to pray.

Philosophy, science, and public opinion say: Christ's teaching is impracticable because man's life depends not on that light of reason by which he can himself illuminate this life, but on general laws; and therefore it is not necessary to illuminate this life by reason and to live in accord therewith, but one must live as one is living, firmly believing that, according to historical, sociological, and other laws of progress, after we have lived badly a very long time, our life will of itself become very good.

People come to a farm, and there find everything necessary for their life: a house with all needful utensils, barns full of corn, cellars, vaults containing all kinds of supplies; in the yard are agricultural implements, tools, harness, horses, cows, sheep, and a complete inventory —all that is needful for a well-supplied life. People from various parts come to this farm and begin to make use of all they find there, each only for himself, not thinking of leaving anything either for those who are there with him in the house or for those who will come later. Each wishes to have everything for himself. Each hastens to make use of what he can seize, and the destruction of everything begins—strife and a struggle for possession. A milch cow, unshorn sheep and sheep bearing young, are killed for meat; fires are fed with benches and carts, and people fight for milk and grain, and spill, scatter, and destroy more than they use. No one eats a morsel quietly; he eats and snarls; a stronger than he comes and takes the piece away, and another takes it from him. Having tormented themselves, these people, beaten and hungry, leave the place. Again the master arranges everything in the place so that people could live quietly in it. Again in the farm there is abundance, and again passers-by come in; but again there is a scrimmage and a fight; all is wasted in vain; and again, tormented and embittered, people go away, scolding, angry with their comrades and also with their host for having prepared the place badly and insufficiently. Again the good host rearranges the place so that people could live in it; and again the same thing occurs, and again, and again, and again. Then in one of the fresh parties a teacher is found who says to the others, 'Brothers, we are not acting rightly. See how many goods there are in the place, and how well it is all arranged! There is enough for us all, and there will be a surplus for those who come after us, only let us live reasonably. We will not snatch from one another, but will help one another. Let us sow, and plough, and tend the cattle, and all will be able to live well.' And it happened that some people understood what the teacher said, and those who understood began to do as he bade them; they ceased fighting and snatching from one another, and began to work. But the rest, who had either not heard the words of the teacher, or had heard but did not believe him, did not follow his advice, but fought as before and spoilt their host's goods and went away. Others came and the same thing occurred. Those who attended to the teacher ever repeated the same thing: 'Do not fight, do not destroy the host's goods, and it will be better for you all. Do as the teacher says.'

But there were still many who had not heard, or did not believe, and matters long went on in the old way. This was all comprehensible, and things might happen so as long as people did not believe what the teacher said. But at last, it is told, a time came when all in the place had heard the teacher's words, all understood them, and not only understood them but acknowledged that it was God Himself who spoke through the teacher, and that the teacher was himself God, and all believed every word the teacher spoke to be sacred. And it is told that after this, instead of all living as the teacher advised, no one any longer refrained from the brawls, and they started thrashing one another, and all began to say that we know now for certain that it should be so and that nothing else is possible!

What does it all mean? Even cattle arrange how to eat their fodder so that one should not disturb another, and men, having learnt how they might live better, and believing that God Himself ordered them to do so, live yet worse, because they say it is impossible to live otherwise. These people have imagined something that is not true. Well, what could these people at the farm have imagined, that they, having believed the teacher's words, should continue to live as before, snatching from one another, fighting, and ruining the goods and themselves? The teacher had told them: 'Your life at this farm is bad; live better and your life will become good;' but they imagined that the teacher had condemned any kind of life at that farm, and had promised them another, a good life, not at that farm but somewhere else. And they decided that this farm was a temporary inn, and that it was not worth while arranging to live well in it, but that it was only necessary to be on the alert not to miss the good life promised in another place. Only so can the strange conduct of these people at the farm be explained who believed the teacher to be God, and of those others who considered him a wise man and his words to be true, but continued to live as before, in contradiction to the teacher's advice.

Men have heard all and understood all; but have let slip past their ears that the teacher said that men must create their own happiness here, at this farm at which they have met; and have imagined that this farm was an inn, and that the real one will be somewhere else. And from this has come their amazing argument that the words of the teacher were very admirable, and were even the words of God Himself, but that it was now difficult to obey them.

If only people would cease from destroying themselves and expecting some one to come and help them—Christ on the clouds with the sound of trumpets, or an historic law, or a law of the differentiation and integration of forces! No one will help them unless they help themselves. Nor need they even help themselves: if only they will cease to expect anything from heaven or from earth, and cease to destroy themselves.

CHAPTER VIII

THE PATH OF LIFE

BUT granting that Christ's teaching is beneficial to the world—granting that it is rational and that one has no reasonable right to reject it—still, what can one man do in a world of those who do not act on Christ's law? If all men suddenly agreed to fulfil Christ's teaching, its observance would be possible; but one man cannot go against the whole world.

'If,' it is generally said, 'I alone in a world of those people who do not fulfil Christ's law fulfil it: give away what I have, turn my cheek to the smiter without defending myself, do not even put in an appearance to take the appointed oaths, or when summoned to war, and if I submit to be plundered; I shall, if I do not die of hunger, get beaten to death, or, if not beaten, imprisoned or shot. So I shall have sacrificed all my happiness in vain, and ruined my whole life.'

This reply is based upon the same misunderstanding as the reply about the impracticability of Christ's teaching.

It is what one usually hears said, and I myself agreed with it until I had quite emancipated myself from Church teaching, and so became able to understand the full meaning of Christ's doctrine about life.

Christ offers his teaching of life to redeem us from the ruinous life people live who do not follow his teaching; and suddenly we declare that we should be glad to follow his teaching were we not sorry to ruin our life. Christ teaches us how to escape from our ruinous life, and we grudge the sacrifice of that ruinous life. It follows that we are far from considering our life ruinous, but consider it something in our possession, real and valuable. In that acknowledgement of our present worldly life as a real thing, and something that is our own, lies the mistake which hinders a comprehension of Christ's teaching. Christ was aware of this mistake, which causes people to consider this worldly life of theirs as something real that belongs to them; and by a whole series of discourses and parables he showed them that they have no right to life, and possess no life till they obtain true life by rejecting the shadow they now call their 'life.'

In order to understand Christ's doctrine of saving one's life, one must first understand what was said by all the prophets, what was said by Solomon, by Buddha, and by all the sages of the world, concerning man's personal life. One may, as Pascal expresses it, disregard the matter and carry a shield before one to hide the abyss of death towards which we are all running; but one need only consider what man's isolated personal life is, to convince oneself that this whole life, if it be only a personal life, has for each separate person no sense or meaning, but is a malicious mockery of one's heart and reason and of all that is good in man. Therefore, to understand Christ's teaching, one has first of all to bethink oneself and to consider. It is necessary that in us *μετάνοια* should take place: that is what Christ's forerunner, John the Baptist, when preaching, said to people who were ensnared like ourselves. He said: 'First of all, repent—that is, bethink yourselves. Even now is the axe laid to the root of the trees to cut them down. Death and destruction are here, beside each one of you. Do not forget it: bethink yourselves.' And Christ, beginning his teaching, says the same thing: 'Repent, or ye will all perish.'

In Luke xiii. 1–5, Christ spoke of the destruction of the Galilæans slain by Pilate, and he said: 'Think ye that these Galilæans were sinners above all the Galilæans because they have suffered these things? I tell you, Nay: but, except ye repent, ye shall all in like manner perish. Or those eighteen, upon whom the tower in Siloam fell, and killed them, think ye that they were offenders above all the men that dwell in Jerusalem? I tell you, Nay: but, except ye repent, ye shall all likewise perish.'

Had he lived in our day, in Russia, he would have said: Think ye that those who were burnt in the circus at Berdichev, or those who perished at the Kukuevsky embankment[1] were worse than others? You will all also perish

1 The reference is to two disasters which occurred in Russia at the time Tolstoy was writing this book.

unless you bethink yourselves, and find that in your life which does not perish. The death of those crushed by the tower, or burnt in the circus, horrifies you; but your death, just as terrible and as unavoidable, awaits you, and in vain do you try to forget it. If it comes unexpectedly it will be all the more terrible.

He says (Luke xii. 54–7): 'When ye see a cloud rising in the west, straightway ye say, There cometh a shower; and so it cometh to pass. And when ye see a south wind blowing, ye say, There will be a scorching heat; and it cometh to pass. Ye hypocrites, ye know how to interpret the face of the earth and the heaven; but how is it that ye know not how to interpret this time? And why even concerning yourselves judge ye not what is right?'

You can forecast the weather by its indications; how is it you perceive not what will befall yourselves? Avoid danger, safeguard your life as much as you please, and all the same, if Pilate does not kill you, a tower will fall on you, or, if neither Pilate nor the tower destroys you, you will die in your bed with yet greater suffering.

Make a simple calculation, as worldly people do when they undertake anything: either to build a tower, or to go to war, or to erect a factory. They plan and toil at an undertaking that may have a reasonable end.

Luke xiv. 28–31: 'For which of you, desiring to build a tower, doth not first sit down and count the cost, whether he have wherewith to complete it? Lest haply, when he hath laid a foundation, and is not able to finish, all that behold begin to mock him, saying, This man began to build and was not able to finish. Or what king, as he goeth to encounter another king in war, will not sit down first and take counsel whether he is able with ten thousand to meet him that cometh against him with twenty thousand?'

Is it not really senseless to work at something which, however much you may try, will never be accomplished? Death will always come sooner than the completion of the tower of your worldly happiness. And if you know in advance that, however you may strive against death, not you, but he, will conquer, is it not better to refrain from struggling against it, and not to devote your life to what will certainly perish, but rather seek some undertaking which will not be destroyed by inevitable death?

Luke xii. 22–7: 'And he said unto his disciples, Therefore I say unto you, Take no thought for your life, what ye shall eat; nor yet for your body, what ye shall put on. For the life is more than the food, and the body than the raiment. Consider the ravens, that they sow not, neither reap; which have no store-chamber, nor barn; and God feedeth them: of how much more value are ye than the birds! And which of you by being anxious can add a cubit unto his stature? If then ye are not able to do even that which is least, why are ye anxious concerning the rest? Consider the lilies, how they grow: they toil not, neither do they spin; yet I say unto you,

Even Solomon in all his glory was not arrayed like one of these.'

However much you may concern yourself about your body and your clothes, no one can add a single hour to his life.[1] Is it not senseless, then, to concern yourself about something you cannot do?

You know very well that your life will end with death, and you exert yourself to safeguard your life by property. Life cannot be safeguarded by property. Understand that this is an absurd deception with which you delude yourself.

The meaning of life cannot consist, Christ says, in what we possess and what we acquire—what is not ourselves; it must consist in something else.

He says (Luke xii. 15–21): 'A man's life consisteth not in the abundance of the things which he possesseth. The grounds of a certain rich man,' he says, 'brought forth plentifully: and he reasoned within himself, saying, What shall I do, because I have not where to bestow my fruits? And he said, This will I do: I will pull down my barns, and build greater; and there will I bestow all my corn and my goods. And I will say to my soul, Soul, thou hast much goods laid up for many years; take thine ease, eat, drink, be merry. But God said unto him, Thou foolish one, this night is thy soul required of thee; and the

[1] The word ἡλικία—age, time of life, is incorrectly translated 'stature.' So the whole expression means: can add an hour to his life.—L. T.

things which thou hast prepared, whose shall they be? So is he that layeth up treasure for himself, and is not rich toward God.'

Death always, every instant, stands over you. And therefore (Luke xii. 35, 36, 38, 39, 40): 'Let your loins be girded about, and your lamps burning; and be ye yourselves like unto men looking for their lord, when he shall return from the marriage feast; that, when he cometh and knocketh, they may straightway open unto him. And if he shall come in the second watch, and if in the third, and find them so, blessed are those servants. But this ye know, that if the master of the house had known in what hour the thief was coming, he would have watched, and not have left his house to be broken through. Be ye also ready: for in an hour that ye think not the Son of man cometh.'

The parable of the virgins awaiting the bridegroom, and of the end of the age and the day of judgement—all these passages, in the opinion of all the commentators, besides relating to the end of the world, also relate to death, which stands always before us every hour.

Death, death, death awaits you every second. Your life passes in the presence of death. If you labour personally for your own future, you yourself know that the one thing awaiting you is—death. And that death ruins all you work for. Consequently life for oneself can have no meaning. If there is a reasonable life it must be found elsewhere; it must be a life the aim of which does not lie in preparing further life for oneself. To live rationally, one must live so that death cannot destroy life.

Luke x. 41: 'Martha, Martha, thou art anxious and troubled about many things: but one thing is needful.'

All the innumerable things we do for our own future are unnecessary: it is all deception with which we delude ourselves. Only one thing is needful.

From the day of man's birth, his position is such that inevitable destruction awaits him—that is to say, a meaningless life and a meaningless death, unless he finds that one thing necessary for true life. It is that one thing which Christ shows to men. He does not invent it, or promise to give it by his divine power; he only shows people that, together with that personal life which is certainly a deception, there must be something that is true and not a deception.

In the parable of the husbandmen (Matt. xxi. 33–42) Christ explains the source of the error which hides that truth from men, and causes them to mistake the phantom of life (their own personal life) for true life.

Men, living in the cultivated garden of a householder, took it into their heads that they owned that garden. And from this false conception flowed a series of insensate and cruel actions performed by them, which ended in their expulsion, in their being ejected from that life. In just such a way have we imagined that the life of each of us is his own personal possession, and that we have a right to it and can do with it as we please, bound by no obligation to any one. And for us, having imagined this, a similar series of insensate and cruel actions and misfortunes is inevitable, resulting in a similar expulsion from life. And as the husbandmen thought that the more cruel they were, the better would they secure themselves (for instance, by killing the messengers and the householder's son), so we also imagine that the more cruel we are, the better we shall be safeguarded.

As the inevitable end of the husbandmen who would not yield the fruit of the garden to any one was that the householder expelled them, so also will be the end of those who imagine personal life to be real life. Death drives them from life, replacing them by others; and this not as a punishment, but merely because they have not understood life. As the dwellers in the garden had either forgotten or wished to ignore the fact that the garden was handed to them ready cultivated, hedged, and supplied with a well, and that some one had laboured there before, and therefore expected them to work; so people living a personal life have forgotten, or wish to forget, all that was done for them before their birth and is being done all the time they are alive, and that something is therefore expected of them: they wish to forget that all the good things of life which they use have been given and are being given, and should therefore be passed on and returned.

This correction of the understanding of life, this μετάνοια is the corner-stone of Christ's teaching, as he said at the end of that parable. According to Christ's teaching, as the husbandmen in the garden they had not planted should have understood and realized that they owed more to the householder than they could repay, so we also should understand and feel that, from the day of our birth to our death, we are overwhelmingly in debt to others, to those who lived before us, those now living, and those who will live, and to that which was, is, and will be—the source of all things. They should understand that each hour of their life, while they retain it, they admit that obligation, and that therefore a man living for himself who denies that obligation uniting him with life and with the source of life, deprives himself of life, and must understand that, by living so, he, while wishing to save his life, destroys it—as was repeatedly said by Christ.

That only is true life which carries on the life of the past, promotes the welfare of the present, and prepares the welfare of the future.

To participate in that life a man must forgo his own will and do the will of the Father of life, who has given life to the Son of man.

In John viii. 35, Christ, again expressing the same thought, says that a slave who follows his own will and not the will of the master abideth not in the house for ever: only the Son, who fulfilleth the will of the Father, abideth for ever.

The will of the Father of life is not the life of an individual man, but of the only Son of man, dwelling within men, and therefore a man preserves his life only when he takes his life as a loan, a talent entrusted to him by the Father for the service of the life of all, and lives not for himself but for the Son of man.

Matt. xxv. 14–46: A master gave part of his property to each of his bondsmen, and, without giving them any instructions, left them alone. Some of the bondsmen, though they had received no orders from their master as to the use of his property, understood that it was not theirs but the master's, and that it should increase; and they worked for their master. And those who worked for their master became partakers in the master's life, but those who did not work were deprived of what had been given them.

The life of the Son of man is given to all men, and they are not told why it is entrusted to them. Some understand that life is not their own, but was received as a gift, and that they should serve the life of the Son of man; and they live accordingly. Others, on the pretext of not understanding the aim of life, do not serve life. And those who serve life merge with the source of life; while those who do not serve life are deprived of it. And (in verses 31 to 46) Christ tells us wherein the service of the Son of man consists, and what the reward of that service is. The Son of man, as Christ expressed it, will say like a king: 'Come, ye blessed of my Father, inherit the kingdom, for ye gave me meat and drink, clothed me, took me in and comforted me, for I am ever one and the same, in you and in these little ones, whom you have pitied and to whom you have done good. You have not lived the personal life, but the life of the Son of man; therefore you have eternal life.'

Only of eternal life of that kind does Christ teach in all the Gospels, and, strange as it may sound to say it of Christ, who personally rose and promised resurrection to all, never did Christ by a single word assert a personal resurrection and personal immortality beyond the grave; and to the restoration of the dead in the kingdom of the Messiah, which the Pharisees taught, he gave a meaning which excluded the conception of personal resurrection.

The Sadducees denied the restoration of the dead. The Pharisees acknowledged it, and it is now acknowledged by orthodox Jews.

The restoration of the dead (and not the resurrection, as the word is incorrectly translated), according to the belief of the Jews, will be accomplished at the coming of the time of the Messiah and the establishment of the kingdom of God on earth. And Christ, encountering this belief in a temporary, local, and corporeal resurrection, denies it, and puts in place of it his teaching of eternal life in God.

When the Sadducees, who did not acknowledge the restoration of the dead, asked Christ, whom they supposed to share the view of the Pharisees, 'To whom will the wife of the seven brothers belong?' he replied clearly and definitely on both points.

He says (Matt. xxii. 29–32; Mark xii. 24–27; Luke xx. 34–38): 'Ye do err, not knowing the Scriptures, nor the power of God.' And, rejecting the Pharisees' view, he says: The restoration of the dead is neither corporeal nor personal. Those who attain to a restoration from the dead become sons of God and live like the angels (the powers of God) in heaven (i.e. with God); and personal questions—such as whose wife a woman will be—cannot exist for them, for they, united with God, cease to be personalities. 'As touching the restoration of the dead,' says he, replying to the Sadducees, who only acknowledged earthly life, 'have ye not read that which was spoken unto you by God?' In the book of Moses it is said that God from the bush spake unto Moses, saying, 'I am the God of Abraham, and the God of Isaac, and the God of Jacob.' If God said to Moses that he is the God of Jacob, then Jacob is not dead for God, since God is the God of the living only, and not of the dead. *For God, all are alive.* And therefore, if there is a living God, that man also lives who has entered into communion with the ever-living God.

Against the Pharisees Christ says that the restoration of life cannot be corporeal and personal. Against the Sadducees he says that, besides a personal and temporary life, there is also a life in communion with God.

Christ denies the personal, the corporeal

resurrection,[1] but acknowledges a restoration of life in a man who merges his life into God's. Christ teaches salvation from personal life and places that salvation in the exaltation of the Son of man and life in God. Uniting this teaching of his with the Jewish doctrine of the coming of a Messiah, he speaks to the Jews of the raising of the Son of man from the dead, meaning by this, not a corporeal and personal restoration of the dead, but an awakening of life in God. He never spoke of a corporeal, personal resurrection. The best proof that he never preached the resurrection of man is furnished by the two solitary passages quoted by the theologians in proof of his having taught the doctrine of resurrection. These two passages are Matt. xxv. 31–46 and John v. 28, 29. The first of these speaks of the coming, i.e. of the restoration, the exaltation, of the Son of

[1] Tolstoy here adopts the views he attributes to Christ. Some years later his opinion on the subject was somewhat modified. He came to lay less stress on the words attributed to Christ; and his own experience was that the more he came to identify his hopes and efforts with doing the will of his Father in heaven, that is to say, with helping right to prevail, the crooked to become straight, and the rough places smooth, here on earth—the less credible did it seem that his existence could cease with the death of the body. But he maintained that we neither know, nor can know, what kind of existence awaits us in the future; whether our personalities will persist, whether we shall merge into the infinite like drops into the ocean, whether we shall be reincarnated, or whether groups of those who have co-operated most closely together may not merge with one another into one larger individuality.

man (just as in Matt. x. 23) and therefore the majesty and power of the Son of man are compared to a king. In the second passage what is spoken of is the restoration of true life here on earth, as it is expressed in the preceding twenty-four verses.

One need only reflect on the meaning of Christ's teaching of eternal life in God, and recollect the teaching of the Hebrew prophets, to understand that if Christ wished to teach the doctrine of the resurrection of the dead, which was then only beginning to find a place in the Talmud and was a subject of dispute, he would have stated that doctrine clearly and definitely; but, on the contrary, not only did he not do so, but he rejected it; and not a single place can be found in any one of the Gospels which confirms that doctrine. The two passages referred to above mean something quite different.

Of his own personal resurrection—strange as this may sound to people who have not themselves studied the Gospels—*Christ never spoke at all!* If, as the theologians teach, the basis of Christian faith lies in the resurrection of Christ, one would think that the least one could wish would be that Christ, knowing that he would rise again and that this would constitute the chief dogma of the Christian faith, should at least once say so clearly and definitely. But not only did he not say so definitely and clearly, he never once, not one single time in all the canonical Gospels, even mentioned it! What Christ taught was to exalt the Son of man;

that is to say, the essential life of man, and to acknowledge oneself a son of God. Christ personified in himself a man acknowledging sonship to God (Matt. xvi. 13–20). He asked the disciples what men said of him—*the Son of man?* The disciples replied that some considered him to be John the Baptist miraculously risen from the dead, or a prophet; others, Elijah descended from heaven. 'But who do you say I am?' asked he. And Peter, understanding Christ as he understood himself, replied: 'Thou art the Messiah, the Son of the living God.' And Christ replied: 'Not flesh and blood hath revealed this unto thee, but our Father which is in heaven.' That is to say, you have understood this not because you believed human explanations, but because you, recognizing yourself to be a son of God, have understood me. And, explaining to Peter that on this sonship to God the true faith rests, Christ warned the other disciples (v. 20) that they should not in future say that he, Jesus, was the Messiah.

And after this Christ says that, notwithstanding the fact that he would be tortured and killed, the Son of man, knowing himself to be God's Son, would nevertheless be re-established and triumph over all. And it is these words that are interpreted as a prediction of his resurrection!

John ii. 19–22; Matt. xii. 40; Luke xi. 30; Matt. xvi. 4–21; Mark viii. 31; Luke ix. 22; Matt. xvii. 23; Mark ix. 31; Matt. xx. 19; Mark x. 34; Luke xviii. 33; Matt. xxvi. 32;

Mark xiv. 28. Those are all the fourteen passages which are understood as being predictions by Christ of his resurrection. In three of them what is spoken of is Jonah in the whale's belly, and in one the reconstruction of the Temple. In the remaining ten passages it is said that the Son of man cannot be destroyed, but nowhere is there one word about the resurrection of Jesus Christ.

In none of these passages, in the original, does the word 'resurrection' even occur. Give a man who does not know the theological interpretation, but who knows Greek, these passages to translate, and he will never translate them as they have been translated. In the original two different words are used in three passages; the one is ἀνίστημι and the other ἐγείρω. One of these words means, 'to upraise'; the other means 'to awaken,' and, in the middle voice, 'to wake up,' 'to rouse oneself.' But neither the one nor the other ever, under any circumstances, can mean 'to raise from the dead.' In order fully to convince oneself that these Greek words, and the corresponding Hebrew word *Kum*, cannot mean 'to raise from the dead,' one need only compare the other passages in the Gospels where these words are used. They are used frequently and never translated by the words 'to raise from the dead' (*auferstehen*, *ressusciter*); such words did not exist in Greek or in Hebrew, nor was there the conception that corresponds to them. To express in Greek, or in Hebrew, the conception of resurrection, one has to employ a circumlocution and say:

'arose from the dead' or 'awoke from the dead.' So in the Gospels (Matt. xiv. 2) where the matter in hand is that Herod assumed the resurrection of John the Baptist, the words used are 'is risen from the dead.' So also in Luke xvi. 31, it is said, in the parable about Lazarus, that if there were a resurrection, the man who returned from the dead would still not be believed, and the expression used is: 'if one rise from the dead.' Where to the words 'to rise,' 'to awaken,' the words 'from the dead' are not added, the words 'rise' and 'awaken' never imply or could imply, 'resurrection.' And, speaking of himself, Christ did not once, in all the passages quoted as proof of his prediction of his resurrection—not one single time did he employ the words, 'from the dead.'

Our conception of the resurrection is so different from the Jewish conception of life that it is impossible even to imagine how Christ could have spoken to the Jews about resurrection and an everlasting, personal life belonging to each man. The conception of a future personal life has come to us neither from Jewish teaching nor from Christ's teaching. It entered church doctrine quite from without. Strange as it may appear, it cannot but be said that a belief in a future personal life is a very low and gross conception (based on a confusion of sleep with death) and one natural to all savage tribes; and that the Hebrew doctrine, not to speak of the Christian doctrine, stood immeasurably above it. We are convinced that this superstition is something very elevated, and seriously try to prove the superiority of our teaching to other doctrines by the fact that we hold this superstition, while others, such as the Chinese and Hindus, do not hold it. This is argued not only by theologians but also by the freethinking, scholarly historians of religion (Tiele, Max Müller and others), who, when classifying religion, reckon those which share this superstition as superior to those which do not share it. The freethinking Schopenhauer plainly calls the Hebrew religion the vilest (*niederträchtigste*) of all religions, because it contains no idea (*keine Idee*) of the immortality of the soul. Actually, in the Hebrew religion, neither that conception nor that word exists. Eternal life, in Hebrew, is *chayi-olam*. *Olam* means endless, immovable in time. *Olam* also means the world, the cosmos, life in general, and especially endless life. *Chayi-olam*, according to the Hebrew doctrine, is an attribute of the one God. God is the God of life, the living God. Man in the Hebrew conception is always mortal; only God is ever-living. In the Pentateuch the words 'live for ever' are twice employed. Once in Deuteronomy, xxxii. 39, 40, God says: 'See now that I, even I, am he, and there is no God but me: I kill, and I make alive; I have wounded and I heal; and there is none that can deliver out of my hand. For I lift up my hand to heaven, and say, As I *live for ever*. . . .' The other time, in Genesis iii. 22, God says: 'Behold, the man has eaten of the fruit of the tree of knowledge of good and evil, and is become as us [one of us]; and now, may he not put forth his hand, and take also of the tree of life, and eat, and *live for ever?'* Except in one chapter of the apocryphal book of Daniel, these are the only two instances of the use of the words 'live for ever' in the Pentateuch or in the whole of the Old Testament, and they clearly define the Jews' conception of life generally and of life eternal. Life itself, in the conception of the Jews, is eternal, and so is life in God; but man is mortal, such is his nature.

Nowhere in the Old Testament is it said, as taught in our Bible-classes, that God breathed into man an *immortal soul*, or that the first man before he sinned was immortal. God created man, as is told in the first story in the book of Genesis (ch. i. 26) just as He created the animals, of the male and female gender: and He ordered them to be fruitful and multiply in just the same way. Just as it is not said of the animals that they are immortal, so it is not said of man. In the following chapters it is plainly said that God drove man out of paradise and warded him off from the way to the tree of life. So that man did not eat of the fruit of the tree of life, and did not obtain *chayi-olam*—that is to say, 'life for ever'—but remained mortal.

According to the Jewish teaching man is man just as we know him—that is to say, he is mortal. Life in him is only life continuing itself in the race from generation to generation. Only the race, according to the teaching of the Jews, has in itself the possibility of life. When God says:

'You shall live and not die,' He speaks to the race. The life breathed by God into man is mortal for each separate man; but this life is continued from generation to generation if men fulfil their covenant with God—that is to say, fulfil the conditions demanded for this by God.

Having set forth all the laws, and said that these laws are not from heaven, but are in their hearts, Moses says in Deuteronomy xxx. 15: 'See, I have set before thee life and good, and death and evil; in that I command thee to love God, to walk in his ways, and to keep his commandments, that thou mayest live.' And in verse 19: 'I call heaven and earth to witness against you this day, that I have set before thee *life and death*, the blessing and the curse: therefore choose life, that thou mayest live, thou and thy seed: to love God, to obey his voice, and to cleave unto him; for from him is thy life and the length of thy days.'

The chief distinction between our understanding of human life and that of the Jews consists in this, that according to our understanding our mortal life, transmitted from generation to generation, is not real life but a fallen life, for some reason temporarily spoilt; but in the Jewish conception this life is the most real, it is the highest good, given to man on condition that he fulfils the will of God. From our point of view, the transmission of that fallen life from generation to generation is the continuation of a curse. From the point of view of the Jews, it is the highest blessing attainable by man, and to be reached only by fulfilling God's will.

It is on that understanding of life that Christ bases his teaching of the true or eternal life, which he contrasts with personal and mortal life. 'Ye search the scriptures,' says Christ to the Jews (John v. 39), 'because ye think that in them ye have eternal life.'

A young man asked Christ (Matt. xix. 16) how to enter into eternal life. Christ, replying to the question of eternal life, says: 'If thou wouldest enter into *life* (he does not say eternal life, but simply life), keep the commandments.' He says the same to the lawyer (Luke x. 28): 'This do, and thou shalt live,' and here also he said *live* simply, without adding 'live eternally.' Christ in both cases defines what would be understood by the words 'eternal life'; when he uses them he says to the Jews what had often been said in their law, namely, that the fulfilment of God's will is eternal life.

Christ, in contradiction to temporal, private, personal life, teaches that eternal life which, in Deuteronomy, God promised to Israel; only with this difference, that, according to the Jewish conception, eternal life endured only in the chosen people of Israel; and to obtain that life it was necessary to observe the exceptional laws God had given to Israel; while, by Christ's teaching, eternal life continues in the Son of man, and what is needed to preserve it is the observance of the laws of Christ, which express God's will for the whole of humanity.

Christ contrasts with personal life, not a life beyond the grave but common life bound up with the past, present, and future, the life of the whole of humanity, the life of the Son of man.

The salvation of personal life from death, according to the teaching of the Jews, lay in the fulfilment of the will of God expressed in the law of Moses by His commandments. Only on that condition did life, as the Jews understood it, not perish but pass on from generation to generation among God's chosen people. The salvation of personal life from death, according to Christ's teaching, lies in a similar fulfilment of the will of God expressed in Christ's commandments. Only on that condition, according to Christ's teaching, does personal life not perish but become ever secure in the Son of man. The difference is only in this, that Moses' service of God is a service of the God of one people, while Christ's service of God is a service of the God of all mankind. The survival of life in the generations of one race was doubtful, for that people itself might disappear, and also because that survival depended on corporeal descendants. The survival of life by Christ's teaching is indubitable, because life, according to his teaching, is transferred to the Son of man, who lives by the will of the Father.

But, even supposing the words of Christ about a day of judgement, the end of the age, and other sayings in John's Gospel have a meaning referring to a life beyond the grave for the souls of those who have died, nevertheless it is unquestionable that his teaching about the light of life and the kingdom of God also has the meaning, comprehensible to his hearers and comprehensible to us, that the only true life is the life of the Son of man according to the will of the Father. It is easier to admit this, since the doctrine of true life according to the will of the Father of life can include the conception of immortality and of life beyond the grave.

It may be more correct to suppose that, after this worldly life lived for the fulfilment of his personal will, an everlasting personal life still awaits a man in paradise with all possible delights: perhaps that is more correct; but to think that it is so, and to try to believe that for good deeds I shall be rewarded with everlasting bliss, and for bad deeds with everlasting torments, does not conduce to an understanding of Christ's teaching. On the contrary, to think so deprives Christ's teaching of its chief basis.

The whole teaching of Christ is that his disciples, having understood the illusory nature of personal life, should renounce it and transfer it into the life of the whole of humanity; the life of the Son of man. The teaching of the immortality of the personal soul, on the other hand, does not call for the renunciation of one's personal life, but rivets that personality for ever.

According to the conception of the Jews, the Chinese, the Hindus, and all the people of the world who do not believe the dogma of the fall of man and his redemption, life is life as we know it. A man copulates, has children, brings them up, grows old, and dies. His children grow up and continue his life, which goes on uninterruptedly from generation to generation, just as all goes on in the world : stones, earth, metals, plants, animals, stars, and everything in the universe. Life is life, and must be used as well as possible. To live for oneself is irrational. Therefore, since people existed, they have sought an aim of life outside themselves ; and live for their child, their family, their tribe, or for humanity, for all that does not die with their personal life.

According to the teaching of our Church, on the contrary, human life, as the greatest good known to us, is represented as being only an atom of the life that is, for a time, held back from us. Our life, according to our view, is not life as God wished to give and should have given it us, but is a spoilt, bad, fallen life, a copy of life, a caricature of the real life we for some reason imagine that God should have given us. The chief aim of our life, according to this view, is not to live this mortal life as the Giver of life desires, nor to make it permanent in the generations of men, as the Jews teach, nor in merging it with the will of the Father, as Christ taught ; but in convincing oneself that after this life true life will begin.

Christ does not speak of this imaginary life of ours which God ought to have given, but for some reason did not give, to man. The theory of the fall of Adam and everlasting life in paradise and an immortal soul breathed into Adam by God, was unknown to Christ, and he did not refer to it, nor by a single word hint at its existence. Christ speaks of life as it is and will always be. But we speak of a life we have imagined for ourselves—such as never existed; how, then, can we understand Christ's teaching?

Christ could not imagine among his disciples such a strange conception. He assumes that every one understands that personal life inevitably perishes, and he shows a life that does not perish. He gives welfare to those who are in evil plight; but to those who have persuaded themselves that they have much more than Christ gives his teaching can offer nothing. I may exhort a man to work, assuring him that for his labour he will receive food and clothing, but suddenly the man becomes convinced that he is a millionaire; evidently he will not listen to my exhortations. The same thing occurs with Christ's teaching. Why should I try to earn, when I can be rich without work? Why should I try to live this life according to the will of God, when I am confident that, without that, I shall have an everlasting personal life?

We are taught that Christ saved people by the fact that he was the Second Person of the Trinity, that he was God and became incarnate, and, having taken on himself the sins of Adam and of all mankind, he redeemed the sins of men before the First Person of the Trinity, and for our salvation established the Church and the sacraments. By believing this we are saved and receive everlasting personal life beyond the grave. But it cannot be denied that he saved and saves people also by the fact that, having shown them the inevitable destruction awaiting them, he, by his words, '*I am the way, the truth, and the life*,' showed them a true path of life in place of the false path of personal life we previously followed.

There may be people who have doubts about life beyond the grave and salvation based on the redemption, but about the salvation of men, individually and collectively, by showing them the inevitability of the destruction of their personal life, and by merging their will with that of the Father, there can be no doubt. Let any rational man ask himself what his life and death is. Can he give to that life and death any other meaning than that which Christ gave ?

Any meaning given to a personal life, if it be not based on the renunciation of self for the service of man, humanity, the Son of man, is a delusion which flies to pieces at the first contact with reason. That my personal life perishes and that the life of the whole world in the will of the Father does not perish, and that only by merging with it can I possibly be saved, of that I can have no doubt. But this is so little in comparison with those exalted religious beliefs in a future life ! Though it be little, it is sure.

We are lost in a snow-storm. A man assures us, and he believes, that there are lights and there is a village; but it only seems so to him and to us because we wish it were so. We have walked towards those lights, and there were none. Another man has walked through the snow; he has reached the road and shouts to us: 'You will get nowhere, the lights are in your eyes; you will go astray and perish. But here is the hard road; I am on it; it will keep us right.' That is very little. When we believed in the lights that glittered in our bewildered eyes, we seemed close to a village and a warm hut, and to safety and rest, and here we have only a firm road. But if we listen to the first man we shall certainly perish, and if we listen to the second we shall certainly reach our destination.

And so what should I do if I alone have understood Christ's teaching and believed in it—alone among people who do not understand it and do not fulfil it?

What am I to do? Live like every one else, or live according to Christ's teaching? I have understood Christ's teaching in his commandments, and I see that their fulfilment offers blessedness to me and to all men. I have understood that the execution of these commandments is the will of that Source of all, from which my life also has come.

I have understood that whatever I may do I shall inevitably perish in a meaningless life and death, with all who surround me, if I do not fulfil the will of the Father, and that in its fulfilment lies the only possibility of salvation.

Doing as all do, I shall certainly counteract

the welfare of all, I shall certainly act contrary to the will of the Father of life, I shall certainly deprive myself of the only possibility of bettering my desperate position. Doing what Christ teaches me, I continue what has been done by people who preceded me: I co-operate in the welfare of all men now living as well as of those who will come after me; I do what is desired of me by Him who brought me into existence, and I do what alone can save me.

The circus at Berdichev is on fire: all push and suffocate one another, pressing against the door, which opens inwards. A saviour appears and says: 'Stand back from the door, turn back; the more you push the less chance you have of being saved. Turn back, and you will find an exit, and will be saved.' Whether many people, or I alone, hear this and believe it—in any case, having heard and believed, what can I do but stand back and call on all to listen to the saviour? They may smother, crush, and kill me; but, all the same, there is no salvation for me except by going the only way that makes an exit possible. And I cannot but go that way. A saviour should really be a saviour—that is to say, should really save. Christ's salvation is really salvation. He came, spoke, and humanity is saved.

The circus has been burning an hour, and one must make haste, and the people may not be in time to escape. But the world has been burning for 1,800 years, since the day when Christ said, 'I have come to bring fire upon earth; and how am I straitened till it is kindled'—and that fire will burn till people save themselves. Is not that why men exist, and is not that why the fire burns, in order that people may have the joy of being saved?

And, having understood this, I understood and believed that Jesus is not only the Messiah, the Christ, but that he is really the Saviour of the world.

I know that there is no other exit either for me or for all those who, together with me, are tormented in this life. I know that for all, and for me, together with them, there is no way of escape except by fulfilling those commands of Christ which offer to all humanity the highest welfare of which I can conceive.

I am not frightened about whether I shall have more unpleasantness or whether I shall die sooner. This may be terrible to one who does not see how senseless and ruinous is his separate, personal life, and who thinks he will not die. But I know that my life, aiming at personal, solitary happiness, is the greatest absurdity, and that at the end of this stupid life there is inevitably nothing but a stupid death. Therefore things cannot be at all terrible for me. I shall die like every one else, like those who do not fulfil the teaching; but, both for me and for all, my life and death will have a meaning. My life and death will serve the salvation and life of all, and that is what Christ taught.

CHAPTER IX

FAITH AND WORKS

WERE all people to fulfil Christ's teaching the kingdom of God would have come on earth; if I alone fulfil it, I do the best that is possible for myself and for all men. Without the fulfilment of the teaching of Christ there is no salvation. 'But how is one to get the faith to fulfil it, always to follow it, and never to be unfaithful to it?' 'Lord, I believe; help Thou my unbelief.'

The disciples asked Christ to confirm their faith; 'I wish to do good, but I do evil,' says the Apostle Paul.

'It is hard to be saved,' men in general say and think.

A man is sinking and asks to be saved; a rope is thrown him which alone can save him, and the drowning man says: 'Confirm my faith that the rope will save me. I believe,' says he, 'that the rope will save me, but help my unbelief.'

What does this mean? If the man does not seize the thing that can save him, it only means that he does not understand his position.

How could a Christian, believing in the divinity of Christ and all his teachings (however he understand them), say that he wishes to believe, but cannot? God himself, coming to earth, said: You have before you everlasting torment, fire, everlasting infernal darkness—and here is your salvation—in my teaching and in its fulfilment.

It is impossible for such a Christian not to believe in the offered salvation, not to fulfil it, and to say, 'Help thou my unbelief.'

In order that man might say that, he must disbelieve in his own destruction, and must believe that he will not perish.

Children jump from a ship into the water. They are still upheld by the current, by their clothes which are not yet soaked, and by their own feeble movements, and they do not understand their peril. From above, from the departing ship, a rope is thrown to them; they are told that they will certainly perish, and are begged by those on the ship to save themselves (the parables of the woman who found a piece of silver, of the shepherd who found a lost sheep, of the supper, and of the prodigal son, speak only of this). But the children do not believe; they disbelieve, not in the rope, but in the fact that they are perishing; other frivolous children, like themselves, have assured them that they will always, even after the ship has gone, continue merrily bathing. They do not believe that their clothes will soon be soaked, that their little arms will be tired, that they will begin to gasp, will be choked, and will go to the bottom; they do not believe in all this, and solely for that reason do not believe in the rope which would save them.

As the children who have fallen from the ship believe that they will not perish, and therefore do not catch at the rope, so people who believe in the immortality of the soul have convinced themselves that they are not perishing, and therefore they do not obey the teaching of Christ-God. They do not believe that which it is impossible to disbelieve, and this simply because they believe in that which it is impossible to believe.

And so they call to some one: 'Confirm in us the belief that we are not perishing.'

But this it is impossible to do; in order that they should have faith that they will not perish they must cease to do the things that destroy them and must begin to do the things that save them– they must catch at the rope which would save them; and they do not wish to do this, but to assure themselves that they are not perishing, despite the fact that one after another their comrades perish before their eyes. And this desire of theirs, to believe in that which is not true, they call faith. It is natural that they always have little faith, and want to have more.

Only when I understood the teaching of Christ did I understand also that what these people call faith is not faith, and that this false faith is what the Apostle James rejected in his Epistle. (That Epistle was long not acknowledged by the Church, and when it was accepted it underwent certain perversions, some words were thrown out, and some transposed or arbitrarily translated. I follow the accepted translation, merely correcting the inaccuracies, in accordance with Tischendorf's text.[1])

James ii. 14–22, 24, 26: 'What doth it profit, my brethren,' says James, 'if a man say he hath faith, and have not works? can that faith save him? If a brother or sister be naked, and in lack of daily food, and one of you say unto them, Go in peace, be ye warmed and filled; and yet ye give them not the things needful to the body; what doth it profit? Even so faith, if it have not works, is dead in itself. Yea, a man may say, Thou hast faith, and I have works: shew me thy faith apart from thy works, and I by my works will shew thee my faith. Thou believest that God is one; thou doest well: the devils also believe, and shudder. But wilt thou know, O vain man, that faith apart from works is barren? Was not Abraham our father justified by works, in that he had offered up Isaac his son upon the altar? Thou seest that faith wrought with his works, and by works was faith made perfect. . . . Ye see that by works a man is justified, and not only by faith. For as the body apart from the spirit is dead, even so faith apart from works is dead.'

James says that the only signs of faith are the works which flow from it, and that therefore faith from which works do not flow is a matter of mere words, which, as they will not feed any one, will also not justify any one or save him, and therefore faith from which works do

[1] The English Revised Version accords with Tolstoy's translation, and has been followed here.

not flow is not faith, but only the desire to believe something: only a mistaken assertion in words that I believe what I do not believe.

Faith, according to this definition, is that which promotes deeds, and deeds are what faith produces—that is to say, that which makes faith really faith. The Jews said to Christ (John vi. 30), 'What then doest thou for a sign, that we may see, and believe thee? What workest thou?'

That is what was said to him when he was on the cross (Mark xv. 32): 'Let the Christ, the King of Israel, now come down from the cross, that we may see and believe.' (Matt. xxvii.42): 'He saved others; himself he cannot save. He is the King of Israel; let him now come down from the cross, and we will believe on him.' And to this demand to increase their faith, Christ replies that their wish is vain, and that nothing can compel them to believe that which they do not believe. (Luke xxii. 67) He said, 'If I tell you, ye will not believe.' (John x. 25-6) 'I told you, and ye believe not. But ye believe not, because ye are not of my sheep.'

The Jews demanded what is demanded by Church Christians, some external sign which would compel them to believe in the teaching of Christ, and he replies and explains to them why it is impossible. He says that they cannot believe because they are not of his sheep—that is to say, do not follow that path of life which he has shown to his sheep. He explained (John v. 44) wherein lies the difference between his sheep and others, explaining what some believe and others do not believe, and on what faith rests. 'How can ye believe,' says he, 'which receive teaching [1] one of another, and the teaching that cometh from the only God ye seek not?'

To believe, says Christ, you must seek that teaching which flows from the only God. He who speaks from himself seeks his own teaching (δόξαν τήν ἴδιαν), but he who seeks the teaching of him who sent me is true, and there is no untruth in him (John vii. 18). The teaching of life is the basis of faith.

Actions all flow from faith, faith comes from *doxa*, that meaning which we attribute to life. There may be innumerable actions; there are also very many faiths; but there are only two *doxa*, doctrines of life. One of these is denied and the other affirmed by Christ. One teaching, that which is denied by Christ, is that personal life is something really existing and belonging to men. This is the doctrine which was held, and is held, by the majority of men, and from which flow all the various faiths held by worldly men and all their actions. The other doctrine is that which was preached by all the prophets and by Christ: it is that our personal life gains meaning only by the fulfilment of the will of God.

If a man has for his *doxa* that the most important thing is his personality, he will

[1] δόξα, as in many other passages, is here quite wrongly translated by the word 'glory'; δόξα, from δοκέω, means opinion, judgement, teaching.—L. T.

consider that his personal welfare is the most important and desirable thing in life, and according to the direction in which he seeks that welfare—whether in obtaining property, or distinction, or fame, or in the satisfaction of his desires—he will have a faith corresponding to that outlook, and all his actions will accord with it.

If his *doxa* is different, if he understands life in such a way that its meaning lies only in the fulfilment of the will of God, as it was understood by Abraham, and as Christ taught, then, according to his perception of the will of God will be his corresponding view of faith, and all his actions will conform therewith.

That is why those who believe that our life is satisfactory cannot believe in the teaching of Christ, and all their efforts to believe it always remain vain. In order to believe, they would have to alter their outlook on life; and until they alter that, their actions will always conform to their belief, and not to what they wish to believe and say they believe.

The desire to believe in the teaching of Christ, in those who asked a sign of him, and in our believers, does not correspond and cannot correspond with their life, however they may try to make it. They may pray to Christ-God, and receive Communion, and do deeds of charity, and build churches, and convert others; all this they do, but they cannot do Christ's deeds, because such deeds flow from faith based on quite another teaching (*doxa*) than that which they hold. They cannot offer up in sacrifice their only son, as was done by Abraham, whereas Abraham could not have hesitated about presenting, or not presenting, his son in sacrifice to God, that God which alone gave meaning and blessedness to his life. And in just the same way Christ and his disciples could not but give up their lives for others, for in that alone lay the meaning and welfare of their life. From this misunderstanding of the essence of faith flows that strange desire people have to believe that it would be better to live according to the teaching of Christ, while with all the strength of their souls, in accordance with their faith in personal life, they seek to live contrary to that teaching.

The basis of faith is the meaning of life, from which flows the valuation of what is important and good and what is unimportant and bad in life. The valuation of all the phenomena of life depends on one's faith. And as now people, having faith based on their own teaching, cannot in any way make it accord with the faith which flows from the teaching of Christ, so was it also impossible for his disciples to do so. And this misunderstanding is frequently and clearly expressed in the Gospels. Christ's disciples often asked him to confirm their faith in what he told them (Matt. xix. 23–8 and xx. 20–8: Mark x. 35–45). According to both the Evangelists, after the sayings—terrible to every believer in personal life and to every one who sees welfare in worldly riches—after the words that the rich will not enter the kingdom of heaven, and the words still more terrible for those who believe only in personal life—that whosoever does not leave all, and life itself, for the sake of Christ's teaching, will not be saved—Peter asks, 'What shall we have who have left all and followed thee?' Afterwards, according to Mark, James and John, they themselves, but, according to Matthew, their mother, asked him to grant that they should sit on each side of him when he will be in his glory. They ask him to confirm their faith by promising a reward. To Peter's question Jesus replied with the parable of the labourers hired at different hours (Matt. xx. 1-16). To James's question he answered: You know not yourself what you ask—that is to say, you ask impossibilities, you do not understand the teaching. The teaching lies in the renunciation of personal life, and you are asking for personal fame, personal reward. You can drink the same cup (live the same life) as I, but to sit on my right and left hand, that is, to be equal with me, is what no one can do. And here Christ says: Only in worldly life do the powerful enjoy and delight in the fame and power of personal life; but you, my disciples, should know that the meaning of human life does not lie in personal happiness, but in serving all, in humiliation before all. Man lives not to be served, but himself to serve and give up his personal life as a ransom for all. Christ, in reply to his disciples' demand, which showed him how completely they failed to understand his teaching, did not tell them to believe—that is to say, to change that valuation of the good and evil in life which flowed from their teaching (he knew that this was impossible) but explained to them the meaning of life on which his faith rested—that is to say, the true valuation of what is good and evil, important and unimportant.

To Peter's question (Matt. xix. 27) 'What shall we have, what reward for our sacrifices?' Christ replies with the parable of the labourers hired at different times and receiving identical payment. Christ explains to Peter his misunderstanding of the teaching, from which his absence of faith results. Christ says: Only in personal and meaningless life is it precious and important that the remuneration for work should accord with the amount of work done. The belief in a remuneration for work according to the amount of work flows from the doctrine of personal life. That belief rests on the assumption that we have a claim to something; but man has no rights and can have none. He is ever in debt for the welfare given him, and therefore can make no demands on any one. Even if he gives up his whole life, he still cannot repay what has been given him, and therefore his master cannot be unjust to him. If a man asserts rights to his life and keeps account with the Source of all things which has given him life, he thereby only shows that he does not understand the meaning of life.

People who had received happiness demanded something more. These people stood in the market-places idle and unhappy, lacking life.

The master took them, and gave them the greatest blessing of life—work. They accepted the kindness of the master, and then remained dissatisfied. They were dissatisfied because they had no clear consciousness of their position; they had come to work holding a false doctrine to the effect that they had rights to their life and to their labour, and that therefore their labour should be rewarded. They did not understand that this labour was the highest blessing, which is freely given to them, and for which they should only try to return a similar blessing, but could not demand reward. And therefore people, having, like these workmen, a perverted understanding of life, cannot have a just and true faith.

The parable of the master and the workman who returned from the field, spoken in reply to the disciples' direct request that he would confirm their faith, defines yet more clearly the foundations of the faith Christ teaches.

(Luke xvii. 3–10) Horrified at the difficulty of fulfilling the rule Christ lays down, that one must forgive one's brother not seven times, but unto seventy times seven, the disciples say: Yes, but . . . in order to fulfil this, one must have faith; confirm, increase, our faith. As previously they had asked: 'What shall we get for it?' so now they ask what all so-called Christians ask to-day: I want to believe, but cannot; confirm our belief that the rope of salvation will save us. They say: Do something to make us believe, just as the Jews had asked of him a sign. By miracles, or by promising rewards, make us believe in our salvation.

The disciples said, as we say: It would be well to arrange so that we, living the personal, self-willed life we do, could also believe that, if we were to fulfil God's teaching, things would be still better for us. We all make that demand, which is one contrary to the whole sense of Christ's teaching, and we are surprised that we are quite unable to believe. And to this most fundamental misunderstanding, which existed then as it exists now, he replies with a parable in which he shows what true faith is. Faith cannot result from credulous acceptance of what is said; faith comes only from recognizing one's position. Faith rests only on reasonable consciousness of what it is best to do, being in the position in which we are. He shows that it is impossible to arouse this faith in others by promising a reward or by threats of punishment, and that this could result only in a weak credulity which would crumble at the first temptation; that the faith which moves mountains—that which nothing can disturb—rests on a consciousness of inevitable impending destruction, and of the only possible means of safety in this position.

To have faith, no promises of reward are necessary. It is only necessary to understand that salvation from inevitable destruction lies in living a common life according to the Master's will. Whoever understands that will not seek for confirmation, but will save himself without any exhortations.

To the disciples' request for a confirmation of their faith Christ says: When a workman returns from the field, his master does not at once tell him to have dinner, but tells him to stall the cattle and serve him, and only then will the workman sit down to table and have dinner. The workman does all this without considering himself ill-used, and does not boast or demand gratitude or reward, but knows that so it should be, and that he is but doing what is needful; that this is a necessary condition both of the service and of the true welfare of his life. So also you, says Christ, when you have done all that is demanded of you, must consider that you have only done your duty. He who understands his relation to the Master will understand that only by submitting to his Master's will can he have life; and he will know wherein his welfare lies, and will have a faith to which nothing will be impossible. This is the faith Christ teaches. Faith, according to Christ's teaching, rests on a reasonable consciousness of the meaning of one's life.

The foundation of faith, according to Christ's teaching, is light.

(John i. 9–12) 'That was the true light, which lighteth every man coming into the world. He was in the world, and the world was made through him, and the world knew him not. He came unto his own, and his own received him not. But as many as received him, even to them that believe on his name, gave he the right to become the children of God.' (iii. 19–21) 'And this is the judgement,[1] that the light is come into the world, but men loved the darkness rather than the light: for their works were evil. For every one that doeth ill hateth the light, and cometh not to the light, lest his works should be reproved. But he that doeth the truth cometh to the light, that his works may be made manifest, because they have been wrought in God.'

For him who has understood the teaching of Christ there cannot be any question of confirming his faith. Faith, according to Christ's teaching, rests on light, on truth. Christ nowhere demands faith in himself: he demands faith in the truth.

(John viii. 40.) He says to the Jews: 'Ye seek to kill me, a man that hath told you the truth, which I heard from God.' (46) 'Which of you convicteth me of sin? If I say truth, why do ye not believe me?' (xviii. 37) He says, 'To this end was I born, and to this end am I come into the world, that I should bear witness unto the truth. Every one that is of the truth heareth my voice.' (xiv. 6) He says, 'I am the way, and the truth, and the life.' (16) 'The Father,' says he to the disciples, 'shall give you another Comforter, that he may be with you for ever.' (17) 'That Comforter is the Spirit of truth, whom the world neither sees nor knows, but whom ye know, for he is with you and shall be in you.'

He says that his whole teaching, and that he himself, is truth.

[1] The judgement (κρίσις) does not mean the *judgement*, but the *division*.—L. T.

The teaching of Christ is the teaching of truth. And therefore faith in Christ is not credulously accepting something concerning Jesus, but is knowledge of the truth. The teaching of Christ is not a thing any one can be induced to believe in, nor is it possible to bribe any one to fulfil it. He who understands the teaching of Christ will also have faith in it, because that teaching is the truth. And he who knows the truth necessary for his welfare cannot but believe it, as a man who has understood that he is really sinking cannot but catch at the rope of salvation. And the question: What must I do to believe? is a question which merely displays a non-comprehension of Jesus Christ's teaching.

CHAPTER X

'MY YOKE IS EASY'

We say, 'It is difficult to live in agreement with the teaching of Christ!' And how can it but be difficult when we ourselves laboriously, by the arrangement of our whole life, hide our position from ourselves and laboriously confirm ourselves in a credulous belief that our position is not at all what it is, but is quite different? And, having called this credulity faith, we make of it something sacred, and by every means—by working on their feelings, by threats, flattery, and deception—we allure men to this false credulity. In this demand for credulous belief in the impossible and unnatural we have reached such a pass that the very irrationality of that for which we demand credulous belief is considered a sign of its validity. A man, 'a Christian,' was found who said, *Credo quia absurdum*,[1] and other Christians repeated this with enthusiasm, assuming that absurdity is the very best method of teaching

[1] The actual words used by Tertullian were, *Credo quia impossibile*. One might amend the above passage to make it read: 'Others have repeated this, assuming that the assertion of impossibilities is the best method of inculcating truth.'

people the truth. Recently I had a conversation with a learned and clever man who told me that Christian teaching, as a moral teaching of life, is unimportant. 'All that,' said he to me, 'could be found among the Stoics and the Brahmins and in the Talmud. The essence of the Christian teaching is not in that, but in the theosophic teaching expressed in its dogmas.' In other words, that is not precious in Christian teaching which is eternal and common to all mankind, necessary for life and reasonable, but that is important and precious which is quite unintelligible and therefore unnecessary, and for the sake of which millions of people have been slaughtered.

We have formed for ourselves a false perception of our life and of the life of the world, based on nothing but our own enmities and personal desires; and belief in this false perception, which is artificially connected with Christ's teaching, we consider to be what is most necessary and important for life. Were it not for this credulous belief in falsehood, which has been maintained among men for centuries, the falsity of our conception of life, and the truth of Christ's teaching, would long ago have become plain.

It is terrible to say, but it sometimes appears to me that if Christ's teaching, with the Church teaching which has grown out of it, had not existed at all, those who now call themselves Christians would have been nearer to the truth of Christ—that is to say, to a reasonable teaching of what is good in life—than they now are. The moral teaching of the prophets of all humanity would have not been closed to them; they would have had their own small preachers of truth, and would have believed in them. But now the whole truth is open to them, and that whole truth has seemed so terrible to those whose deeds were evil, that they have reinterpreted it into falsehood, and people have lost their belief in what is true. In our European civilized society, in reply to Christ's statement that he came into the world to witness to the truth, and that therefore every one who is of the truth hears him—people have long ago answered in the words of Pilate, 'What is truth?' Those words, which express the profound and sad irony of a single Roman, we have accepted seriously and have adopted as our belief. All in our world live, not merely without the truth, not merely without a desire to know it, but with a firm conviction that, of all useless occupations, the most useless is the search for truth defining human life.

The teaching of life—which among all nations, before the age of European society, was always considered the most important thing, that about which Christ said that it was the one thing needful—this one thing is excluded from our life and from the whole activity of humanity. With this matter the institution which calls itself the Church is occupied: an institution in which all, including even those who compose it, have long ceased to believe. The solitary window towards the light, to which are directed the eyes of all who think or who suffer, has been boarded up. In reply to the question, 'What am I?' and 'What am I to do? Can I not aid my life by the teaching of that God who, you say, came to save me?' I am told, 'Obey the demands of the powers that be, and believe in the Church.' 'But why is it so hard for me to live in this world?' asks a despairing voice; 'Why is there all this evil? Is it not possible for me in my own life to abstain from participating in this evil? Can it be that it is impossible to lessen this evil?' They reply: 'It is impossible. Your wish to live your life well and to help others to do the same is pride and a snare. The one thing you can do is to save yourself; that is, to save your soul for a future life. If you do not wish to participate in the evil of the world, retire from it; that path is open to every one,' says the teaching of the Church. 'But know that, on choosing that path, you must not take part in the life of the world, but cease to live and must slowly kill yourself.' There are two paths, say our teachers: (1) to believe and to obey us, and the powers that be, and participate in the evil we have organized, or (2) to retire from the world and go into a monastery, not sleeping and not eating, rotting your flesh on the top of a column,[1] bending and unbending, and doing nothing of any use to men. Either admit the teaching of Christ to be impracticable, and therefore acquiesce in the lawlessness of life the Church has

[1] Like St. Simeon Stylites and the other Stylites, who are more highly honoured in the Eastern than in the Western world.

sanctified, or renounce life—which is equivalent to slow suicide.

Astonishing, to any one who understands Christ's teaching, as is the delusion which admits Christ's teaching to be very good for men, but impracticable, still more amazing is that delusion which acknowledges that a man who wishes to carry out the teaching of Christ not in words only, but in deeds, ought to retire from the world.

The delusion that it is better for men to withdraw from the world is an old delusion, familiar long ago to the Jews, but quite foreign to the spirit, not only of Christianity, but even to that of Judaism. Against that fallacy, long before the time of Christ, was written the story of the prophet Jonah, of which Christ was so fond, and which he so often quoted. The thought of that story from beginning to end is identical. Jonah, the prophet, wishes personally, by himself alone, to be a just man, and he withdraws from among depraved people, but God shows him that he is a prophet and that therefore it is necessary that he should impart his knowledge to the people who are in error, and so he should not flee from the erring people, but should live in contact with them. Jonah despises the depraved Ninevites and flees from them; but, however much he runs away from his destiny, God brings him back to the Ninevites by means of the whale, and that is accomplished which God desires, namely, the Ninevites receive God's teaching from Jonah, and their life becomes better. But Jonah, far from being glad that he is the instrument of God's will, is discontented, and is jealous of God's favour to the Ninevites, and would like to be reasonable and good alone by himself. He withdraws into the desert, weeps over his fate, and reproaches God: then a gourd grows up in one night over him and shields him from the sun, and in another night a worm eats the gourd, and Jonah reproaches God still more desperately because the gourd he valued has been lost. Then God says to him, 'You regret the gourd you call yours, which grew up in one night; but do I not regret the great people which was perishing, living like beasts unable to distinguish their right hand from their left? Your knowledge of the truth was only of value if it was communicated to those who had it not.'

Christ knew the story and frequently quoted it, and we are also told in the Gospels how Christ himself, after visiting John the Baptist, who had withdrawn into the desert, underwent that same temptation before commencing his own preaching, and how he was led away by the devil (by a deception) into the desert to be tempted, and how he conquered that deception and in the strength of his spirit returned into Galilee, and how from that time on, without avoiding any depraved people, he spent his life among publicans, Pharisees, and sinners, teaching them the truth (Luke iv. 1).[1]

[1] Christ was led into the wilderness in order there to be tempted (Matt. iv. 3–7). The deception told Christ that he was not a Son of God if he could not turn stones into bread. Christ replied: 'I can

According to Church teaching, Christ, the God-Man, gave us an example of life. The whole of the life of Christ known to us was led in the very whirlpool of life among publicans and adulterers in Jerusalem, and with the Pharisees. The chief injunctions of Christ were love of one's neighbour and the preaching of the truth to others: the one and the other demand continual intercourse with the world. Suddenly out of this is deduced the conclusion that, according to the teaching of Christ, one should withdraw from everything, have nothing to do with any one, and stand on a column. In order to follow the example of Christ, it appears that one must do exactly the opposite of what he taught, and of what he did. The teaching of Christ, according to Church commentators, is presented both for worldly people and also for the Religious Orders, not as a teaching of life—how to make it better for

live without bread; I live by that which was breathed into me by God.' Then the deception said: 'If you live by that which was breathed into you by God, throw yourself down from this high place; you will kill your flesh, but the spirit breathed into you by God will not perish.' Christ replied: 'It is the will of God that I should live in the flesh; to kill my flesh means to act contrary to the will of God—to tempt God' (Matt. iv. 8–11). Then the deception said: 'If that is so, then serve your flesh as all men do, and your flesh will reward you.' Christ replied: 'I am not the owner of my flesh. My life is in the spirit; but I cannot destroy my flesh, because my spirit is in my flesh by the will of God, and therefore only by living in the flesh can I serve my Father, God.' And Christ departed from the wilderness into the world.

ourselves and for others—but as a teaching of what the worldly people should believe, in order, by living badly, to save themselves in the next world; and, for the Religious Orders, how to make this life still worse for themselves than it is.

But that is not what Christ taught. Christ taught truth, and, if abstract truth is truth, it will also be true in practice; and if life in God is the only true life blessed in itself, then it is true and blessed here on earth amid all the possible accidents of life. If life here did not confirm the teaching of Christ about life, that teaching would be untrue.

Christ does not call us to something worse instead of something better, but, on the contrary, to something better instead of something worse. He pities people who appeared to him like lost sheep, perishing without a shepherd, and he promises them a shepherd and good pasture. He says that his disciples will be persecuted for his teaching and will have to suffer and to endure worldly persecution with fortitude, but he does not say that by following his teaching they will suffer more than by following the world's teaching; on the contrary, he says that those who follow the teaching of the world will be unhappy, and those who follow his teaching will be blessed.

Christ does not teach salvation by faith or by asceticism—that is, by a deception of the imagination or by voluntarily tormenting oneself in this life; but he teaches life in which, besides salvation from the loss of personal life, there will, here in this world, be less of suffering and more of joy than by a personal life.

Christ, revealing his teaching, says to people that, by following it, even among those who do not follow it, they will not be more unhappy than before, but, on the contrary, will be happier than those who reject it. He says that there is true worldly advantage in not taking thought for the worldly life.

'And Peter began to say unto him: Behold we have left all and followed thee; what shall we receive?' Jesus answered him and said, 'Verily, I say unto you, there is not one who has left home, or brother, or sister, or father, or mother, or wife, or child, or lands, for my sake and the Gospel's, who will not receive now, in this time, amid persecutions, a hundred times more houses, and brethren, and sisters, and fathers, and mothers, and children, and lands, and in the age to come, life eternal.' (Matt. xix. 27, 29; Mark x. 28-30; Luke xviii. 28-30.)

Christ, it is true, says that those who follow him will be persecuted by those who do not listen to him, but he does not say that the disciples will lose anything thereby; on the contrary, he says that his disciples will here, in this world, have more of joy than those who do not follow him.

That Christ says and thinks this is shown beyond possibility of doubt by the clearness of his words and the drift of his whole teaching, as well as by his way of life and that of his disciples. But is it true?

Examining the abstract question whether the position of the disciples of Christ or of the disciples of the world is the better, one cannot but see that the position of the disciples of Christ should be better, because they, doing good to all men, would not evoke hatred. The disciples of Christ, doing harm to no one, would only be persecuted by evil men, but the disciples of the world would be persecuted by all, since the law of their life is the law of strife—that is to say, the persecution one of another. The chances of suffering are the same for these as for those, with only this difference, that Christ's disciples will be prepared for the sufferings, but the world's disciples will employ all the powers of their souls to escape them; and that Christ's disciples, when suffering, will think that the world needs their sufferings; but the world's disciples, when suffering, will not know why they suffer. Arguing in the abstract, the position of Christ's followers should be better than that of those of the world. But is it so in reality?

To verify this let every one remember all the painful moments of his life, all the physical and spiritual sufferings he has endured and still endures, and ask himself for what has he borne all these misfortunes, for the sake of the world's teaching, or for that of Christ's? Let every sincere man remember well his whole life, and he will see that never, not once, has he suffered from obeying the teaching of

Christ, but that most of the misfortunes of his life have come about because, contrary to his own inclination, he has followed the world's teaching which constrained him.

In my own life, exceptionally fortunate in a worldly sense, I can recall sufferings borne by me in the name of the world's teaching, which would be sufficient to supply a good Christian martyr. All the bitterest moments of my life, from the drunkenness and debauchery of student-days, the duels, war, and so on, to that ill-health and those unnatural and trying conditions of life in which I now live—all this was martyrdom in the name of the world's teaching.

And I speak of my own life, which is exceptionally fortunate in a worldly sense. But how many martyrs are there who have endured, and are now enduring, for the sake of the world's teaching, sufferings which I cannot even vividly imagine to myself!

We do not see all the difficulty and danger of obeying the world's teaching, merely because we consider that all we endure for it is unavoidable.

We have assured ourselves that all these misfortunes which we inflict on ourselves are necessary conditions of our life, and therefore we are unable to grasp the fact that Christ teaches just how we should free ourselves from these misfortunes, and live happily.

To be in a condition to discuss the question which life is happier, we should, if only in thought, dismiss that false notion, and look without prejudice within ourselves and around us.

Go among a large crowd of people, especially townsfolk, and notice the wearied, distressed, sickly faces, and then remember your own life and the lives of people about whom you have known; remember all the violent deaths, all the suicides of which you have heard, and ask yourself for whose sake was all this suffering, death, and suicidal despair? And you will see, strange as it at first seems, that nine-tenths of these sufferings are endured for the sake of the world's teaching; that all these sufferings are unnecessary, and need not exist; and that the majority of people are martyrs to the world's teaching.

Recently, one rainy autumn Sunday, I went by tram through the Bazaar at the Sukharev Tower. For nearly half a mile the car made its way through a dense crowd of people, who immediately closed in again behind it. From morning to night these thousands of people, of whom most were hungry and ragged, swarm here in the dirt, scolding, cheating, and hating one another. The same thing occurs in all the bazaars of Moscow. The evening is passed by these people in the dram-shops and taverns, the night in their corners [1] and hovels. Sunday is the best day in their week. On Mon-

[1] It was common for Moscow workmen to live in a corner of a room or passage, generally not even screened off from the rest of the room in which other people, besides the owner and his family, had other corners.

day, in their infected dens, they will again resume the work they detest.

Consider the life of all these people in the positions they left to choose that in which they have placed themselves, and remember the unceasing toil these people voluntarily endure—men and women—and you will see that they are real martyrs.

All these people have left their home, field, fathers, brothers, and often their wives and children, and have abandoned everything, even their very lives, and have come to town to acquire that which, according to the teaching of the world, is considered indispensable for each of them. And they all—not to mention those tens of thousands of unfortunate people who have lost everything and struggle along on garbage and vodka in the doss-houses—they all, from the factory hands, cabmen, seamstresses, and prostitutes, to the rich merchants and Ministers of State, with their wives, endure the most trying and unnatural manner of life, and yet fail to acquire what, according to the teaching of the world, they need.

Search among these people for a man, poor or rich, for whom what he earns secures what he considers necessary according to the world's teaching, and you will not find one in a thousand. Every one struggles with his whole strength to obtain what he does not need, but what is demanded of him by the teaching of the world, and the absence of which therefore makes him unhappy. And as soon as he obtains what is required, something else, and again something else, is demanded of him, and so this work of Sisyphus continues endlessly, ruining the life of men. Take the ladder of wealth of people who spend from £30 to £5,000 a year, and you will rarely find one who is not tormented and worn out with work to obtain £40 when he has £30, and £50 when he has £40, and so on endlessly. And there is not one who, having £50, would voluntarily exchange into the way of life of one having £40, or, if there are such cases, the exchange is made not to live more easily, but to save money and hide it away. They all have more and more to burden their already overladen life with work, and to devote their life and soul entirely to the service of the world's teaching. To-day I obtain a coat and goloshes, to-morrow a watch and chain, after to-morrow a lodging with a sofa and a lamp, then carpets in the sitting-room and velvet clothes, then racehorses and pictures in gilt frames, then finally, I fall ill from my excessive labours and die. Another continues the same labour and also sacrifices his life to that same Moloch; he too dies, and also does not know why he did what he did. But perhaps the life itself during which a man does all this is happy?

Test that life by the measure of what all men have always described as happiness, and you will see that this life is terribly unhappy. Indeed, what are the chief conditions of earthly happiness—those which no one disputes?

One of the first conditions acknowledged by everyone is that man's union with nature should not be infringed—that is to say, that he should live under the open sky, in the light of the sun and in the fresh air, in contact with the earth, with vegetation, and with animals. All men have always considered that to be deprived of those things was a great misfortune. Men confined in prison feel this deprivation more than anything else. But consider the life of people who live according to the teaching of the world : the more they achieve success according to the world's teaching, the more are they deprived of this condition of happiness. The higher they climb in the scale of worldly fortune the less do they see of the light of the sun, of the fields and the woods, and of wild or domestic animals. Many of them, almost all the women, live on to old age seeing the rising of the sun only once or twice in their lives, and never seeing the fields and the woods except from a carriage or a railway train, and not only without having sown or planted anything, or fed or reared cows, horses, or hens, but without even having an idea of how those animals are born, grow, and live. These people only see textiles, stone, and wood shaped by human toil, and that not by the light of the sun, but by artificial light. They only hear the sounds of machines, vehicles, cannons, and musical instruments ; they smell scents and tobacco-smoke ; under their feet and hands they have only textiles, stone, and wood ; for the most part, on account of their weak digestions, they eat food that smells and is not fresh. Their movements from place to place do not save them from these deprivations. They move about in closed boxes. In the country and abroad, wherever they go, they have the same textiles and wood under their feet, the same curtains hiding the light of the sun from them, the same footmen, coachmen, and porters depriving them of contact with the earth, with plants, and with animals. Wherever they may be they are deprived, like prisoners, of this condition of happiness. As prisoners console themselves with a tuft of grass that grows in the prison yard, with a spider or a mouse, so these people sometimes console themselves with puny indoor plants, a parrot, or a monkey, and even these they do not themselves rear.

Another undoubted condition of happiness is work; in the first place voluntary work which one is fond of, and, secondly, physical work which gives one an appetite and sound, restful sleep. Again, the more good fortune people have secured according to the world's teaching, the more are they deprived of this second condition of happiness. All the fortunate ones of the world, the men in important places, and the rich, either live like prisoners, quite deprived of work and vainly struggling with diseases that arise from the absence of physical labour, and still more vainly with the ennui which overcomes them (I say vainly, because work is only joyous when it is undoubtedly needful—and they need nothing), or they do work they hate, as bankers, public prosecutors, governors, or ministers, while their wives arrange drawing-rooms, china, and costumes for themselves and their children. (I say hateful because I have never yet met one of them who praised his occupation, or did it with even as much pleasure as that with which a porter clears away the snow from before the house.) All these fortunate people are either deprived of work or are burdened with work they dislike—that is to say, they find themselves in the position in which prisoners are placed.

The third indubitable condition of happiness is a family. And again, the further people have advanced in worldly success the less is that happiness accessible to them. Most of them are adulterers, and consciously renounce the happiness of a family, submitting only to its inconveniences. If they are not adulterers, still their children are not a joy to them, but a burden, and they deprive themselves of them, trying in every way—often by most tormenting means—to make their marital unions barren. Or, if they have children, they are deprived of the joy of intercourse with them. They, by their rules, have to hand them over to strangers, for the most part quite alien people; first to foreigners,[1] and then to the Government instructors[2]; so that their family only causes them grief, their children from infancy becoming as unhappy as their parents, and having only one feeling towards their parents—a desire

[1] This is a reference to the common Russian practice of having a foreign nurse, governess, or tutor for young children, that they may learn a foreign language in the nursery.

[2] The Russian schools are State institutions.

for their death in order to inherit their property.[1] They are not shut up in prison, but the consequences of their life, in regard to their family, are more tormenting than the deprivation of family life to which prisoners are exposed.

The fourth condition of happiness is free, amicable intercourse with all the different people in the world. And again, the higher the rank attained by men of the world the more are they deprived of this chief condition of happiness: the higher, the narrower, and the more restricted is the group of people with whom it is possible for them to associate, and the lower in mental and moral development are the few people who form the enchanted circle from which there is no escape. For a peasant and his wife intercourse is open with the whole world of mankind, and if one million people do not wish to have intercourse with him he still has eighty millions of people such as himself, labouring people, with whom, from Archangel to Astrakhan,

[1] The defence of such a life which one often hears from parents is amazing. 'I want nothing,' say the parents; 'this kind of life is hard for me, but, as I love my children, I bear it for their sakes.' That is to say, I know by undoubted experience that our life is unhappy, and therefore . . . I educate my children so that they should be as unhappy as I am. And therefore, out of my love for them, I place them in the full physical and moral contagion of a town; I hand them over to strangers who have only a mercenary aim in educating them; and so physically, morally, and mentally I take pains to injure my children. And this contention has to serve as justification for the irrational life the parents themselves lead!—L. T.

without waiting for visits or introductions, he can at once enter into the closest brotherly relations. For an official with his wife there are hundreds of people on the same level as himself; but those above him do not receive him, and those below him are all separated from him. For a rich man of the world and his wife a few dozen worldly families are accessible; all the rest are cut off from him. For a Minister of State, or a millionaire, and his family, there are a single dozen similarly important or wealthy people. For Emperors and Kings the circle is yet more restricted. Is not this a form of imprisonment, in which the prisoner can only have intercourse with two or three warders?

Finally, a fifth condition of happiness is a healthy and painless death. And again, the higher people stand on the social ladder the more are they deprived of this condition of happiness. Take, for example, a moderately rich man and his wife and an average peasant and his wife, notwithstanding all the hunger and excessive toil which, not by his fault but by the cruelty of man, a peasant has to bear, and you will see that the lower the healthier, and the higher the sicklier are men and women.

Count over in your memory the rich men and their wives you have known or now know, and you will notice that most of them are ill. Among them a healthy man, who is not undergoing treatment continually or periodically summer after summer, is as much an exception as is a sick man among the peasantry. All these fortunate people, without exception, begin with onanism (which has become in their class a natural condition of development), they all have bad teeth, are all grey or bald at an age when a workman is just reaching his full strength. They are nearly all subject to nervous, digestive, and sexual illnesses from gluttony, drunkenness, debauchery, and doctoring, and those who do not die young spend half their life in being doctored and taking injections of morphia, or are shrivelled cripples, unfitted to live by their own exertions and capable of existing only like parasites or like those ants who are fed by slave-ants. Consider their deaths: this one shot himself; that one rotted with syphilis; another old man died from the effects of a stimulant, while another died young from a flogging to which he submitted in his desire for sex-stimulation; one was eaten alive by lice, another by worms; one drank himself to death, another died of over-eating; one from morphia, and another from producing an abortion. They perish one after another for the sake of the world's teaching. And the crowd throngs after them and seeks, like martyrs, for suffering and destruction.

One life after another is flung under the chariot-wheels of that god: the chariot passes on tearing them to pieces, and fresh and fresh victims, with groans, cries, and curses, fall beneath it!

To fulfil the teaching of Christ is hard! Christ says: 'Let him that would follow me leave house, and fields, and brothers, and follow me, God, and he shall receive in this world a hundred times more houses, fields, and brothers, and besides that shall gain eternal life.' And no one follows him. But the teaching of the world says: 'Abandon house, and fields, and brothers, and go from the village to the rotten town. Live all your life as a naked bath-attendant, soaping other people's backs amid the steam, or serve in a money-changer's basement-office, all your life counting other people's pence; or live as a public prosecutor, spending your whole life in the courts, over law-papers, and devoting yourself to making miserable people's fate yet worse; or as a Minister of State, signing unnecessary papers in a hurry all your life; or as a colonel, killing people all your life—live such a monstrous life as this, always ending in a painful death, and you will neither get anything in this world nor will you receive life eternal.' And every one follows this course. Christ said: 'Take up your cross and follow me'—that is to say, endure submissively the fate that has befallen you and obey me, God; and no one follows him. But the first abandoned man wearing epaulets, and fit for nothing but murder, into whose head it enters, says: 'Take, not a cross, but a knapsack and rifle, and follow me to all kinds of torment and to certain death'—and all follow him.

Having abandoned their families, parents, wives, and children, and having been dressed up like fools and submitted themselves to the authority of the first man of higher rank that they happened to meet: cold, hungry, and exhausted by forced marches, they go like a herd of bullocks to the slaughter; yet they are not bullocks, but human beings. They cannot but know that they are being driven to slaughter with the question unanswered—Why? And with despair in their hearts they go, and die of cold, hunger, and infectious diseases, till they are placed under a shower of bullets and cannon-balls and ordered to kill people who are unknown to them. They slay and are slain. And no one of the slayers knows why or wherefore. The Turks roast them alive on the fire, skin them, and tear out their entrails. And to-morrow some one will again whistle, and again all will follow to horrible sufferings, to death, and to obvious evil. And no one considers this hard! Neither those who endure the sufferings, nor their fathers and mothers, consider this difficult. The parents even themselves advise their children to go. It seems to them that not only is this necessary and unavoidable, but that it is also good and moral.

It would be possible to believe that the fulfilment of Christ's teaching is difficult and terrible and tormenting, if the fulfilment of the world's teaching were easy, safe, and pleasant. But, in fact, the fulfilment of the world's teaching is much more dangerous and tormenting than the fulfilment of Christ's teaching.

There used, it is said, to be Christian martyrs,

but they were the exception; they have been reckoned at 380,000—voluntary and involuntary, in 1,800 years. But count the worldly martyrs, and for each Christian martyr you will find a thousand worldly martyrs whose sufferings are a hundred times more terrible. Those slain in war, during the present century, are reckoned at 30,000,000.[1]

Now these were all martyrs to the world's teaching, who needed not even to follow the teaching of Christ but simply to abstain from following the teaching of the world, in order to have escaped from suffering and death.

A man need only do what he wishes to do—refuse to go to war,—he will be set to dig trenches: but will not be tormented in Sevastopol or Plevna. A man need but disbelieve the world's teaching that he must wear overshoes[2] and a watch-chain and have a drawing-room he does not need, and that he must do all the stupid things demanded of him by the world's teaching, and he will not be exposed to excessive toil and suffering, never-ending cares, and work without rest or aim; he will not be deprived of intercourse with nature, will not be deprived of congenial work, of family, and of health, and will not perish by a senseless and tormenting death.

[1] This book was written in 1884; and the figures relate to the nineteenth century.

[2] The wearing of over shoes or goloshes to keep one's feet dry and warm, and to be able, on entering a house, to kick them off and have clean feet, is here instanced as a sign of distinction from the peasant, who usually wears nothing over his high boots.

It is not necessary to be a martyr in Christ's name—that is not what he teaches. He only bids us cease to torment ourselves in the name of the world's false teaching.

Christ's teaching has a profound metaphysical meaning, it has an all-human meaning, and it has the simplest, clearest, and most practical meaning for the life of every single man. That last meaning can be expressed thus: Christ teaches men not to commit stupidities. Therein lies the simplest meaning of Christ's teaching, accessible to all.

Christ says: Do not be angry, do not consider any one your inferior—to do so is stupid. If you get angry and insult people it will be the worse for you. Christ also says: Do not run after women, but unite with one woman and live with her—it will be better for you so. He also says: Do not promise anything to any one,[1] or else they will oblige you to do stupid and evil actions. He also says: Do not return evil for evil, or the evil will return to you yet more bitterly than before: like the heavy log suspended over the store of honey, which kills the bear.[2] He also says: Do not consider

[1] We have here one of Tolstoy's sweeping conclusions, and one which caused a great deal of trouble in the Tolstoy movement and among those who arranged Tolstoy Colonies. These all fell to pieces largely for lack of definite understanding as to what each man might expect of his fellow-colonists.

[2] The reference is to the practice of hanging a heavy block, or log, over a deposit of honey. When a bear tries to take the honey he knocks himself against the log, which swings back and hits him.

men foreign to you merely because they live in another country and speak another language. If you consider them as enemies, and they consider you such, it will be worse for you. So do not commit all these stupidities, and it will be better for you.

'Yes,' people reply, 'but the world is so arranged that to resist its arrangements is more painful than to live in accord with them. If a man refuses military service he will be sent to a fortress, and perhaps shot. If a man does not safeguard his life by acquiring the property he and his family need, he and they will die of hunger.' So people say, trying to defend the world's arrangement, but they do not think so themselves. They only speak so because they cannot deny the justice of the teaching of Christ, in whom they are supposed to believe, and they must justify themselves in some way for not fulfilling that teaching. They not only do not think this, but they have never even thought about the matter at all. They believe the world's teaching and merely employ the excuse the Church has taught them, to the effect that if one fulfils Christ's teaching one must endure great suffering; and therefore they have never even tried to fulfil it. We see the innumerable sufferings people endure for the sake of the world's teaching, but in our time we never see sufferings for the sake of

The bear then strikes the log more fiercely, and it, rebounding, strikes him still more heavily, and so on, until, it is said, the bear is sometimes killed by the blows he receives.

Christ's teaching at all. Thirty millions have perished for the world's teaching in warfare; thousands of millions have pined in a tormenting life for the sake of the world's teaching, while not only no millions, but not even thousands or dozens, or even one single man, do I know who has perished by death or by a painful life of hunger and cold for the sake of Christ's teaching. It is only a ridiculous excuse, showing to what a degree Christ's teaching is unknown to us. Not only do we not share it; we have never even seriously considered it. The Church has been at pains to explain Christ's teaching so that it has appeared to us not as a teaching of life, but as a bugbear.

Christ calls men to a spring of water which is there beside them. Men are tormented by thirst, eat dirt, and drink one another's blood, but their teachers tell them that they will perish if they go to the spring to which Christ directs them. And people believe this; they suffer and die of thirst at two steps from the water, not daring to go to it. But it is only necessary to believe Christ, that he has brought blessing on earth, and that he gives us who thirst a spring of living water, and to come to him, to see how insidious is the Church's deception, and how insensate are our sufferings when salvation is so near at hand. It is only necessary to accept Christ's teaching, simply and plainly, for the terrible deception in which we all and each are living to become clear.

Generation after generation we labour to

secure life by means of violence and by safeguarding our property. Our happiness seems to us to lie in obtaining the maximum of power and the maximum of property. We are so accustomed to this that Christ's teaching that a man's happiness cannot depend on his power or his estate, and that a rich man cannot be happy, seems to us like a demand to make a sacrifice for the sake of future bliss. But Christ did not think of calling us to sacrifice; on the contrary, he teaches us not to do what is worse, but to do what is better for us, here in this life. Christ, loving men, teaches them to refrain from securing themselves by violence and by property, just as others who love men teach them to refrain from brawling and drunkenness. He says that men, if they live without resisting others and without property, will be happier; and by the example of his own life he confirms this. He says that a man living in accord with his teaching must be prepared to die at any moment by the violence of others, by cold or hunger, and cannot be sure of a single hour's life. And we imagine this to be a terrible demand of sacrifice; but it is only a declaration of the conditions in which every man always and inevitably lives. Christ's disciple must be prepared at any moment for suffering and death. But is not a disciple of the world in the same position? We are so accustomed to our pretence that all we do for the imaginary security of our life—our armies, fortifications, stores, clothes, and doctoring, our property and our money—seems to us real, and as something that seriously secures our life. We forget, though it is obvious to every one, what happened to the man who planned to build barns in order to be safe for many years. He died that same night. Indeed all we do to safeguard our life is just what an ostrich does, standing still and hiding its head in order not to see how it is being killed. We do worse than the ostrich: doubtfully to safeguard our doubtful life in a doubtful future, we certainly destroy our certain life in the certain present.

The deception consists in the false conviction that our life can be secured by strife against others. We are so accustomed to this deception —an imaginary safeguarding of our life and property—that we do not notice all we lose by it. And we lose all—our whole life. Our whole life is absorbed in cares for this safeguarding of life, this preparation for life, so that no life at all is left us.

We need but for a moment discard our habits and regard our life from outside, to see that all we do for the supposed safeguarding of our life we really do not at all to safeguard our life, but only, by busying ourselves with these things, to forget that life is never secured. But not only do we deceive ourselves and spoil our real life for the sake of an imaginary one; we generally in this effort to make ourselves safe, ruin the very thing we wish to secure. The French armed themselves to secure their life in 1870, and in consequence of this safeguarding hundreds of thousands of Frenchmen perished.

The same is done by all nations that arm themselves. The rich man secures his life by having money, and that very money attracts a robber who kills him. A nervous man safeguards his life by undergoing a cure, and the cure itself slowly kills him, or, if it does not kill him, certainly deprives him of life, like that sick man who did not live for thirty-eight years, but waited for the angel at the pool (John v. 2–8).

Christ's teaching that life cannot be made safe, but that one must always, at each moment, be ready to die, is certainly better than the world's teaching that one must secure one's life: it is better because the inevitability of death and the insecurity of life remain the same whether one adopts the world's teaching or that of Christ; but life itself, by Christ's teaching, is not all absorbed without any remainder, in the useless occupation of pseudo-safeguarding one's life, but becomes free and can be devoted to its one natural aim, the welfare of one's self and one's fellows. A disciple of Christ will be poor. Yes; that is to say, he will always make use of all those blessings which God has given him. He will not ruin his life. We have called poverty,[1] which is a happiness, by a word that indicates misfortune, but the reality of the matter is not altered thereby. To be poor means that a man[2]

[1] Poverty, in Russian, is *bednost*, from the same root as *beda*, a misfortune.

[2] Tolstoy has in mind a Russian country peasant, whom he contrasts with a rich townsman, and the description relates to things as they were under the Tsars in the pre-Revolutionary days.

will not live in a town but in a village, and will not sit at home but will work in the woods or fields; will see the light of the sun, the earth, the sky, and animals; will not consider what he can eat to arouse his appetite, and how to get his bowels to move, but will be hungry three times a day; will not toss about on soft cushions, wondering how he is to escape from sleeplessness, but will sleep; he will have children and will live with them; will have free intercourse with all men, and above all will not do things he does not wish to do, and will not be afraid of what will happen to him. He will sicken, suffer, and die as every one does (though, to judge by the way poor men sicken and die, it will be better for him than it is for the rich); but he will certainly live more happily. To be poor, to be indigent and a vagrant (πτωχός means vagrant) is what Christ taught; that without which it is impossible to enter the kingdom of God, without which it is impossible to be happy here on earth.

'But no one will feed you, and you will die of hunger,' is said in reply to this. To the objection that a man living according to Christ's teaching will die of hunger Christ replied by one brief sentence (the one which is interpreted as a justification for the idleness of the clergy, Matt. x. 10; Luke x. 7).

He said: 'Take no wallet for your journey, neither two coats, nor shoes, nor staff: for the labourer is worthy of his food.' 'In that same house remain, eating and drinking such things as they give, for the labourer is worthy of his hire.'

The labourer is worthy,[1] literally means: can and should have his subsistence. It is a very short saying; but for any one who understands it as Christ did, it admits of no further argument to the effect that a man who has no property will die of hunger. To understand these words in their real meaning one must first of all quite renounce the supposition (which has become so common among us as a consequence of the dogma of the redemption) that man's welfare consists in idleness. One must return to the conception natural to all unperverted people, that the necessary condition of happiness for man is not idleness, but work; that a man cannot reject work; that not to work is dull, wearisome, and hard, as it is dull and hard for an ant, a horse, or any other animal not to work. One must forget our savage superstition that the position of a man with an inexhaustible purse—that is to say, with a Government post, the ownership of land, or of bonds bearing interest, which make it possible for him to do nothing—is a naturally happy condition. One must restore in one's imagination that view of work which all unperverted

[1] In both the Geneva and Christchurch editions of the Russian the word ἔξεστι is here inserted. It does not occur in either of the Gospel texts referred to, and it perplexes the present translator, who omits it as meaningless. If anyone can furnish a clue to its presence, such assistance will be much appreciated. Possibly, as the work could not be printed in Russia, the proofs may have been passed with inadequate revision. Tolstoy's MS. was often untidy and rather illegible, and an error may have crept in which cannot now be traced to its source.

people have, and which Christ had when he said that the labourer was worthy of his subsistence. Christ could not imagine people who would regard work as a curse, and therefore could not imagine a man who did not work, or did not wish to work. He always supposes that his disciples work. And therefore he says: 'If a man works, then his work will feed him.' If another man takes the produce of this man's labour, then the other man will feed the worker, just because he reaps the advantage of his labour. And so the worker will receive his subsistence. He will not have property, but there can be no doubt about his subsistence.

The difference between Christ's teaching and the teaching of our world about work lies in this, that, according to the world's teaching, work is man's peculiar merit for which he keeps account with others, and considers that he has a right to the more subsistence the more he works; while, according to Christ's teaching, work is a necessary condition of man's life, and subsistence is the inevitable consequence of work. Work produces food, food produces work, that is the unending circle: the one is the consequence and the cause of the other. However evil a master may be, he will feed his workman as he will feed the horse that works for him; and will feed him so that the workman may produce as much as possible; in other words, can co-operate in that which provides the welfare of man.

'The Son of man came not to be ministered

unto, but to minister, and to give his life a ransom for many.' According to the teaching of Christ each individual man, independently of what the world may be like, will have the best kind of life if he understands that his vocation is not to demand work from others, but to devote his own life to working for others, and to give his life a ransom for many. A man who acts so, says Christ, is worthy of his subsistence—that is to say, cannot but receive it. In a word, man does not live that others should work for him, but that he should work for others. Christ sets up the basis which undoubtedly ensures man's material existence, and by the words, 'The labourer is worthy of his subsistence,' he sets aside that very common objection to the possibility of fulfilling his teaching which says that a man carrying out Christ's teaching among people who do not carry it out will perish of hunger and cold. Christ shows us that a man ensures his subsistence, not by taking it from others, but by doing what is useful and necessary for others. The more necessary he is to others the more safe will be his existence.

Under the existing arrangements of the world people who do not fulfil Christ's law, but who work for their neighbours and have no property, do not die of hunger. How, then, can one make it an objection to Christ's teaching that those who obey it—that is to say, those who work for their neighbours—will die of hunger? A man cannot die of hunger while the rich have bread. In Russia, at any given moment, there are always millions of people living without any property, simply by their labour.

Among the heathen a Christian will be provided for as among Christians. He works for others, consequently they need him, and therefore he will be fed. Even a dog that is wanted is fed and cared for; how then should a man not be fed and cared for, who is of use to every one?

But a sick man, one with a family and children, is not wanted and cannot work—so people will cease to feed him, say those who are bent on making out a case for a bestial life. They will and do say this, and do not notice that they themselves, who say so and would like to act so, cannot do it, but behave quite otherwise. Those very people who do not acknowledge the practicability of Christ's teaching, follow it! They do not cease to feed a sheep, a bull, or a dog which falls ill. They do not even kill an old horse, but give it such work as it can do; they feed their family, as well as lambs, little pigs, and puppies, expecting them to be of use. So how should they not feed a useful man when he is ill, and how should they fail to find work within their strength for the old and the young, or cease to rear those who will one day work for them?

They not only will do this, but they are doing this very thing. Nine-tenths of the people—the common labourers—are fed like working cattle by the one-tenth who are not common people, but are rich and powerful. And, however gross the delusion in which that one-tenth lives, however much they may despise the other nine-tenths, this one-tenth of powerful people never deprives the nine-tenths of necessary subsistence, though they have the power to do so. In order that they may have offspring who should labour for them, they do not deprive the common people of what is necessary for them. Latterly this one-tenth have consciously endeavoured to arrange for the nine-tenths to be properly fed, that as large an output of work may be got from them as possible, and that fresh workmen may be produced and reared. Even the ants breed and rear their own milch-cows, so how should men not do as much, and breed those who will work for them? Workers are needed. And those who make use of their work will always be much concerned to see that the workers do not die out.

The objection to the practicability of Christ's teaching which says that if I do not acquire for myself, and do not retain what I have acquired, no one will feed my family, is correct, but only in relation to idle, useless, and therefore harmful, people such as the majority of our wealthy class. No one except stupid parents will bring up idle people; because idle people are of no use to any one, not even to themselves; but even the worst men will feed and rear workers. Calves are reared, and man, as a working animal, is more valuable than a bull, as the prices in the slave-markets have always proved. That is why children will never be left without care.

Man does not live that others should serve him,

but that he should himself serve others. He who labours will be fed.

That is a truth confirmed by the life of the whole world.

Till the present time, always and everywhere, where man has worked he has obtained sustenance, as every horse receives his feed. And such sustenance was received by the workers involuntarily, against the grain, for they only desired to free themselves from toil, to get as much as possible, and to seat themselves on the neck of those who were sitting on their necks. Such an involuntary, unwilling worker, envious and angry, was not left without sustenance, and was even more fortunate than the man who did not work, but lived on the labour of others. How much more fortunate still will he be who works according to Christ's law, and whose aim is to work as much as he can and to take as little as possible! And how much more happy will his position be when around him there will be at least some, and perhaps even many, men like himself, who will serve him!

Christ's teaching of work and its fruits is expressed in the story of the feeding of the five and the seven thousand with two loaves and five fishes. Humanity will reach the highest happiness possible for it on earth when people do not try to swallow and consume everything themselves, but when they do as Christ taught them by the sea-shore.

Some thousands of people had to be fed. A disciple told Christ that he had seen a lad who had some fishes, the disciple also had some loaves. Jesus understood that some of the people, coming from a distance, would have brought food, but that others would not. (That some had supplies with them is shown by the fact that in all four Gospels it is mentioned that when the meal was ended remnants were collected in twelve baskets. If no one but the lad had brought anything, there would not have been those twelve baskets in the field.) If Christ had not done what he did, namely, performed the miracle of feeding the thousands of people with five loaves, what happens in our world would have happened there. Those who had supplies would have eaten what they had. They would have eaten it all, and even over-eaten themselves, so as not to leave anything over. The mean ones, perhaps, would have carried home their surplus. Those who had nothing would have remained hungry, watching the eaters with angry envy, and perhaps some of them would have snatched from those who saved, and there would have been quarrels and fights, and some would have gone home satiated, others hungry and angry. It would have been as it is in our life.

But Christ knew what he wanted to do (as is said in the Gospels). He bade them all sit round, and he told his disciples to offer to others what they themselves had, and to bid others do the same. And then it appeared that, when all who had supplies had done like Christ's disciples—that is to say, had offered what they had to others—all ate moderately, and, after going round the circle, there was food enough left for those who had at first not eaten. And all were satisfied, and much food remained over; so much that they gathered up twelve baskets full.

Christ taught men that they should deliberately behave in this way in life, because such is the law of man and of all humanity. Work is a necessary condition of man's life. Work also gives welfare to man. And therefore the withholding from others of the fruits of one's labour, or of other people's labour, hinders the welfare of man. Giving one's labour to others promotes man's happiness.

'If people do not take away property from one another they will die of hunger,' we say. It would seem that we should rather say the contrary: if people take by force from one another there will be some who will die of hunger—and this actually occurs.

Really every man, however he lives, whether according to Christ's teaching or to the world's—is alive only thanks to the work of other people. Others have protected him, and given him drink and fed him, and still protect him and feed him, and give him drink. But by the world's teaching man, by violence and threats, obliges others to continue to feed him and his family. By Christ's teaching equally man is protected, nourished, and supplied with drink by others; but in order that others should continue to guard, to feed, and to give him drink, he does not bring force to bear on any one, but tries himself to serve others and to be useful to all men as he can, and thereby he becomes necessary to all. Worldly people will always wish to cease to feed one who is unnecessary to them and who compels them by force to feed him, and at the first opportunity they not only cease to feed him, but kill him as unnecessary. But all men, always, evil as they may be, will carefully feed and safeguard one who works for them.

In which way, then, is it safer, more reasonable, and more joyous to live: according to the world's teaching or according to Christ's?

CHAPTER XI

THE DEAD CHURCH

THE teaching of Christ establishes the kingdom of God on earth. It is not true that the fulfilment of this teaching is difficult ; it is not only not difficult, but it is inevitable for a man who has comprehended it. This teaching supplies the only possible salvation from the inevitably impending destruction of personal life. Finally, not only does the fulfilment of this teaching not call us to sufferings and deprivations in this life, but it releases us from nine-tenths of the sufferings we endure for the sake of the world's teaching.

And, having understood this, I asked myself, Why, till now, have I not fulfilled this teaching which offers me welfare, salvation, and happiness, but have followed quite a different teaching—that which has made me unhappy ? And the only answer that could be given was : I did not know the truth ; it was hidden from me.

When the meaning of Christ's teaching revealed itself to me for the first time I had no idea that the elucidation of that meaning would cause me to repudiate the teaching of the Church ; it merely seemed to me that the Church had not reached the conclusion which flows from Christ's teaching; but I did not suspect that the new meaning of Christ's teaching which had revealed itself to me, and the deductions which followed therefrom, would separate me from the teaching of the Church. I was afraid of that, and therefore, during my researches, far from seeking for mistakes in the Church's teaching, I on the contrary intentionally shut my eyes to the propositions which seemed to me obscure and strange, but which did not contradict what I considered to be the essence of the Christian teaching.

But the further I travelled in the study of the Gospels and the more clearly the meaning of Christ's teaching revealed itself to me, the more inevitable became the choice between the teaching of Christ—reasonable, clear, accordant with my conscience and giving me salvation—and the directly opposite teaching, disagreeing with my reason and conscience and giving me nothing except a consciousness of destruction for myself and others; and I could not help rejecting the Church's propositions one after another. I did this unwillingly, with a struggle, and with a desire as far as possible to soften my disagreement with the Church, not to separate from it, and not to deprive myself of that most joyous support to one's faith—community with many people. But when I had finished my work I saw that, try as I might to retain at least something of the Church's teaching, nothing remained. Not only did nothing remain, but I was convinced that nothing could remain. During the conclusion of my work the following incident occurred. My young son told me that two quite uneducated and scarcely literate people, who were our servants, had had a dispute about a passage in a religious book in which it was said that it is not a sin to kill criminals or kill people in war. I did not believe that this could have been printed, and I asked to have the book shown to me—the booklet which had provoked the dispute was called *An Explanatory Prayer-book* (3rd edition, 80th thousand, Moscow, 1879). On page 163 of that booklet is said :

'What is the sixth of God's commandments ? Thou shalt not kill. What does God forbid in this commandment ? He forbids us to kill—that is to say, deprive men of life. Is it a sin legally to punish a criminal with death, or to kill one's enemies in war ? It is not a sin. A criminal is deprived of life in order to stop the great evil which he commits ; enemies are killed in war because in war one fights for one's ruler and country.' And to those words is limited the explanation of why the commandment of God is repealed. I did not believe my eyes.

The disputants asked my opinion about their difference. I told the one who considered that what the book said was right that the explanation was incorrect.

'How is it that people print what is wrong and contrary to the law ?' said he. I had no reply to give him. I kept the book and looked it all through. The book contains (1) thirty-one prayers, with instructions about genuflections, and how to hold one's fingers when crossing oneself; (2) an explanation of the Creed; (3) a quite unexplained extract from the fifth chapter of St. Matthew, which for some reason is called, 'Commands for obtaining bliss;' (4) the Ten Commandments of Moses with explanations, which for the most part annul them; (5) hymns for Church Festivals.

As I have said, I not only tried to avoid condemning the faith of the Church, but I tried to see it in the best light, and therefore did not seek for its weaknesses, and, though well acquainted with its academic, I was quite unacquainted with its pedagogic, literature. The circulation of such an enormous number of copies of a prayer-book in 1879 which evoked the doubts of the simplest people amazed me. I could not believe that the plainly pagan contents of the prayer-book (having nothing in common with Christianity) were the teaching the Church deliberately disseminated among the people. To verify this, I bought all the books published by the Synod or with its blessing, and containing brief statements of the Church's faith, for children and the common people; and I read them through.

Their contents were for me almost new. When I had Scripture lessons, such matter did not exist. There were then, so far as I can remember, no 'Commands for obtaining Bliss,' nor was there the teaching that to kill is *not a sin*. It is not found in any of the old Russian catechisms. It is not in the catechisms of

Peter Mogila, nor in the catechism of Platon, nor in the catechism of Balyakov, nor in the short Catholic Catechisms. This novelty was introduced by Filaret, who also drew up a catechism for the use of the Army. The *Explanatory Prayer-book* is drawn up in accord with that catechism. The fundamental book is the 'Long *Christian* Catechism of the Orthodox Church, for the use of *all* Orthodox *Christians*, published by order of His Imperial Majesty.'

That book is divided into three parts: On Faith, On Hope, and On Love. In the first part is an analysis of the Nicene Creed. In the second part an analysis of the Lord's Prayer, and the eight verses of the fifth chapter of Matthew forming an introduction to the Sermon on the Mount, and for some reason called 'Commands for obtaining bliss.' (Both these parts treat of Church dogmas, of prayers and sacraments, but give no teaching at all about life.) In the third part the duties of a Christian are set forth. In this part, called 'On Love,' are set out, not the commandments of Christ, but the Ten Commandments of Moses, and these are set out as though only to teach people not to fulfil them but to act in opposition to them; as, after each commandment, there is a reservation which cancels it. With reference to the first commandment, which orders us to honour one God, the catechism teaches us to honour angels and saints, besides, of course, the Mother of God and the three Persons of the Trinity (*Long Catechism*, pp. 107,

108). With reference to the second commandment, not to make to oneself idols, the catechism teaches the obeisance before icons (p. 108). With reference to the third commandment, not to take oaths in vain, the catechism teaches people to swear on any demand of the *legal* authorities (p. 111). With reference to the fourth commandment, to observe Saturday, the catechism teaches us to keep not Saturday, but Sunday, and thirteen great holidays and a multitude of smaller ones, and to observe all the Fasts, including Wednesdays and Fridays (pp. 112–15). With reference to the fifth commandment, to honour one's father and mother, the catechism teaches us to honour the Tsar and the Fatherland, one's spiritual pastors '*and those in various positions of authority*' (sic) and on honouring those in authority there are three pages with an enumeration of all kinds of authorities: '*Those in authority in schools, the civil authorities, the judges*, the *military authorities, one's masters* (sic). *This last injunction refers to those who serve them and whom they command*' (sic—pp. 116–19).

I am quoting from the 1864 edition of the Catechism. Twenty years have passed since the abolition of serfdom, and no one has taken the trouble even to strike out the sentences which, with reference to the commandment of God to honour one's parents, were included in the Catechism for the maintenance and justification of slavery. With reference to the sixth commandment, 'Thou shalt not kill,' one is taught from the first lines to kill.

Q. What is forbidden in the sixth commandment ?

A. Murder, or the taking of life from one's neighbour in any manner.

Q. Is every taking of life a sinful murder ?

A. It is not sinful murder when life is taken *in the fulfilment of one's duties*, for instance : (i) When a criminal is *punished* with death by legal sentence. (ii) When enemies are killed *in war* for ruler and country. (The italics are in the original.) And further :

Q. What occasions can be regarded as criminal murder ?

A. . . . When anyone *hides or releases* a murderer.

And this is printed in hundreds of thousands of copies, and forcibly, with threats and under fear of punishment, is instilled into all Russian people under the guise of Christian doctrine. This is what the whole of the Russian people are taught ; this is what all the innocent angel children are taught—those children whom Christ wished not to have driven away from him because 'theirs is the kingdom of God' ; —those children whom we must resemble in order to enter the kingdom of God (resemble by not knowing such teaching) ; those children, in defence of whom Christ said, 'Woe unto him who causeth one of these little ones to stumble.' And it is these children to whom this is forcibly taught, and who are told that this is the only and the sacred law of God.

This is not a proclamation circulated secretly under fear of imprisonment, but a proclamation disagreement with which is punished by imprisonment. I now write this, and I am frightened that I even allow myself to say that one cannot repeal God's chief law, written in all the codes and in all our hearts, by words which explain nothing, 'in the fulfilment of one's duties to King and country,' and that people should not be taught so.

Yes, that has come about which Christ foretold (Luke xi. 35, 36; Matt. vi. 23): 'Look therefore whether the light that is in thee be not darkness. If the light that is in thee be darkness, how great is the darkness!'

The light that is within us is become darkness, and the darkness in which we live has become terrible.

'Woe unto you,' says Christ, 'woe unto you, scribes and Pharisees, hypocrites! because ye shut the kingdom of heaven against men: for ye enter not in yourselves, neither suffer ye them that are entering in to enter. Woe unto you, scribes and Pharisees, hypocrites! for ye devour widows' houses, even while for a pretence ye make long prayers: therefore ye shall receive greater condemnation. Woe unto you, scribes and Pharisees, hypocrites! for ye compass sea and land to make one proselyte; and when he is become so, ye make him worse than before. Woe unto you, ye blind guides!

'Woe unto you, scribes and Pharisees, hypocrites! for ye build the sepulchres of the prophets, and garnish the tombs of the righteous and say, If we had been in those days when the prophets were tortured, we should not have been partakers in their blood. Ye are witnesses against yourselves, that ye are sons of them that slew the prophets. Fill ye up then the measure begun by those who were like yourselves. I will send unto you prophets and wise men; some of them ye will kill and crucify; and some of them ye will scourge in your assemblies, and expel from city to city; that upon you may come all the righteous blood shed on the earth since Abel.' 'Every blasphemy [libel] will be forgiven to men, but the libel against the Holy Spirit cannot be forgiven.' All this reads as though it had been written yesterday against those who now no longer compass the sea and the land, libelling the Holy Spirit and leading people to a belief which makes them worse, but directly, by violence, oblige them to accept that belief, and persecute and destroy all those prophets and wise men who attempt to expose their fraud.

And I became convinced that the Church's teaching, although it calls itself Christian, is that very darkness against which Christ strove and ordered his disciples to strive.

Christ's teaching, like every religious teaching, has two sides: (i) The teaching of conduct —of how we should live, each separately and all together—the ethical teaching; and (ii) the explanation of why people should live in that way, and not otherwise—the metaphysical teaching. The one is the result, and at the same time the cause, of the other. Man should live so, because such is his destiny: or the destiny of man is such, and therefore he should live so—these two sides of Christ's teaching are to be found in all the religions of the world. Such is the religion of the Brahmans, Confucius, Buddha, and Moses, and such is the religion of Christ. He teaches life, how to live, and he gives the explanation why that is how one should live. But, as it was with all other teachings—Brahmanism, Judaism, Buddhism—so was it with the teaching of Christ. People lapse from the teaching of life, and among them some are found who undertake to justify that lapse. These people, seating themselves, to use Christ's expression, in the seat of Moses, explain the metaphysical side of the teaching in such a way that the ethical demands cease to be obligatory and are replaced by an external service of God—by ritual. This phenomenon is common to all religions, but never, I think, has it been displayed so sharply as in Christianity. It has been displayed with such exceptional sharpness because the teaching of Christ is the highest teaching; and it is the highest because the metaphysics and ethics of Christ's teaching are so inseparably united and are so defined by one another, that to separate them is impossible without depriving the whole teaching of its meaning; and also because Christ's teaching is in itself a Protestantism—that is to say, a denial not merely of the ritual observances of Judaism, but of every external worship of God. And therefore in Christianity of necessity this tearing asunder completely perverts the teaching and deprives it of any meaning. And so it was. The sundering of the teaching of life from the explanation of life began with the preaching of Paul, who did not know the ethical teaching expressed in the Gospel of Matthew, and who preached a metaphysical-cabalistic theory foreign to Christ; and this separation was finally completed at the time of Constantine, when it was found possible to clothe the whole heathen order of life in a Christian dress, and therefore to accept it as Christianity without altering it.

From the time of Constantine a heathen of the heathen whom the Church, for all his crimes and vices, numbers with the company of the saints—begin the Ecclesiastical Councils, and the centre of gravity of Christianity was transferred completely to the metaphysical side of the teaching. And that metaphysical teaching, with the ceremonies that accompany it, diverging ever more and more from its fundamental meaning, reaches its present stage—a teaching which explains the most incomprehensible mysteries of life in heaven, and gives a most complex ritual of divine service, but supplies *no* religious teaching concerning our life on earth.

All religions except Church Christianity demand from their adherents, besides ceremonies, the performance of certain good actions and abstention from certain bad ones. Judaism demands circumcision, the keeping of the Sabbath, the giving of alms, the observance of the Jubilee year, and much else. Mohammedanism demands circumcision, prayer five times a day, tithes for the poor, worship at the prophet's tomb, and much else. And so with all the other religions. Whether these demands are good or bad, at any rate they demand certain actions. Only pseudo-Christianity demands nothing. There is nothing that it is definitely obligatory for a Christian to do, or from which he must definitely abstain, if one does not count fasts and prayers which the Church itself admits to be non-obligatory. All that is necessary for the pseudo-Christian are the sacraments. But the sacrament is not done by the believer himself, it is performed over him by others. A pseudo-Christian is not bound to do anything, and is not bound to abstain from anything, in order to be saved, but all that is necessary is performed over him by the Church: he is baptized, and anointed, and communion is given him, as well as extreme unction, and absolution is even granted on an inarticulate confession, and he is prayed for—and saved! The Christian Church since the time of Constantine has not demanded any actions from its members. It has not even put forward any demands of abstinence from anything. The Christian Church recognized and sanctified everything that existed in the heathen world: it recognized and sanctified divorce, and slavery, and courts of justice, and all the state authorities that existed, and wars and executions, and it only demanded at baptism a verbal renunciation of evil, and that only at first; afterwards, with the introduction of infant baptism, it ceased even to demand that.

The Church, acknowledging Christ's teaching in words, directly rejected it in life.

Instead of guiding the life of the world, the Church, to make itself agreeable to the world, interpreted Christ's metaphysical teaching in such a way that no demands relating to life result from it; so that it did not prevent people from living as they had done before. The Church yielded to the world, and, having done so once, it followed the world's way. The world did whatever it liked, allowing the Church, as best it could, to shape its explanations of the meaning of life accordingly. The world in everything arranged its life contrary to Christ's teaching, and the Church devised allegories to show that people, while living contrary to Christ's law, live in accord with it. And finally the life of the world became worse than heathen life had been, and the Church not merely justified that life, but asserted that it was in agreement with Christ's teaching.

But a time came when the light of Christ's true teaching which was in the Gospels, despite the fact that the Church, feeling its own falsity, tried to hide it (by forbidding translations of the Bible)—a time came when this light (through those who were called sectarians, and even through worldly freethinkers) made its way among the people and the falsity of the Church's teaching became evident to men, and they began to alter their way of life (which the Church had justified) to life on the basis of Christ's teaching, which had made its way to them independently of the Church.

So people themselves, apart from the Church, abolished slavery, which the Church had justified, and religious executions,[1] and abolished the power (sanctified by the Church) of the Emperors and Popes, and have now begun the task which presents itself next in turn: the abolition of property and of the State.[2] And the Church did not defend, and cannot defend, any of these things, because the abolition of these wrongs in life took place, and is now taking place, on the basis of that same Christian teaching which was preached and is preached by the Church, however it tries to pervert it.

The guidance of the life of man has emancipated itself from the Church and established itself independently of the Church.

The Church retains an explanation, but an explanation of what? The metaphysical explanation of a teaching has significance when the teaching of life which it explains exists. But the Church has no teaching of life left. It had only an explanation of a life it instituted once upon a time, and which no longer exists. If the Church still retains an explanation of that life which used to exist (like the explanation in the Catechism that officials ought to kill) no

[1] Such as the *autos-da-fé* of the Inquisition.

[2] This sentence is remarkable, not only because it was written thirty-three years before the Bolshevik Revolution (which in theory, though not in practice, contemplated the abolition of the State); but also because it shows that in this (almost the first of his didactic works) Tolstoy went to the ultimate limit of his theory of Christian Anarchy, which he spent the remaining twenty-six years of his life in elaborating.

one any longer believes it. And the Church has nothing left but cathedrals, icons, brocaded vestments, and words.[1]

The Church carried the light of Christian teaching of life through eighteen centuries, and, wishing to hide it under its garments, has itself been burnt up by that flame. The world, with its arrangements, sanctified by the Church, has repudiated the Church in the name of those very principles of Christianity which the Church has reluctantly borne; and the world now lives without the Church. That fact is accomplished, and to hide it is impossible. All that is really alive—and does not linger on in angry dejection, not really living but merely hindering others from doing so—all that really lives in our European world has rejected the Church, and all churches, and lives its own life independently of the Church. And let it not be said that this is so in 'rotten western Europe'[2]; our Russia, with its millions of rationalist Christians, educated and uneducated, who have rejected Church teaching, proves beyond dispute that Russia, in regard to the repudiation of the Church, is, thank God, far more 'rotten' than the rest of Europe.

[1] Before the generation had passed away to whom Tolstoy first issued this book the Church in Russia had been disendowed and disestablished, and the words 'Religion is the people's opium' were painted, by order of the authorities, in large letters on the walls of the churches.

[2] A favourite phrase of the Slavophils, a Stephen-Graham-like folk, who regarded Russia and her institutions as far superior to anything existing in the democratic West.

All that is alive is independent of the Church.

The power of Government rests on tradition, on science, on popular election, on brute force, and on what you will, only not on the Church.

Wars and the relations of the Powers are arranged on the principle of race, balance of power, or what you will, but not on Church principles.

The State institutions plainly ignore the Church. The idea that the Church could, in our times, be the foundation of the law or of property is merely ridiculous.

Science not only does not co-operate with the Church teaching, but inadvertently, involuntarily, in the course of its development is always hostile to the Church.

Art, which formerly served the Church exclusively, has now quite departed from it.

It is not enough that life has completely emancipated itself from the Church. Life has no relation to the Church; it feels merely contempt for her so long as she does not meddle in the affairs of life, and nothing but hatred as soon as she tries to remind it of her former rights. If the form which we call the Church still exists, it is only because people fear to smash a vessel which once held precious contents; only so is it possible to explain the existence in our century of the Catholic, the Orthodox, and the various Protestant Churches.

All the Churches—the Catholic, Orthodox, and Protestant—stand like sentinels laboriously on guard over a prisoner who has long since escaped, and is now walking about among the sentinels and even fighting them. Everything that now really animates the world—Socialism, Communism, theories of political economy, utilitarianism, the freedom and equality of individuals, of classes, and of women, all man's moral conceptions, the sanctity of labour, the sanctity of reason, of science and of art, all that moves the world, and that the Church regards as inimical, all are parts of that teaching which the Church herself has unwittingly handed on together with the teaching of Christ which she sought to conceal.

In our time the life of the world goes its own way quite independently of the Church's teaching. That teaching has lagged so far behind that the men of the world no longer hear the voices of church teachers. Nor is there anything to hear, for the Church only offers explanations of an arrangement of life which the world has already outgrown, and which has already ceased to exist or is now being irresistibly destroyed.

People went rowing in a boat, and a helmsman steered them. The people came to believe in their helmsman, and he guided them well; but the time came when the good helmsman was replaced by another, who did not steer. But the boat glided on quickly and easily. At first it was not noticed that the new helmsman was not steering, and the people were only pleased that the boat moved quickly. But afterwards, having realized that the new helmsman was useless, they began to laugh at him, and dismissed him.

This would not have mattered, but the trouble was that people, moved by their annoyance with the useless helmsman, forgot that without a helmsman one does not know which way one is going. That is what has happened in our Christian society. The Church does not direct, and it is easy to drift, and we have gone far; and all the successes of science that our nineteenth century is so proud of are but the mileage we have gone without a rudder. We advance, but know not whither. We live and get through our life, and positively do not know why. But it does not do to drift and row not knowing one's direction, and one must not live and pass through life not knowing why.

If men did nothing themselves but were placed by some external force in the position they occupy, they might, in reply to the question, 'Why are you in this position?' quite reasonably reply, We do not know, but we find ourselves placed as we are. But people make their position for themselves, for others, and in particular for their children; and therefore they must reply to the questions: Why do you enroll others, and have been yourselves enrolled, into armies of millions, with which you kill and mutilate one another? Why have you spent, and why are you spending, tremendous human energies, expressed in milliards, on the building of towns unnecessary and harmful to you? Why do you arrange your absurd law-courts, and send people you consider criminals from France to Cayenne, from Russia to Siberia, and from

England to Australia,[1] knowing yourselves that this is unreasonable? Why do you abandon the field-work you love for work in factories and workshops which you yourselves dislike? Why do you educate your children so that they should continue this life of which you do not approve? Why do you do all this?

These questions cannot be left unanswered. Even had all these things been pleasant things you like doing, you should have given a reason for doing them. But as they are terribly difficult things, and you do them only with effort and with murmurs, it is impossible for you not to consider why you do them all. It is necessary either to cease to do all this or else to explain why we do it. Without a reply to that question, people never have lived, and never can live. And such a reply people have never been without.

The Jews lived as they did—that is to say, fought, executed people, built the temple, and arranged their whole life in one way and not in another, because this was all prescribed by their law which, according to their conviction, had come down to them from God Himself. So it is with a Hindu or a Chinaman, and so it was with a Roman, and is with a Mohammedan; and the same was the case with a Christian till a hundred years ago; and so now it is for the

[1] As a matter of fact, banishment to Australia had ceased some twenty years before Tolstoy wrote this, but the memory of legal barbarities committed in distant countries lingers long in men's minds, as is illustrated by frequent references in England to the knout, the use of which was abolished generations ago.

masses of ignorant Christians. To those questions these ignorant Christians now reply that army-service, wars, law-courts and executions, all exist by God's law, given to us by the Church. This world is a fallen world. All the evil that exists, exists by the will of God as a punishment for the sins of the world, and we therefore cannot remedy this evil.[1] We can only save our souls by faith, sacraments, prayers, and by submission to the will of God, as taught us by the Church. The Church teaches us that every Christian should submit absolutely to the Tsar, the anointed of God, and to all officials appointed by him, and should defend by violence their own and other people's property, and should fight, execute, and endure execution, at the will of those God-appointed authorities.

Whether such explanations be good or bad, they explained for a believing Christian—as was the case for a Jew, a Buddhist, or a Mohammedan—all the peculiarities of life; and a man did not renounce his reason when living according to the law he accepted as divine. But now a time has come when only the most ignorant people believe in these explanations, and the number of such people diminishes every day and every hour. It is quite impossible to

[1] The amazing submission shown by the Russian people to the misrule they suffered under the Tsars for centuries, and, stranger still, to the greater oppression they have endured for three years since the Bolsheviks seized power and organized the Extraordinary Committee (which is a twentieth-century Inquisition), may be partly explained by the habit of submission deeply engrained in them, to which Tolstoy alludes.

arrest this movement. All men irresistibly follow those who go in advance, and all will reach the place where the advanced people now stand. But the advanced people are standing at the brink of a precipice. Those in front are in a terrible position; they are shaping life for themselves and preparing life for all who follow them, and are completely ignorant of why they do what they do. Not one civilized and progressive man is now in a position to reply to the plain question, Why do you live the life you are living? Why are you doing all that you are doing? I have tried to ask about this, and have questioned hundreds of people, and have never received a direct reply. Always, instead of a direct reply to the personal question, Why do you live so, and do so? I have received an answer, not to my question, but to one I had not put.

A believing Catholic, Protestant, or Orthodox Churchman, in reply to the question why he lives as he is living—that is to say, in contradiction to that teaching of the Christ-God which he professes, always, instead of a straight answer, begins to speak of the woful extent of incredulity in the present generation; about the bad people who promote infidelity, and of the significance and the future of the true Church. But why he himself does not do what his faith bids him do he does not say. Instead of replying about himself, he speaks about the general condition of humanity, and about the Church just as though his own life was of no importance to him at all, and he was concerned only with the salvation of the whole of humanity and with what he calls the Church.

A philosopher, of whatever denomination—idealist, spiritualist, pessimist, or positivist—in reply to the question why he lives as he does, that is to say, not in accord with his philosophical teaching, will always, instead of replying to that question, speak about the progress of humanity, the historic law of that progress, which he has discovered and in accord with which mankind strives towards its welfare. But he never replies directly to the question why he himself, in his own life, does not do what he considers reasonable. The philosopher, like the believer, seems as though he were not concerned with his own life, but only with observing the general laws of humanity.

An average man, one of the immense majority of semi-believing, semi-sceptical civilized people, those who always without exception complain of their life and of the organization of our life, and anticipate the ruin of everything, this average man, in reply to the question why he himself lives this life he condemns and does nothing to improve it, will always, instead of a direct reply, begin to speak not of himself but on some general question: the law, trade, the State, or civilization. If he is a policeman or a public prosecutor he will say: 'But how will law and order get on if I, to improve my life, cease to take part in them?' 'And how about trade?' says he, if he is a commercial man. 'And how about civilization if I, to improve my own life, do not co-operate in it?' He always speaks as though the aim of his life were not to secure the good for which he always yearns, but to serve the State, or trade, or civilization. The average man replies exactly like the believer and the philosopher. For the personal question he substitutes a general question, and, like the believer and the philosopher, the average man makes this substitution because he has no reply to the question concerning his personal life, since he possesses no real philosophy of life. And he feels ashamed.

He is ashamed because he feels himself to be in the humiliating position of one who has no philosophy of life; whereas man never has lived, and cannot live, without a philosophy of life. Only in our Christian world. instead of a philosophy of life and an explanation why life should be such and not other—that is to say, instead of a religion, we have merely an explanation of why life should be such as it once used to be, and something is called religion which is of no sort of use to anybody; and life itself has become emancipated from any sort of teaching—that is to say, it lacks any definition.

Nor is that all: as always occurs, science has accepted this accidental, monstrous position our society is in, as a law for all humanity. Tiele, Herbert Spencer, and others treat of religion quite seriously, understanding by it a metaphysical teaching concerning the origin of all things, and without suspecting that they are talking, not of the whole of religion, but of only a part of it.

From this has arisen the amazing phenomenon that in our age we see wise and learned people most naïvely convinced that they are free from all religion, merely because they do not acknowledge the metaphysical explanations of the origin of things, which at some period and for some people served as an explanation of life. It does not enter their heads that they have got to live somehow and do live somehow, and that whatever it is that induces them to live so and not otherwise is their religion. These people imagine that they have very elevated convictions, but no faith. But, whatever they may say, they have a faith if they perform any reasonable actions. For reasonable actions are always defined by one's faith. And the actions of these people are defined solely by the faith that one must always do what one is ordered to do. The religion of these people who do not acknowledge religion, is the religion of submission to all that is done by the powerful majority, or, more briefly, it is the religion of submission to the existing authorities.

One may live according to the world's teaching—that is to say, live an animal life, not acknowledging anything higher and more obligatory than the decrees of the powers that be. But he who lives so cannot assert that he is living rationally. Before asserting that we live rationally, one must answer the question, What teaching about life do we consider rational? And we unfortunates not merely have no such teaching, but have even lost the consciousness that any reasonable teaching about life is necessary.

Ask men of our day, believers or sceptics, what teaching they follow in their lives. They will have to confess that they follow only one teaching, the laws which are written by officials in the Judicial Department or in the Legislative Assemblies, and which are enforced by the police. That is the only teaching our European people acknowledge. They know that that teaching has not come down from heaven, nor from the prophets, nor from sages; they constantly condemn the regulations made by those officials or Legislative Assemblies, but all the same they acknowledge that teaching, and submit to its executors—the police; and they implicitly obey its most terrible demands. If the officials or the Assemblies have written that every young man must be ready to be abused, to be killed, and to murder others—all the fathers and mothers who have reared sons submit to this law, written yesterday by a venal official and capable of alteration to-morrow.

The conception of law indubitably rational and made obligatory on every one by his inner conviction has been so lost in our society that the existence among the Jewish people of a law which defines their whole life, a law made obligatory not by compulsion but by the inner consciousness of every one—is considered an exceptional characteristic of the Jewish race alone. That the Jews only obeyed what they in the depth of their souls considered to be the undoubted truth received direct from God—that is to say, obeyed only what was accordant with their conscience—is considered to be a Jewish peculiarity. It is considered to be the normal condition, natural to an educated man, that he should obey what is notoriously written by contemptible people and put into operation by policemen armed with pistols—things which each of them, or at least the majority of them, consider to be wrong—that is to say discordant with their conscience.

Vainly have I sought in our civilized world for any clearly expressed moral principles for life. There are none. There is not even a recognition that they are needed. There is even a strange conviction that they are not needed, that religion consists only in certain words about a future life, about God, in certain ceremonies very useful in the opinion of some people for saving one's soul, and of no sort of use at all in the opinion of others, and that life goes on of itself, and needs no principles or rules; only one must do what is ordered! Of what forms the essence of belief—the teaching about life and the explanation of its meaning—the first is considered as unimportant, and as not appertaining to belief; while the second, namely, the explanation of a life that used to be lived, or discussions and guesses at the historic course of life, is considered most important and serious. In all that forms the life of man—how to live; whether to go or not to go to kill people; to go or not to go to try people; whether to educate one's children in this way or in that

—the people of our world submit absolutely to others, who are also in the position of not themselves knowing why they live and why they oblige others to live this way and not that.

And such a life people consider rational, and they do not feel ashamed of it.

The divergence between the explanation of the faith which we call faith, and faith itself, which is called social or political life, has now reached the utmost limit, and all the civilized majority of mankind are left with no guidance for life, except a faith in the gendarme and the policeman.

The position would be terrible if it were quite like that. But fortunately there are, even in our day, men, the best men of our time, who are not satisfied with such a faith, and who have a belief of their own as to how men should live.

These people are considered the most harmful, dangerous, and, above all, irreligious people; yet they are the only faithful people of our time, and are not only believers in general, but believers in the teaching of Christ, or if not in his whole teaching, at least in a small part of it.

These people often have no knowledge of Christ's teaching, do not accept it, and often, like their opponents, do not accept the chief groundwork of the Christian faith—non-resistance to him that is evil. They often even hate Christ; but their whole belief of what life should be like is drawn from the teaching of

Christ.[1] However much these people may be persecuted, however much they may be slandered, they are the only people who do not unmurmuringly submit to all that is decreed; and therefore they are the only people in our world who are living not an animal, but a rational life—they are the only believers.

The thread connecting the world with the Church that used to give the world a meaning has become ever weaker and weaker as the essence, the sap of life, has more and more flowed over to the world. And now, when the sap has all flowed over, the connecting cord has become a mere hindrance.

That is the mysterious process of birth, which is being performed before our eyes. At one and the same time the last bond with the Church is being dissolved and the independent process of life is being established.

Church teaching (with its dogmas, councils, and hierarchy) is undoubtedly connected with Christ's teaching. That connection is as evi-

[1] At the time Tolstoy was preparing this work, V. I. Alexeyev was his son's tutor. Alexeyev had been an active Socialist agitator at the time when the movement was still new in Russia. He says: 'Sometimes we' (Tolstoy and he) 'started a conversation on economics and social themes. I had a copy of the Gospels, left from the days of my Socialist propaganda among the people. Passages relating to social questions were underlined in it, and I often pointed these out to Tolstoy.' It is to the Socialist propaganda on behalf of the poor that Tolstoy refers in this passage. (See Maude's *Life of Tolstoy*, vol. ii, pp. 5–6, Constable.)

dent as the connection of a new-born babe with its mother's womb. But if the navel-cord and the after-birth become unnecessary bits of flesh, which (from respect for what they have preserved) must be carefully buried in the earth, so also the Church has become an unnecessary, obsolete organ, which, merely from respect for what it once was, should now be hidden away somewhere far off. Directly the breathing and the circulation of the blood has been established, the bond which was formerly the source of nourishment becomes a hindrance. And efforts to maintain that connection and compel the babe that has now come into the world to nourish itself through the navel-cord, and not to live by means of its own mouth and lungs, are irrational.

But the babe's emancipation from its mother's womb is not yet life. The life of the child depends on the setting up of a new connection with its mother for the supply of nutriment. And the same must be accomplished for our Christian world. Christ's teaching has borne our world and brought it to life. The Church—one of the organs of Christ's teaching—has done its part, and has become unnecessary and a hindrance. The world cannot be guided by the Church, but the emancipation of the world from the Church is not yet life. Its life will come when it realizes its impotence and feels the necessity of fresh nourishment. And this must occur with our Christian world: it must cry out with consciousness of its impotence. Only consciousness of its impotence, consciousness of the impossibility of receiving nourishment as heretofore, and of the impossibility of obtaining any other nourishment than that of its mother's milk (Christ's teaching) will bring it to its mother's breasts, swollen as they are with milk.

In our European world, superficially self-confident, bold and resolute, but in the depth of its consciousness frightened and perplexed, the same thing is occurring as happens with a new-born babe: it flings itself about, fidgets, cries, pushes as though it were angry, and it does not understand what it has to do. It feels that its former source of nourishment has dried up, but it does not know where to seek fresh nourishment.

A new-born lambkin moves his eyes and his ears, shakes his tail, jumps, and kicks. To judge by his assurance it seems as though he knew everything; but he, poor little thing, knows nothing. All this confidence and energy is the result of his mother's juices, the transfer of which has now ceased and cannot be renewed. He is in a happy, but at the same time a desperate, condition. He is full of freshness and strength; but he is lost unless he takes to his mother's teats.

The same is occurring with our European world. See what a complex, seemingly reasonable, energetic life is seething in the world. It is as if all these people knew what they were doing and why they were doing it all. See how resolutely, confidently, and briskly the men of our world undertake all that they do. Art, science, industry, social and state activities—all is full of life. But it lives only because it has been till recently nourished by its mother's juices through its navel-cord. There used to be a Church which transmitted Christ's reasonable teaching to the life of the world. All the energies of the world were nourished by it, and grew and developed. But the Church has played its part and dried up. All the organs of the world are alive, the source of their former nourishment is exhausted, and they have not yet found a fresh one. They seek it everywhere, only not from the mother from whom they have been released. They, like the lambkin, still live by the former nourishment, but have not yet come to understand that only from their mother can food be had, but that it must be got in a different way than formerly.

The business that now awaits the world consists in understanding that the former process of unconscious feeding is done with, and that a new, conscious process is necessary.

That new process consists in conscious acceptance of those truths of the Christian teaching which were formerly unconsciously imbibed by humanity through the instrumentality of the Church, and by which humanity still lives. Men must raise once more that light by which they lived but which was hidden from them, and they must lift it high before themselves and before others, and must consciously live by that light.

The teaching of Christ, as a religion defining life and explaining the life of man, stands now, as it stood 1,800 years ago, before the world. But formerly the world had the Church's explanations, which, though they hid the teaching, nevertheless seemed to suffice for the world's former life; now, however, a time has come when the Church has been outlived and the world lacks explanation of its new life, and cannot but feel its impotence and therefore can no longer avoid accepting Christ's teaching.

Christ teaches, first of all, that men should believe in the light while the light is yet in them. Christ teaches that men should set that light of reason above all else, and should live in accord with it, not doing things they themselves consider irrational. If you consider it irrational to go to kill Turks or Germans—do not go [1]; if you consider it unreasonable forcibly to take the labour of the poor in order to wear a silk hat or to tie yourself up in a corset, or to arrange a drawing-room that will incommode you—do not do it; if you consider it unreasonable to put men, corrupted by idleness and bad company, into prison, that is, into the very worst company and the completest idleness—do not do it; if you consider it

[1] Tolstoy's anti-war teaching had a considerable effect in preparing the way for Lenin's disintegration of the Russian army in 1917. Cheap reprints of Tolstoy's works, liberally subsidized by the Soviet Government, were issued when they seized power. The fact that they were willing to make use of these works for propaganda purposes did not, however, prevent their enrolling a Red Army and energetically contesting a series of civil wars during the following years.

irrational to live in an infected town atmosphere when it is possible to live in pure air; or if you consider it unreasonable to teach your children first of all, and most of all, dead languages—do not do it. Only do not do what is done now by the whole of our European world, namely, live a life you consider unreasonable; act while considering your actions unreasonable; disbelieve in your reason, and live in discord with it.

Christ's teaching is light. The light shines and the darkness comprehendeth it not. One cannot refuse to accept the light when it shines. One cannot dispute with it; it is impossible to dispute with it. With Christ's teaching one cannot dispute, because it envelops all the errors in which people live, and does not collide with them, but, like the ether about which the physicists talk, it permeates them all. The teaching of Christ is equally unavoidable for every one in our world, whatever his circumstances may be. Christ's teaching cannot but be accepted by men, not because it is impossible to deny the metaphysical explanation of life it gives (it is possible to deny it), but because it alone supplies those rules of life without which humanity has not lived, and cannot live, and without which no man has lived or can live if he wishes to live as a man—that is to say, to live a reasonable life.

The strength of Christ's teaching lies not in its explanation of the meaning of life, but in what flows therefrom—the teaching of life. Christ's metaphysical teaching is not new. It is still the same teaching of humanity which is written in the hearts of men, and which has been taught by all the true sages of the world. But the strength of Christ's teaching lies in the application of that metaphysical teaching of life.

The metaphysical basis of the ancient teaching of the Jews and of Christ is one and the same: love of God and of one's neighbour. But for the application of that teaching of life according to Moses, as the Jews understood it, the fulfilment of 613 commandments was necessary, many of them senseless and cruel, and all resting on the authority of the Scriptures. According to Christ's law, the teaching of life which flows from that same metaphysical basis is expressed in five commandments, which are reasonable, beneficent, carry in themselves their meaning and justification, and embrace the whole life of man.

Christ's teaching cannot but be accepted by those believing Jews, Buddhists, Mohammedans, and others who have begun to doubt the validity of their own law. Still less can it be rejected by those of our Christian world who now lack any moral law whatever.

Christ's teaching does not dispute with the men of our world about their conception of the world; it agrees with it in advance, and, including this in itself, gives them what they lack, what is indispensable to them, and what they are searching for; it gives them a way of life, and one not novel to them, but long familiar and akin to all.

You are a believing Christian, of whatever

sect or confession. You believe in the creation of the world, in the Trinity, in the fall and redemption of man, in the sacraments, in prayers, and in the Church. Christ's teaching not only does not argue with you, but fully agrees with your outlook on the world; it only gives you what you have not got. Retaining your present belief, you feel that the life of the world, and your own life, is filled with evil, and you do not know how to avoid it. Christ's teaching (obligatory for you, because it is the teaching of your God) gives you simple, practicable rules of life, which will free you and other people from the evil that torments you. Believe in the resurrection, in heaven and hell, in the Church, in sacraments, in the redemption, and pray as your faith demands, fast, and sing psalms—all this does not prevent you from fulfilling what Christ has revealed to be necessary for your welfare: do not be angry; do not commit adultery; do not bind yourself by oaths; do not defend yourself by violence; and do not go to war.

Perhaps you will fail to keep some one of these rules and will be tempted to infringe one of them, as now in moments of temptation you infringe the rules of your faith, the rules of the civil law, or the laws of politeness. Similarly in moments of temptation you may perhaps infringe the laws of Christ; but in your quiet moments do not do what you do now—do not arrange your life so that it should be difficult not to be angry, not to commit adultery, not to take oaths, not to defend yourself, and not to fight; but in such a way that it should be hard to do these things. You cannot but acknowledge this, for God commands it of you.

You are an unbelieving philosopher, no matter of what denomination. You say everything comes about in the world according to a law you have discovered. Christ's teaching does not dispute with you, and fully admits the law you have discovered. But then, besides that law of yours by which thousands of years hence that welfare will come to pass which you desire and have prepared for mankind, there is also your own life, which you can live either in accord with reason or in contradiction to reason; and for that same life of yours you have now no rules, except those which are written by men you do not respect and are put in execution by the police. Christ's teaching gives you rules that will certainly accord with your law, for your law of altruism or the common will, is nothing else than a paraphrase of Christ's teaching.

You are an average man, half a believer, half a sceptic, who has no time to immerse himself in the meaning of human life, and you have no definite outlook on life; you do what everybody else does. Christ's teaching does not dispute with you. It says: 'Very well, you are unable to argue and to verify the truths of the doctrine taught you; it is easier for you to act as everybody else does. But, however modest you may be, you yet are conscious in yourself of that inward judge, who sometimes approves your action that accords with everybody's, and sometimes does not approve of it. However humble your lot may be, it yet occurs to you to ponder, and to ask yourself: Shall I do this thing as they all do it, or in my own way? And just in these cases—that is to say, just when you have occasion to decide that question—the laws of Christ will present themselves to you in all their strength. And they will certainly furnish a reply to your question for they embrace the whole of your life, and they will reply in accord with your reason and your conscience. If you are nearer to belief than to unbelief, then, acting in this way, you will be acting in accord with the will of God. If you are nearer to free-thought, then, acting in this way, you will act in accord with the most reasonable rules that exist in the world, of which you can convince yourself, for Christ's rules bear in themselves their own reason and justification.

Christ said (John xii. 31): '*Now is the judgement of this world:* now shall the prince of this world be cast out.'

He also said (John xvi. 33): 'These things have I spoken unto you, that in me ye may have peace. In the world ye have tribulation: but be of good cheer; *I have overcome the world.*'

And really the world—that is, the evil of the world, is conquered.

If there still exists a world of evil, it only exists inertly; it no longer possesses the roots of life. It does not exist for one who believes in the laws of Christ. It has been conquered in the reasonable consciousness of the son of man. The runaway train still moves forward, but all the rational work on it has long since been directed the contrary way.

'For whatsoever is begotten of God overcometh the world: and *this is the victory that hath overcome the world, even our faith*' (1 Epistle of John v. 4).

The faith that overcomes the world is faith in the teaching of Christ.

CHAPTER XII

WHAT IS FAITH?

I BELIEVE Christ's teaching; and this is what I believe.

I believe that my welfare in the world will only be possible when all men fulfil Christ's teaching.

I believe that the fulfilment of that teaching is possible, easy, and joyful.

I believe that before that teaching is universally followed, even were I alone in fulfilling it, there is still nothing for me to do to save my life from inevitable ruin but to fulfil that teaching; just as there is no alternative way of escape from a burning house for a man who has found the door leading to safety.

I believe that the life I lived in accord with the world's teaching was tormenting, and that only life in accord with Christ's teaching gives me in this world the welfare the Father of life intended for me.

I believe that this teaching confers blessedness on all humanity, saves me from inevitable destruction, and gives me here the greatest possible welfare. Therefore I cannot but accept it.

'The law was given by Moses; grace and

truth came by Jesus Christ' (John i. 17). Christ's teaching is welfare and truth. Formerly, not knowing the truth, I did not know welfare. Mistaking evil for good, I fell into evil, and doubted the rightness of my strivings after goodness. Now I have understood and believed that the goodness towards which I strove is the will of the Father, and is the most legitimate essence of my life.

Christ has said to me: Live for goodness, but do not trust those snares (σκάνδαλοες) which, tempting you with a simulacrum of what is good, deprive you of goodness, and trap you into evil. Your welfare lies in your unity with all men; evil is the infringement of that unity of the son of man. Do not deprive yourself of that welfare which is given you.

Christ has shown me that the unity of the son of man, the love of men among themselves, is not, as it formerly seemed to me, an aim towards which people should strive, but that this unity, this love of men among one another, is their natural condition, in which children are born according to Christ's words, and in which all men live until this condition is infringed by fraud, error, or temptation.

But Christ not only showed me that; he clearly, beyond possibility of error, enumerated for me, in his commandments, all the temptations which had deprived me of that natural condition of unity, love, and blessedness and had drawn me into evil. The commands of Christ give me the means of salvation from the temptations which have deprived me of my welfare, and therefore I cannot but believe in those commandments.

I was given the blessing of life, and I myself ruined it. Christ, by his commandments, showed me the temptations through which I ruin my happiness, and therefore I cannot continue to do what ruins it. In that, and in that alone, is my whole belief.

Christ showed me that the first temptation which destroys the good of life is enmity, anger against other men. I cannot but believe this, and therefore can no longer deliberately bear ill-will to others; I cannot, as I used to do formerly, take pleasure in my anger, be proud of it, inflame it, and justify it by considering myself important and wise and other people insignificant, *lost*, and senseless. I can now no longer, at the first indication that I am giving way to anger, fail to acknowledge that I alone am guilty, and to seek reconciliation with those who strive against me.

But that is not enough. If I now know that my anger is an unnatural condition, harmful for me, I also know what temptation brings me to it. That temptation consists in the fact that I have separated myself from other people, considering only some of them to be my equals, and all the rest to be mere ciphers, not real men (*raca*) or stupid and uneducated (irrational). I now see that this separation of myself from others, and this estimation of others as *raca* and senseless, was the chief cause of my enmity against men. Remembering my former life,

I now see that I never allowed my hostile feeling to flame up against those I considered to be my superiors, and never insulted them; but that the smallest action that was unpleasant to me from a man I considered beneath me provoked my anger, and caused me to insult him, and the more I thought myself above such a man the more ready was I to insult him; sometimes even my imagination of the inferiority of a man's position caused me to insult him. Now I remember that that man alone is superior to others who humbles himself before others and is the servant of all. I now understand why that which is exalted among men is an abomination before God, and why woe befalls the rich and famous, and the poor and humble are blessed.

Only now do I understand this and believe it, and this belief has changed my whole appreciation of what is good and lofty, and what is bad and mean in life. All that formerly appeared to me good and lofty—honours, fame, education, riches, the complexity and refinement of life and of its surroundings, food, dress, and outward manners—all this has become for me bad and mean; while peasant life, obscurity, poverty, roughness, simplicity of surroundings, food, dress, and manners, has all become for me good and noble. And therefore if now, knowing all this, I still, in moments of forgetfulness, yield to anger and insult my brother-man, yet, when I am calm, I can no longer yield to that temptation which, placing me above my fellows, deprives me of my true welfare, unity and love; just as a man cannot reset for himself a trap into which he has formerly fallen, and which nearly destroyed him. Now I cannot participate in anything that would outwardly place me above others, separating me from them; I cannot, as formerly, recognize, either for myself or for others, any titles, ranks, or distinctions, beyond claiming to be a man; I cannot seek for fame or praise; I cannot seek such knowledge as would separate me from others, and cannot but seek to free myself from my wealth which separated me from others, and I cannot, in my life and its surroundings, in food, clothing and external manners, fail to seek for all that will not divide me from, but unite me with, the majority of men.

Christ has shown me that another snare ruining my welfare is lustfulness—that is to say, desire for another woman and not for her with whom I have united. I cannot but believe this, and therefore cannot, as I used to, consider adulterous lust a natural and noble quality in a man. I cannot justify it to myself by my love of beauty, by being enamoured, or by defects in my wife. I cannot but, at the first intimation that I am yielding to adulterous desire, recognize that I am in an unhealthy and unnatural state, or fail to seek for all the means which can free me from that evil.

But, knowing now that adulterous lust harms me, I also know the temptation which formerly led me into it, and therefore I cannot serve it; I now know that the chief cause of temptation is not that people cannot refrain from fornication, but that most men and women have been deserted by those with whom they first came together. I now know that every desertion of a man or woman by him or her with whom they first had connection is that very divorce which Christ forbids ; because the husbands and wives abandoned by their first mates cause all the depravity in the world. Remembering what it was that led me into lechery, I now see that, besides the barbarous education by which the lust of fornication in me was physically and mentally inflamed, and was excused by all sorts of subtleties, the chief snare that entangled me arose from my having abandoned the first woman with whom I had connection, and the condition of women who had been abandoned and who surrounded me. I now see that the chief strength of the temptation was not in my lust, but in the fact that my lust, and that of the women who had been deserted and who surrounded me, was unsatisfied. I now understand the words of Christ : God at first created man, male and female, so that the two were one, and therefore man may not and should not divide that which God hath joined. I now understand that monogamy is the natural law of humanity, which must not be infringed. I now fully understand the saying that whoso divorceth his wife (i.e. the woman with whom he has first come together) for another, causes her to become dissolute, and brings fresh evil into the world to his own detriment. I believe this, and that belief alters my whole former evaluation of what is good and lofty and what is bad and mean in life. What formerly seemed to me the best—a refined, elegant life, with passionate and poetic love, extolled by all the poets and artists—all this has come to appear to me bad and repulsive. On the contrary, what seems to me good is a laborious, frugal, rough life which moderates the lusts. High and important seems to me, not so much the human institution of marriage, affixing the external seal of legality on a certain union of a man and woman, as the union itself of any man and woman, which, once it has been accomplished, cannot be infringed without infringing the will of God. If I may, even now, in a moment of forgetfulness, yield to adulterous desire, I can at any rate no longer, knowing the temptation which led me into that evil, serve it as I did formerly. I cannot desire and seek for physical idleness and a life of repletion, which inflamed in me excessive desire; I cannot seek those amusements which inflame amatory lust—novels, verses, music, theatres, and balls, which formerly seemed to me not merely harmless but very noble amusements. I cannot leave my wife, knowing that leaving her is the first snare for me, for her, and for others; I cannot take part in the idle life of repletion led by others, I cannot take part in or promote those lustful amusements, novels,[1] theatres, operas, balls,

[1] This book appeared when de Vogue was writing his work *Le roman Russe*, and not having before him Tolstoy's subsequent pronouncements on Art, nor of course the stories, novels, and plays Tolstoy was yet to produce, he made too much of these few words,

etc.—which serve as a snare for me and for others. I cannot encourage unmarried life for people who are ripe for marriage; I cannot be a party to the separation of husbands and wives; I cannot make distinctions between unions called marriages and those not so called; I cannot but consider holy and obligatory only the first marital union which a man has formed.

Christ has shown me that a third temptation ruining my welfare is the temptation of the oath. I cannot but believe this, and therefore cannot now, as I did formerly, myself take an oath to any one, or about anything, and I cannot now, as I did formerly, justify myself for taking an oath by saying that it does no one any harm, that everybody does it, that it is necessary for the State, or that it will be worse for me and for others if I refuse this demand. I now know that it is an evil for me and for others, and I cannot do it.

But not only do I know this, I now also know the temptation which led me into that evil, and I cannot serve it. I know that the deception consists in this, that people promise in advance to obey what some man, or some men, order; whereas man must never obey any one but God. I now know that the most terrible evils in the world, by their results, are murder in war, imprisonments, executions, and tortures, which

and by his comments misled a whole string of French, English, and American critics, who, since then, instead of reading Tolstoy for themselves, have put forth what profess to be original criticisms, but are really re-hashes of what de Vogue had said, and represent Tolstoy as having 'abandoned art.'

are performed, thanks only to this temptation whereby responsibility is lifted from those who commit the evil. Remembering many and many evils which made me blame and dislike people, I now see that they were all caused by the oath—the acknowledgement of an obligation to submit oneself to the will of others. I now understand the meaning of the words: Whatever is more than a simple assertion or denial, 'Yes' or 'No,' all that is beyond that, every promise given in advance,[1] is evil. Understanding that, I believe that the oath ruins my welfare and that of others; and this belief changes my valuation of what is good and evil, lofty and mean. All that formerly seemed to be good and lofty, the duty of loyalty to the Government confirmed by an oath of allegiance, the extortion of such oaths from others, and all actions contrary to conscience, performed under the influence of such oaths—all this now appears to me both bad and mean. And therefore I cannot now any longer depart from Christ's com-

[1] Here again Tolstoy introduces an extension of the teaching, which may be a logical deduction but which was certainly not stated by Christ. Tolstoy, as usual, aims at the absolute right, ignoring the complexity of life, and the fact that, when seeking the best of the paths open to us, we often have to weigh pros and cons. To give no promise in advance would have the advantage that one would be free from day to day to change one's mind as to one's work; but it would seriously hinder one's taking part in any large undertaking requiring forethought and the assured co-operations of many people for a considerable period. Yet such undertakings are often greatly needed, and may be of great service to one's fellow men.

mand, which forbids the oath. I cannot any longer swear to any one, or compel others to swear, or take part in making other people either themselves swear or compel others to swear, and I cannot look upon the oath as either valuable or necessary, or even innocuous, as many suppose it to be.

Christ has shown me that a fourth temptation depriving me of welfare is resistance to evil by means of violence applied to other people. I cannot but believe that this is an evil to me and to others, and therefore I cannot consciously employ it, and cannot, as I used to, justify this evil on the ground that it is necessary for my defence and for that of others[1]; nor can I now,

[1] Tolstoy overlooks the fact that there may be reasons for using physical force, other than a desire to protect the lives and property of oneself or of one's fellow-countrymen. To refer once again to the American War of 1861–4: the questions at issue were not at all those Tolstoy gives as the causes of the use of violence. At the root of the matter then lay the question whether the Government of the United States should not merely acquiesce in the holding of some millions of negroes in a state of slavery, but also in such a manipulation of political power by the Slave States as would ultimately give them control of the machinery of Government in the United States, and lead to an enlargement of the area of slave territory and to the permanence of that peculiar institution. That war was fought on a question of right and wrong; and Lincoln held, as I hold, that when a supreme issue of that kind presents itself a man has no right to say, 'I will use such mental powers as I possess to help the right to prevail, but will stop short of using my physical powers to that end,' for this is eventually to assert that the body is more important than the mind or soul.

at the first reminder that I am committing violence, do other than refrain from it and stop it.

But not only do I know this, I now also know the snare which led me into this evil. I now know that that temptation consists in the delusion that my life can be secured by defending myself and my property from other people.

I now know that a large part of the ills of mankind proceed from the fact that. instead of giving work to one another, not only do men not give it, but they deprive themselves of work and seize by violence the work of others. Remembering now all the evil I have done to myself and to others, and all the evil that the others did, I see that a large part of that evil proceeded from the fact that we considered it possible to secure and improve our lives by defending them. I also now understand the words : Man is born, not that others may work for him, but that he should work for others ; and also the meaning of the words : the labourer is worthy of his subsistence. I now believe that my welfare, and that of other people, is only possible when each one labours not for himself, but for others, and not only ceases to withhold his work from others, but gives it to any one who needs it. This belief has changed my valuation of what is good and evil and mean. All that formerly seemed to me good and lofty—riches, property of all kinds, honours, consciousness of one's own dignity and rights, has all become evil and mean ; while all that seemed to me evil and mean—work done for others, poverty, humiliation, renunciation of all property and all rights—has become good and lofty in my eyes. If now I may, in moments of forgetfulness, be tempted to use violence to defend myself and others, or my own or other people's property, I can at any rate no longer calmly and consciously serve this temptation which ruins me and others, and cannot acquire property. I cannot employ any kind of physical force against any one, except a child, and then only in order to save it from immediately impending danger.[1] I cannot take part in any Governmental activity that has for its aim the defence of people and their property by violence; I cannot be a judge, or take part in trials, or be an official, or serve in any Government office[2]; nor can I help others to take part in law-courts and Government offices.

Christ showed me that the fifth temptation which deprives me of welfare is the separation we make of our own from other nations. I cannot but believe this, and therefore if, in a moment of forgetfulness, feelings of enmity to-

[1] Tolstoy's conclusions were, naturally, largely shaped by the conditions and experiences of his own life, and it is noticeable that he wrote this when he had young children to safeguard, and never repeated this very serious limitation of his favourite precept after his own children had reached an age at which they no longer needed the constant physical protection demanded by childhood.

[2] This is a logical and quite inevitable conclusion from the non-resistant position—that the use of physical force to prevent men doing what they please is immoral. It is therefore very necessary that that position should be refuted if, as I suppose, it can be controverted.

wards a man of another nation may arise within me, yet I can no longer, in my calm moments, fail to acknowledge that feeling to be a false one, and I cannot justify myself, as I used to do, by claiming the superiority of my own people to others, basing this on the errors, cruelties, and barbarities of another nation, nor can I, at the first reminder of this, fail to try to be more friendly to a foreigner than to a compatriot.

But not only do I now know that my separation from other nations is an evil, ruining my welfare, but I also know the temptation that led me into that evil, and I can no longer, as I did formerly, consciously and quietly serve it. I know that that temptation lies in the delusion that my welfare is bound up only with that of the people of my own nation, and not with that of all the peoples of the earth. I now know that my union with other people cannot be severed by a line of frontier and by Government decrees about my belonging to this or that nation. I now know that all men everywhere are equals and brothers. Remembering now all the evil I have done, suffered, and seen, resulting from the enmity of nations,[1] it is clear to me that the cause of it all lay in the gross fraud called patriotism and love of one's country. Remembering my education, I now see that a feeling of hostility to other nations, a feeling of separation from them, was never really natural

[1] Some of Tolstoy's most vivid recollections related to the Crimean War, in which he fought against the French and the English, and of which he wrote a remarkable account in his book, *Sevastopol.*

to me, but that all these evil feelings were artificially inoculated into me by an insane education. I now understand the meaning of the words: Do good to your enemies; behave to them as to your own people. You are all children of one Father; so be like your Father, i.e. do not make distinctions between your own people and other peoples; be the same with them all. I now understand that my welfare is only possible if I acknowledge my unity with all the people of the world without exception. I believe this. And that belief has changed my whole valuation of what is good and evil, lofty and mean. What seemed to me good and lofty—love of fatherland, of one's own people, of one's State, and service of it to the detriment of the welfare of other peoples,[1] the military achievements of men, all this now appears to me repulsive and pitiable. What seemed to me bad and shameful—rejection of fatherland, and

[1] This sentence seems to mark a peculiar obliquity of vision on Tolstoy's part. With all his great qualities, he suffered from an over-readiness to attribute evil intention to all existing institutions, and he here assumes that the fundamental purpose of the division of mankind into separate nations is to inflict harm on one another. Plausibility is given to this assumption by the frequency with which different nations do misunderstand and injure one another; but the ultimate ground of the division of mankind into separate States is not to inflict mutual injuries, but to organize men into units sufficiently homogeneous to admit of their working with a minimum of friction and violence. That they should be so organized should tend, not to the detriment, but to the ultimate advantage, of other lands.

cosmopolitanism[1]—now appears to me, on the contrary, good and noble. If now, in a moment of forgetfulness, I can co-operate with a Russian rather than with a foreigner and can desire the success of the Russian State or nation, I can no longer, in calm moments, serve that temptation which ruins me and other people. I cannot acknowledge any States or nations, cannot take part in the quarrels between nations and States, either by writings or (still less) by serving any Government. I cannot take part in all those affairs which are based on the diversity of nations, not in custom-houses and the collection of taxes, nor in the preparation of military stores and ammunition, nor in any activity for creating armaments, nor in military service, nor (still less) in war itself against other nations—and I cannot help other people to do so.

I have now understood wherein my welfare lies; I believe in this, and therefore cannot do what undoubtedly deprives me of welfare.

But not only do I believe that I ought to live thus; I also believe that if I live so my life will receive for me the only possible, reasonable, and joyful meaning, indestructible by death.

[1] One sees how Tolstoy unwittingly prepared the ground for Lenin's defeatist activity, when the latter, in 1914–17, published *The Social Democrat* advocating the desirability of Russia's defeat in the war: an event which was achieved by the disintegration of the Russian Army which followed on his propaganda, and resulted in the break-up of Russia, and in the war being very nearly won by the military imperialist Power of Germany.

I believe my rational life, my light, was only given me in order to shine before men, not by words but by good works, that men may praise the Father (Matt. v. 16). I believe that my life and knowledge of truth is a talent given me to use ; and this talent is a fire, which is only a fire when it burns. I believe that I am Nineveh in relation to other Jonahs from whom I have learnt and am still learning the truth, but that I too am a Jonah in relation to other Ninevites to whom I must convey the truth. I believe that the sole meaning of my life lies in living by that light which is within me, and in not hiding it under a bushel, but holding it high before men that they may see it. And this belief gives me fresh strength to fulfil Christ's teaching, and destroys those hindrances which formerly blocked my path.

The very thing which formerly militated against the truth and practicability of Christ's teaching and drove me away from it—the possibility of privations, sufferings, and death inflicted by those who do not know his teaching—that very thing now confirms for me the truth of the teaching, and attracts me to it.

Christ said, 'When you exalt the son of man you will all be drawn to me,' and I felt that I was irresistibly drawn to him. He also said, 'The truth will make you free,' and I felt myself completely free.

'If a hostile army, or wicked people, attack me,' thought I formerly, 'and I do not defend myself, they will despoil me, shame me, and torment and kill me and my neighbours,' and this seemed to me terrible. But now all that formerly disturbed me seems to me joyful and confirms the truth. I now know that I and the enemy and the so-called criminals and robbers are all men, all just sons of man as myself, who love good and hate evil as I do, and who also live on the eve of death as I do, seeking salvation and with no possibility of finding it except in Christ's teaching. All evil that they do me will be evil for themselves, and therefore they should do me good. If the truth is unknown to them and they do evil considering it good, I know the truth only in order to show it to those who do not know it. But I cannot show it them except by renouncing participation in evil and acknowledging the truth by my actions.

'Enemies will come: Germans, Turks, savages, and if you do not fight they will slaughter you!' That is not true. If there were a society of Christians doing no harm to any one and giving the whole surplus of their work to others, no enemies—neither Germans, nor Turks, nor savages—would kill and torture such people. They would take for themselves all that those people (for whom no distinction existed between Russians, Germans, Turks, or savages) were in any case giving away. If Christians are living in a non-Christian Society which defends itself by war, and the Christians are called on to take part in the war, then an opportunity occurs for those Christians to help those who do not know the truth. A Christian only knows the truth in order to testify to it before those who know it not. And they can only testify by actions. That action is, the repudiation of war and the doing of good to people without distinguishing between so-called enemies and one's own people.

'But if the foreign enemy does not, then his own wicked neighbours will, attack the Christian's family, and will pillage, torture, and kill him and those dear to him if they do not defend themselves.' This, again, is not true. If all the members of the family are Christians, and therefore devote their lives to serving others, no man so senseless will be found as to deprive of food, or to kill, those who serve him. Miklukha-Maklay [1] settled among the most bestial savages, so it is said, and they not only did not kill him, but grew fond of him, and submitted to him, merely because he was not afraid of them, demanded nothing of them, and did them good. If a Christian lives with an un-Christian family and relations who defend themselves and their property by violence, and the Christian is called on to take part in that defence, this demand is for him a call to the fulfilment of his duty in life. A Christian knows the truth only to show it to others, and most of all to those near him and bound to him by ties of relationship and friendship, and a Christian can show the truth by not falling into the error others have fallen into, by not ranging himself either on the side of the attackers or on the

[1] N. N. Miklukha-Maklay was a distinguished Russian explorer (1846–88) who investigated the manners and customs of the inhabitants of New Guinea and Micronesia.

side of the defenders, but by giving all to others and showing by his life that he wants nothing except to fulfil the will of God, and that he fears nothing except to depart from that will.

'But the Government cannot allow members of society to refuse to acknowledge the foundations of the State organization, and to evade the performance of the duties of every citizen. The Government demands from Christians, oaths, participation in legal proceedings, and military service, and for a refusal of these things subjects them to punishment, banishment, imprisonment, or even execution.' And again, this demand, made by Government, will only serve for a Christian as a call to fulfil the business of his life. For a Christian the Government's demand is the demand of people who do not know the truth. And therefore a Christian, who knows it, cannot but bear witness to it before those who know it not. Violence, imprisonment, or execution, to which a Christian is subjected in consequence of this, affords him the possibility of witnessing, not in words, but in deeds. Every violence by war, robbery, or execution, is not a result of the irrational forces of nature, but is perpetrated by erring people, deprived of knowledge of the truth. And, therefore, the greater the evil these people do to a Christian, the further they are from the truth, the more unfortunate are they, and the more do they need a knowledge of the truth. But a Christian cannot impart to men that knowledge otherwise than by refraining from the error in which those dwell who do him evil, and by returning good for evil. And that alone is the whole business of a Christian's life, and its whole meaning, which death cannot destroy.

People bound together by a delusion form, as it were, a collective cohesive mass. The cohesion of that mass is the world's evil. All the reasonable activity of humanity is directed towards the destruction of this cohesion.

All revolutions are attempts to break up that mass by violence. It seems to people that if they break up that mass it will cease to be a mass, and therefore they strike at it; but, by trying to break it, they only forge it closer. The cohesion of the particles is not destroyed until the inner force passes from the mass to the particles and obliges them to separate from it.

The strength of that cohesion of people lies in a falsehood, a fraud. The force freeing each particle of the human cohesive mass is truth. Man can hand on the truth only by deeds of truth.

Only deeds of truth bringing light into man's consciousness destroy the cohesion of deception and separate men, one after another, from the mass bound together by the cohesion of deception.

And this work has been going on already for 1,800 years. From the time the commandments of Christ were laid before humanity that work began, and it will not end until all has been accomplished, as Christ said (Matt. v. 18).

The Church formed of those who thought to unite people into one by asserting of themselves, with oaths, that they possessed the truth has long since died. But the Church formed of men joined in union, not by promises nor by anointings but by deeds of truth and goodness, this Church has always lived, and will live. This Church now, as heretofore, is formed, not of those who say, Lord, Lord! yet work iniquity (Matt. vii. 21, 23), but of those who hear these words and do them. The members of this Church know that it is only necessary for them not to infringe the unity of the son of man for their life to be a blessing, and that this blessedness is only infringed by the non-fulfilment of the commandments of Christ. And therefore members of the Church cannot but fulfil those commandments and teach others to fulfil them.

Whether there are now few or many such people, that is the Church which nothing can overcome, and to which all men will be united.

'Fear not, little flock, for it is your Father's good pleasure to give you the kingdom' (Luke xii. 32).

MOSCOW,
January 22, 1884.

A LIST OF THE
WORLD'S CLASSICS

Oxford University Press

THE WORLD'S CLASSICS

A SERIES in constant progress, containing over four hundred volumes, and offering in a size adapted for the pocket, and at a low price, the most famous works in the English language, with more than a few translations. Many of the volumes contain introductions by the best modern writers.

POCKET SIZE, $6 \times 3\frac{3}{4}$ inches (as this list). Large type, on thin opaque paper, in superfine art cloth.

A NUMBER of the volumes are also obtainable in Pebble grain Moroccoette; also in Sultan-red Leather or Natural grain Morocco. These are specially recommended for presentation.

THE VOLUMES are obtainable only through the booksellers.

IN THE FOLLOWING LIST the books are classified as below:

Anthologies	*Letters*
Autobiography	*Literary Criticism*
Biography	*Philosophy and Science*
Classics–Greek and Roman	*Poetry*
Drama	*Politics, Political Theory, and Political Economy*
Essays and Belles Lettres	*Religion*
Fiction (Short Stories are grouped separately)	*Short Stories*
History	*Travel and Topography*

AN INDEX OF AUTHORS is given at the end of the list.

LATEST ADDITIONS

¶ *Biography*

CRABBE, LIFE OF. By his Son. Introduction by *E. M. Forster* (404).

TREVELYAN (SIR G. O.). Life of Macaulay. With a new Introduction by *G. M. Trevelyan*. 2 vols. (401, 402).

¶ *Essays, &c.*

ENGLISH CRITICAL ESSAYS. (Twentieth Century.) Selected and edited by *Phyllis M. Jones* (405).

MODERN ENGLISH ESSAYS. Selected by *H. S. Milford*. Second Series (406).

READING AT RANDOM. A 'World's Classics' Anthology (410).

¶ *Fiction*

AUSTEN (JANE). Northanger Abbey. Introduction by *Michael Sadleir* (355). Persuasion. Introduction by *Forrest Reid* (356). Sense and Sensibility. Introduction by *Lord David Cecil* (389).

FRENCH SHORT STORIES. Selected and translated by *K. Rebillon Lambley* (396).

GERMAN SHORT STORIES. Translated by *E. N. Bennett*, with an Introduction by *E. K. Bennett* (415).

HOLME (CONSTANCE). Crump Folk going Home (419). The Lonely Plough (390). The Old Road from Spain (400). The Splendid Fairing (416). The Trumpet in the Dust (409).

LA MOTTE FOUQUÉ. Undine, Sintram, Aslauga's Knight, and The Two Captains. With an Introduction by *Sir Edmund Gosse* (408).

RABELAIS. Gargantua and Pantagruel. Translated by *Urquhart* and *Motteux*, with notes. 3 vols. (411–13).

SCOTT. Short Stories. With an Introduction by *Lord David Cecil* (414).

TOLSTOY. Nine Stories (1855–63) (420). War and Peace. A revised translation by *Louise* and *Aylmer Maude*, embodying Tolstoy's final amendments. 3 vols. (233–5).

TROLLOPE. Orley Farm. 2 vols. (423, 424). *In preparation.*

¶ *Poetry*

DANTE'S DIVINE COMEDY. Italian text and English translation, by *Melville B. Anderson*, on facing pages, with notes and full index. 3 vols. (392–4).

English translation only, with notes and full index, in 1 vol. (395).

GOETHE. Faust, Parts I and II. Translated by *Bayard Taylor*. Intro. by *Marshall Montgomery* and notes by *Douglas Yates* (380).

¶ *Politics, &c.*

SPEECHES AND DOCUMENTS ON THE BRITISH DOMINIONS (1918–1931), from Self-Government to National Sovereignty. Selected, with an Introduction, by *A. Berriedale Keith* (403).

COMPLETE LIST OF THE SERIES

¶ *Anthologies*

A Book of Narrative Verse. Compiled by *V. H. Collins*. Introduction by *Edmund Blunden* (350).
A Book of Scottish Verse. Compiled by *R. L. Mackie* (417).
American Criticism. Representative Literary Essays. Chosen by *Norman Foerster* (354).
English Essays, chosen and arranged by *W. Peacock* (32).
English Essays, 1600–1900, chosen by *S. V. Makower* and *B. H. Blackwell* (172).
English Essays, Modern. Two Series. Selected by *H. S. Milford* (280, 406).
English Prose from MANDEVILLE to RUSKIN, chosen and arranged by *W. Peacock* (45).
English Prose, chosen and arranged by *W. Peacock* in 5 volumes: I, WYCLIFFE to CLARENDON; II, MILTON to GRAY; III, WALPOLE to LAMB; IV, LANDOR to HOLMES; V, MRS. GASKELL to HENRY JAMES (219–23).
English Prose, Narrative, Descriptive, Dramatic (MALORY to STEVENSON), compiled by *H. A. Treble* (204).
English Songs and Ballads, compiled by *T. W. H. Crosland*. New edition, with the text revised, and additional poems (13).
English Short Stories (Nineteenth and Twentieth Centuries), selected by *H. S. Milford*. Three Series (193, 228, 315).
English Verse. Edited by *W. Peacock*. Vol. I, Early Lyrics to SHAKESPEARE (308). Vol. II, CAMPION to the Ballads (309). Vol. III, DRYDEN to WORDSWORTH (310). Vol. IV, SCOTT to ELIZABETH BROWNING (311). Vol. V, LONGFELLOW to RUPERT BROOKE (312).
Letters Written in War-time (Fifteenth to Nineteenth Centuries), selected and arranged by *H. Wragg* (202).
A Miscellany of Tracts and Pamphlets. Sixteenth to Nineteenth Centuries. Edited by *A. C. Ward* (304).
Palgrave's Golden Treasury, with 190 pages of additional poems by *FitzGerald*, *Tennyson*, the *Brownings*, *Arnold*, &c. (133).
Reading at Random. A 'World's Classics' Anthology (410).

¶ *Autobiography*

Aksakoff (Serghei). Trans. by *J. D. Duff*. A Russian Gentleman (241). Years of Childhood (242). A Russian Schoolboy (261).
Cellini (Benvenuto) (300).
De Quincey (Thomas). Confessions of an Opium-Eater (23).
Franklin (Benjamin). The Autobiography, edited from his original manuscript by *John Bigelow* (250).
Gibbon (Edward). Autobiography. Intro. *J. B. Bury* (139).

HAYDON (BENJAMIN ROBERT). The Autobiography. Introduction and Epilogue by *Edmund Blunden* (314).
HOLCROFT (THOMAS). Memoirs, continued by *W. Hazlitt* (302).
HUNT (LEIGH). Autobiography. Intro. *Edmund Blunden* (329).
MILL (JOHN STUART). Autobiography. Introduction by *Harold J. Laski* (262).
MORITZ (C. P.). Anton Reiser. Intro. *P. E. Matheson* (299).
TOLSTOY. A Confession, and What I believe. Translated by *Aylmer Maude* (229).
TRELAWNY (E. J.). Adventures of a Younger Son. Introduction by *Ethel Colburn Mayne* (289).
TROLLOPE (ANTHONY). Autobiography. Introduction by *Michael Sadleir* (239).

¶ *Biography*

CARLYLE. The Life of John Sterling. Introduction by *W. Hale White* (*'Mark Rutherford'*) (144).
CRABBE, LIFE OF. By his Son. Intro. *E. M. Forster* (404).
DOBSON (AUSTIN). Four Frenchwomen: Charlotte Corday, Madame Roland, Princess de Lamballe, Madame de Genlis (248).
EMERSON. Representative Men. (With *English Traits*) (30).
FRANCIS OF ASSISI (ST.). The Little Flowers; and The Life of Brother Giles. Translated into English verse by *James Rhoades* (265).
GASKELL (MRS.). The Life of Charlotte Brontë (214).
HOUGHTON (LORD). Life of Keats (364).
JOHNSON (SAMUEL). Lives of the Poets. 2 vols. (83, 84).
MAUDE (AYLMER). Life of Tolstoy. 2 vols. (383, 384).
SCOTT (SIR WALTER). Lives of the Novelists. Introduction by *Austin Dobson* (94).
SMITH (J. T.). Nollekens and his Times. With Introduction by *Walter Sichel* (322).
TREVELYAN (SIR G. O.). Life of Macaulay. With a new Introduction by *G. M. Trevelyan*. 2 vols. (401, 402).
WALTON (IZAAK). Lives of Donne, Wotton, Hooker, Herbert, Sanderson. Introduction by *George Saintsbury* (303).

¶ *The 'Classics', Greek and Roman*

AESCHYLUS. The Seven Plays. Translated into English Verse by *Lewis Campbell* (117).
ARISTOPHANES. The Acharnians, Knights, Birds, and Frogs. Translated by *J. Hookham Frere*. Intro. *W. W. Merry* (134).
HOMER. Translated by *Pope*. Iliad (18). Odyssey (36).
SOPHOCLES. The Seven Plays. Translated into English Verse by *Lewis Campbell* (116).
VIRGIL. The Aeneid, Georgics, and Eclogues. Translated by *John Dryden* (37).
—— The Aeneid, Georgics, and Eclogues. Translated by *James Rhoades* (227).

¶ *Drama*

BROWNING (ROBERT). Poems and Plays, 1833–42 (58).
CONGREVE (WILLIAM). Complete Works. 2 vols. Introduction by *Bonamy Dobrée*. Vol. I, The Comedies. Vol. II, The Mourning Bride, with Letters, Poems, and Miscellanies (276, 277).
EIGHTEENTH CENTURY COMEDY. FARQUHAR'S Beaux' Stratagem, STEELE'S Conscious Lovers, GAY'S Beggar's Opera, FIELDING'S Tom Thumb, GOLDSMITH'S She Stoops to Conquer (292).
EIGHTEENTH CENTURY, LESSER COMEDIES OF THE. Edited by *Allardyce Nicoll*. The five comedies are ARTHUR MURPHY'S The Way to keep him, GEORGE COLMAN'S The Jealous Wife, MRS. INCHBALD'S Everyone has his Fault, THOMAS MORTON'S Speed the Plough, and FREDERICK REYNOLDS'S The Dramatist (321).
FIVE PRE-SHAKESPEAREAN COMEDIES. Edited by *F. S. Boas*. Contains MEDWALL'S Fulgens and Lucrece, HEYWOOD'S The Four PP., UDALL'S Ralph Roister Doister, the anonymous Gammer Gurton's Needle, and GASCOIGNE'S Supposes (418).
FIVE ELIZABETHAN COMEDIES. Edited by *A. K. McIlwraith*. Contains GREENE'S Friar Bacon and Friar Bungay, PEELE'S The Old Wives Tale, LYLY'S Campaspe, DEKKER'S Shoemaker's Holiday, and the anonymous Merry Devil of Edmonton (422).
MARLOWE'S Dr. Faustus (with GOETHE'S Faust, Part I, trans. *J. Anster*). Introduction by *Sir A. W. Ward* (135).
RESTORATION TRAGEDIES. DRYDEN'S All for Love, OTWAY'S Venice Preserved, SOUTHERNE'S Oronooko, ROWE'S Fair Penitent, and ADDISON'S Cato. Introduction by *Bonamy Dobrée* (313).
SHAKESPEARE. Plays and Poems. Preface by *A. C. Swinburne*. Introductions by *Edward Dowden*. 9 vols. Comedies. 3 vols. (100, 101, 102). Histories and Poems. 3 vols. (103, 104, 105). Tragedies. 3 vols. (106, 107, 108).
SHAKESPEARE, Six Plays by Contemporaries of. DEKKER, The Shoemaker's Holiday; WEBSTER, The White Devil; BEAUMONT and FLETCHER, The Knight of the Burning Pestle, and Philaster; WEBSTER, The Duchess of Malfi; MASSINGER, A New Way to pay Old Debts. Edited by *C. B. Wheeler* (199).
SHERIDAN. Plays. Introduction by *Joseph Knight* (79).
TOLSTOY. The Plays. Complete edition, including the posthumous plays. Translated by *Louise* and *Aylmer Maude* (243).

¶ *Essays and Belles Lettres*

BACON. The Essays, Civil and Moral (24).
BROWN (DR. JOHN). Horae Subsecivae (Rab and His Friends, &c.). Introduction by *Austin Dobson* (118).
CARLYLE. On Heroes and Hero-Worship (62). Past and Present. Introduction by *G. K. Chesterton* (153). Sartor Resartus (19).

DOBSON (AUSTIN). At Prior Park, &c. (259). Eighteenth-Century Vignettes. Three Series (245–7). Four Frenchwomen (248). Old Kensington Palace, &c. (258). A Paladin of Philanthropy, &c. (256). Rosalba's Journal, &c. (260). Side-Walk Studies (257).

EMERSON. English Traits, and Representative Men (30). Essays, Two Series (6). Nature, and Miscellanies (236).

ENGLISH CRITICAL ESSAYS. 3 volumes. I, Sixteenth to Eighteenth Centuries. II, Nineteenth Century. III, Twentieth Century (240, 206, 405).

ENGLISH ESSAYS, chosen and arranged by *W. Peacock* (32).

—— (A BOOK OF), 1600–1900 (172).

—— MODERN. Two Series. Selected by *H. S. Milford* (280, 406).

ENGLISH PROSE. MANDEVILLE to RUSKIN. Chosen by *W. Peacock* (45). Also a selection in 5 volumes by the same editor; WYCLIFFE to CLARENDON (219); MILTON to GRAY (220); WALPOLE to LAMB (221); LANDOR to HOLMES (222); MRS. GASKELL to HENRY JAMES (223).

ENGLISH PROSE. Narrative, Descriptive, and Dramatic (MALORY to STEVENSON). Compiled by *H. A. Treble* (204).

FROUDE (J. A.). Short Studies on Great Subjects. Series I (269).

HAZLITT (WILLIAM). Characters of Shakespeare's Plays. Introduction by *Sir Arthur Quiller-Couch* (205). The English Comic Writers. Introduction by *R. B. Johnson* (124). Sketches and Essays. Essays on Men and Manners (15). Table-Talk (5). The Spirit of the Age (57). Winterslow (25).

HOLMES (OLIVER WENDELL). The Autocrat of the Breakfast-Table (61). The Poet at the Breakfast-Table. Introduction by *Sir W. R. Nicoll* (95). The Professor at the Breakfast-Table. Introduction by *Sir W. R. Nicoll* (89).

HORNE (R. H.). A New Spirit of the Age. Introduction by *W. Jerrold* (127).

HUNT (LEIGH). Essays and Sketches. Introduction by *R. B. Johnson* (115).

IRVING (WASHINGTON). The Sketch Book of Geoffrey Crayon, Gent. Introduction by *T. Balston* (173).

LAMB. Essays of Elia, and The Last Essays of Elia (2).

LANDOR. Imaginary Conversations. Selected, with Introduction, by *Prof. E. de Sélincourt* (196).

MILTON. Selected Prose. Intro. *Malcolm W. Wallace* (293).

MONTAIGNE'S ESSAYS. Florio's translation. 3 vols. (65, 70, 77).

REYNOLDS (SIR JOSHUA). The Discourses, and the Letters to 'The Idler'. Introduction by *Austin Dobson* (149).

RUSKIN. (*Ruskin House Editions, by arrangement with Messrs. Allen & Unwin, Ltd.*) 'A Joy for Ever', and The Two Paths. Illustrated (147). Sesame and Lilies, and Ethics of the Dust (145). Time and Tide, and The Crown of Wild Olive (146). Unto this Last, and Munera Pulveris (148).

RUTHERFORD (MARK). Pages from a Journal (358).

SMITH (ALEXANDER). Dreamthorp, &c. (200).

SMOLLETT. Travels through France and Italy (90).
STERNE (LAURENCE). A Sentimental Journey. Introduction by *Virginia Woolf* (333).
STEVENSON (R.L.). Virginibus Puerisque, & Across the Plains (296).
THACKERAY. The Book of Snobs, &c. (50).
THOREAU. Walden. Introduction by *Theodore Watts-Dunton* (68).
TOLSTOY. Translated by *A. Maude*. Essays and Letters (46). 'What is Art?' and Essays on Art (331).
TRACTS AND PAMPHLETS, from JOHN KNOX to H. G. WELLS (304).
WHITE (GILBERT). The Natural History of Selborne (22).
WHITMAN. Specimen Days in America (371).

¶ *Fiction* (For SHORT STORIES see separate heading)

AINSWORTH (W. HARRISON). The Tower of London (162).
AUSTEN (JANE). Emma (129). Pride and Prejudice (335). Mansfield Park (345). Northanger Abbey (355). Persuasion (356). Sense and Sensibility (389).
BETHAM-EDWARDS (M.). The Lord of the Harvest (194).
BLACKMORE (R.D.). Lorna Doone. Intro. *Sir Herbert Warren* (171).
BORROW (GEORGE). Lavengro (66). The Romany Rye (73).
BRONTË (ANNE). Agnes Grey (141). Tenant of Wildfell Hall (67).
BRONTË (CHARLOTTE). Jane Eyre (1). Shirley (14). Villette (47). The Professor, and the Poems of the Brontës (78).
BRONTË (EMILY). Wuthering Heights (10).
BUNYAN. The Pilgrim's Progress (12). Mr. Badman (338).
CERVANTES. Don Quixote. 2 volumes (130, 131).
COBBOLD (REV. RICHARD). Margaret Catchpole (119).
COLLINS (WILKIE). The Moonstone. Introduction by *T. S. Eliot* (316). The Woman in White (226).
COOPER (J. FENIMORE). The Last of the Mohicans (163).
DEFOE. Captain Singleton (82). Robinson Crusoe. Part I (17).
DICKENS. Barnaby Rudge (286). Christmas Books (307). Edwin Drood (263). Great Expectations (128). Hard Times (264). Old Curiosity Shop (270). Oliver Twist (8). Pickwick Papers. 2 volumes (120, 121). Tale of Two Cities (38).
DISRAELI (BENJAMIN). Coningsby (381). Sybil (291).
ELIOT (GEORGE). Adam Bede (63). Felix Holt (179). The Mill on the Floss (31). Romola (178). Scenes of Clerical Life (155). Silas Marner, &c. (80).
FIELDING. Jonathan Wild (382). Joseph Andrews (334).
GALT (JOHN). The Entail. Introduction by *John Ayscough* (177).
GASKELL (MRS.). Cousin Phillis, and Other Tales, &c. (168). Cranford, The Cage at Cranford, and The Moorland Cottage (110). Lizzie Leigh, The Grey Woman, and Other Tales, &c. (175). Mary Barton (86). North and South (154). Right at Last, and Other Tales, &c. (203). Round the Sofa (190). Ruth (88). Sylvia's Lovers (156). Wives and Daughters (157).

GISSING. Veranilda (349). Will Warburton (348).
GOLDSMITH. The Vicar of Wakefield (4).
HARRIS (JOEL CHANDLER). Uncle Remus (361).
HAWTHORNE. House of the Seven Gables (273). The Scarlet Letter (26). Tales (319).
HOLME (CONSTANCE). Crump Folk going Home (419). The Lonely Plough (390). The Old Road from Spain (400). The Splendid Fairing (416). The Trumpet in the Dust (409).
KINGSLEY (HENRY). Geoffry Hamlyn (271). Ravenshoe (267). Austin Elliot (407).
LE FANU (J. S.). Uncle Silas. Introduction by *Montague R. James* (306).
LA MOTTE FOUQUÉ. Undine, Sintram, &c. (408).
LESAGE. Gil Blas. Ed. *J. Fitzmaurice-Kelly*. 2 volumes (151, 152).
LYTTON. The Coming Race, &c. (327). Harold (165).
MARRYAT. Mr. Midshipman Easy (160).
MEINHOLD. The Amber Witch. Intro. by *J. W. Mackail* (325).
MELVILLE (HERMAN). Moby Dick (225). Typee (274). Omoo (275). White Jacket (253).
MORIER (J. J.). Hajji Baba (238). Hajji Baba in England (285).
MORITZ (C. P.). Anton Reiser. Intro. *P. E. Matheson* (299).
PEACOCK (T. L.). Headlong Hall; and Nightmare Abbey (339). Misfortunes of Elphin; and Crotchet Castle (244).
RABELAIS. Gargantua and Pantagruel. Translated by *Urquhart* and *Motteux*, with notes. 3 volumes (411–13).
SCOTT. Ivanhoe (29).
SMOLLETT. Roderick Random (353). Humphry Clinker (290).
STERNE. Sentimental Journey (333). Tristram Shandy (40).
STEVENSON (R. L.). Treasure Island (295). Kidnapped; and Catriona (297).
SWIFT. Gulliver's Travels (20).
TAYLOR (MEADOWS). Confessions of a Thug (207).
THACKERAY. Henry Esmond (28).
TOLSTOY. Translated by *Louise* and *Aylmer Maude*. Anna Karenina. 2 volumes (210, 211). Childhood, Boyhood, and Youth (352). The Cossacks, &c. (208). The Kreutzer Sonata, &c. (266). Resurrection, trans. by *L. Maude* (209). Twenty-three Tales (72). War and Peace. 3 volumes (233–5).
TRELAWNY (E. J.). Adventures of a Younger Son (289).
TROLLOPE. American Senator (391). Ayala's Angel (342). Barchester Towers (268). The Belton Estate (251). The Claverings (252). Cousin Henry (343). Doctor Thorne (298). Dr. Wortle's School (317). The Eustace Diamonds (357). Framley Parsonage (305). The Kellys and the O'Kellys (341). Last Chronicle of Barset. 2 vols. (398, 399). Miss Mackenzie (278). Orley Farm. 2 vols. (423, 424). Rachel Ray (279). Sir Harry Hotspur (336). Tales of all Countries (397). The Three Clerks (140). The Warden (217). The Vicar of Bullhampton (272).
WATTS-DUNTON (THEODORE). Aylwin (52).

¶ *History*

BARROW (SIR JOHN). The Mutiny of the *Bounty* (195).
BUCKLE. The History of Civilization. 3 volumes (41, 48, 53).
CARLYLE. The French Revolution. Introduction by *C. R. L. Fletcher*. 2 volumes (125, 126).
FROUDE (J. A.). Short Studies on Great Subjects. Series I (269).
GIBBON. Decline and Fall of the Roman Empire. With Maps 7 volumes (35, 44, 51, 55, 64, 69, 74).
IRVING (WASHINGTON). Conquest of Granada (150).
MACAULAY. History of England. 5 vols. (366–70).
MOTLEY Rise of the Dutch Republic. 3 volumes (96, 97, 98).
PRESCOTT (W. H.). The Conquest of Mexico. 2 vols. (197, 198).

¶ *Letters*

BURKE. Letters. Selected, with Introduction, by *H. J. Laski* (237).
CHESTERFIELD. Letters. Selected, with an Introduction, by *Phyllis M. Jones* (347).
CONGREVE. Letters, in Volume II. See under *Drama* (277).
COWPER. Letters. Selected, with Intro., by *E. V. Lucas* (138).
DUFFERIN (LORD). Letters from High Latitudes. Illustrated (158).
ENGLISH LETTERS. Fifteenth to Nineteenth Centuries (192).
GRAY (THOMAS). Letters. Selected by *John Beresford* (283).
JOHNSON (SAMUEL). Letters. Selected, with Introduction, by *R. W. Chapman* (282).
LETTERS WRITTEN IN WAR-TIME. Fifteenth to Nineteenth Centuries. Selected and arranged by *H. Wragg* (202).
SOUTHEY. Selected Letters (169).
TOLSTOY. Essays and Letters. Trans. by *L.* and *A. Maude* (46).
WHITE (GILBERT). The Natural History of Selborne (22).

¶ *Literary Criticism*

AMERICAN CRITICISM. Representative Literary Essays. Chosen by *Norman Foerster* (354).
COLERIDGE (S T.) Lectures on Shakespeare (363).
ENGLISH CRITICAL ESSAYS. Selected and edited by *Edmund D. Jones*. 2 volumes. I, Sixteenth to Eighteenth Centuries. II, Nineteenth Century (240, 206).
HAZLITT (WILLIAM). Characters of Shakespeare's Plays. Introduction by *Sir A. T. Quiller-Couch* (205). Lectures on the English Comic Writers. Introduction by *R. Brimley Johnson* (124). Lectures on the English Poets (255). The Spirit of the Age. (Essays on his contemporaries) (57).
HORNE (R H.). A New Spirit of the Age (127).
JOHNSON (SAMUEL). Lives of the Poets. 2 volumes (83, 84).
SAINTE-BEUVE. Causeries du Lundi. (In English.) Two Series (372–3).
SHAKESPEARE CRITICISM. (HEMINGE and CONDELL to CARLYLE.) Selected and Introduced by *D. Nichol Smith* (212).

¶ *Philosophy and Science*

(For POLITICAL THEORY and RELIGION see separate headings)

AURELIUS (MARCUS). Thoughts. Translated by *John Jackson* (60).

BACON. The Advancement of Learning, and the New Atlantis. Introduction by *Professor Case* (93). Essays (24).

CARLYLE. Sartor Resartus (19).

DARWIN. The Origin of Species. With a new preface by *Major Leonard Darwin* (11). Voyage of a Naturalist (360).

REYNOLDS (SIR JOSHUA). Discourses, &c. Intro. *A. Dobson* (149).

TOLSTOY. What then must we do? Trans. by *A. Maude* (281).

WHITE (GILBERT). The Natural History of Selborne (22).

¶ *Poetry*

(For AESCHYLUS and ARISTOPHANES see 'Classics' on p. 5)

ARNOLD (MATTHEW). Poems, 1849–67 (85).

BARHAM (RICHARD). The Ingoldsby Legends (9).

BLAKE (WILLIAM). Selected Poems (324).

BRONTË SISTERS, THE. The Professor, by CHARLOTTE BRONTË, and Poems by CHARLOTTE, EMILY, and ANNE BRONTË (78).

BROWNING (ELIZABETH BARRETT). Poems. A Selection (176).

BROWNING (ROBERT). Poems and Plays, 1833–42 (58). Poems, 1842–64 (137).

BURNS (ROBERT). Poems (34). Complete and in large type.

BYRON. Poems. A Selection (180).

CHAUCER, The Works of. 3 volumes. Vol. I (42); Vol. II (56); Vol. III, containing the whole of the Canterbury Tales (76).

COLERIDGE. Poems. Introduction by *Sir A. T. Quiller-Couch* (99).

CONGREVE (WILLIAM). Complete works in 2 volumes. Introductions by *Bonamy Dobrée*. I, The Comedies. II, The Mourning Bride, Poems, Miscellanies and Letters (276, 277).

DANTE. Italian text and English verse-translation by *Melville B. Anderson*, on facing pages, with notes. 3 vols. (392–4). Translation only, with notes, in one volume (395).

DOBSON (AUSTIN). Selected Poems (249)

ENGLISH SONGS AND BALLADS. Compiled by *T. W. H. Crosland*. New edition, with revised text and additional poems, 1927 (13).

ENGLISH VERSE. Vols. I–V: Early Lyrics to SHAKESPEARE; CAMPION to the Ballads; DRYDEN to WORDSWORTH; SCOTT to E. B. BROWNING; LONGFELLOW to RUPERT BROOKE. Edited by *William Peacock* (308–312).

FRANCIS OF ASSISI (ST.). The Little Flowers of St. Francis. Translated into English Verse by *James Rhoades* (265).

GOETHE. Faust, Parts I and II. Translated by *Bayard Taylor*. Intro. by *Marshall Montgomery* and notes by *Douglas Yates* (380).

GOLDEN TREASURY, THE. With additional Poems (133).

GOLDSMITH. Poems. Introduction by *Austin Dobson* (123).

HERBERT (GEORGE). Poems. Introduction by *Arthur Waugh* (109).

HERRICK (ROBERT). Poems (16).

HOMER. Translated by *Pope*. Iliad (18). Odyssey (36).
HOOD. Poems. Introduction by *Walter Jerrold* (87).
KEATS. Poems (7).
KEBLE. The Christian Year (181).
LONGFELLOW. Evangeline, The Golden Legend, &c. (39): Hiawatha, Miles Standish, Tales of a Wayside Inn, &c. (174).
MACAULAY. Lays of Ancient Rome; Ivry; The Armada (27).
MARLOWE. Dr. Faustus (with GOETHE's Faust, Part I, trans. *J. Anster*). Introduction by *Sir A. W. Ward* (135).
MILTON. The English Poems (182).
MORRIS (WILLIAM). The Defence of Guenevere, Life and Death of Jason, and other Poems (183).
NARRATIVE VERSE, A BOOK OF. Compiled by *V. H. Collins*. With an Introduction by *Edmund Blunden* (350).
NEKRASSOV. Trans. by *Juliet Soskice*. Who can be happy and free in Russia? A Poem (213). Poems (340).
PALGRAVE. The Golden Treasury. With additional Poems (133).
ROSSETTI (CHRISTINA). Goblin Market, &c. (184).
SCOTT (SIR WALTER). Selected Poems (186).
SHAKESPEARE. Plays and Poems. Preface by *A. C. Swinburne*. Introductions by *Edward Dowden*. 9 volumes. Comedies. 3 volumes (100, 101, 102). Histories and Poems. 3 volumes (103, 104, 105). Tragedies. 3 volumes (106, 107, 108).
SHELLEY. Poems. A Selection (187).
SOPHOCLES. The Seven Plays. Translated into English Verse by *Lewis Campbell* (116).
TENNYSON. Selected Poems. Intro. *Sir Herbert Warren* (3).
VIRGIL. The Aeneid, Georgics, and Eclogues. Translated by *Dryden* (37). Translated by *James Rhoades* (227).
WELLS (CHARLES). Joseph and his Brethren. A Dramatic Poem. Intro. *A. C. Swinburne*, and Note by *T. Watts-Dunton* (143).
WHITMAN. A Selection. Introduction by *E. de Sélincourt* (218).
WHITTIER. Poems: A Selection (188).
WORDSWORTH. Poems: A Selection (189).

¶ *Politics, Political Economy, Political Theory*

BAGEHOT (WALTER). The English Constitution. With an Introduction by the *Earl of Balfour* (330).
BUCKLE. The History of Civilization. 3 volumes (41, 48, 53).
BURKE (EDMUND). Letters. Selected, with an Introduction, by *Harold J. Laski* (237). Works. 6 volumes. Vol. I: A Vindication of Natural Society; The Sublime and Beautiful, &c. (71). II: The Present Discontents; and Speeches and Letters on America (81). III: Speeches on India, &c. (111). IV: Writings on France, 1790–1 (112). V: Writings on Ireland, &c. (113). VI: A Letter to a Noble Lord; and Letters on a Regicide Peace (114).
ENGLISH SPEECHES, from BURKE to GLADSTONE. Selected and edited by *E. R. Jones* (191).

MACHIAVELLI. The Prince. A revised translation (43).
MAINE (SIR HENRY). Ancient Law (362).
MILL (JOHN STUART). On Liberty, Representative Government, and the Subjection of Women (170).
MILTON (JOHN). Selected Prose. Intro. *Malcolm W. Wallace* (293).
RUSKIN. 'A Joy for Ever', and The Two Paths. Illustrated (147). Time and Tide, and The Crown of Wild Olive (146). Unto this Last, and Munera Pulveris (148).
SMITH (ADAM). The Wealth of Nations. 2 volumes (54, 59).
SPEECHES AND DOCUMENTS ON BRITISH COLONIAL POLICY (1763–1917). Ed. *A. B. Keith*. 2 volumes (215, 216).
SPEECHES AND DOCUMENTS ON THE BRITISH DOMINIONS, 1918–31. Selected, with Introduction, by *A. B. Keith* (403).
SPEECHES AND DOCUMENTS ON INDIAN POLICY (1756–1921). Edited, with Introduction, by *A. B. Keith* (231, 232).
SPEECHES ON BRITISH FOREIGN POLICY (1738–1914). Edited by *Edgar R. Jones, M.P.* (201).
TRACTS AND PAMPHLETS, A Miscellany of. Sixteenth to Nineteenth Centuries. Edited by *A. C. Ward* (304).
TOLSTOY. What then must we do? Translated, with an Introduction, by *Aylmer Maude* (281).

¶ *Religion*

THE OLD TESTAMENT. Revised Version. 4 vols. (385–8).
APOCRYPHA, THE, in the Revised Version (294).
THE FOUR GOSPELS, AND THE ACTS OF THE APOSTLES. Authorized Version (344).
THE NEW TESTAMENT. Revised Version (346).
À KEMPIS (THOMAS). Of the Imitation of Christ (49).
AURELIUS (MARCUS). Translated by *John Jackson* (60).
BUNYAN. The Pilgrim's Progress (12). Mr. Badman (338).
KORAN, THE. Translated by *E. H. Palmer*. Introduction by *Reynold A. Nicholson* (328).
TOLSTOY. A Confession, and What I believe. Translated by *Aylmer Maude* (229).

¶ *Short Stories*

AFRICA, STORIES OF. Chosen by *E. C. Parnwell* (359).
AUSTRIAN SHORT STORIES. Selected and translated by *Marie Busch* (337).
CRIME AND DETECTION. Two Series (301, 351). Stories by H. C. BAILEY, ERNEST BRAMAH, G. K. CHESTERTON, SIR A. CONAN DOYLE, R. AUSTIN FREEMAN, W. W. JACOBS, EDEN PHILPOTTS, 'SAPPER', DOROTHY SAYERS, and others.
CZECH TALES, SELECTED. Translated, with a Preface, by *Marie Busch* and *Otto Pick* (288). Nine stories, including two by the BROTHERS CAPEK.
DICKENS. Christmas Books (307).

ENGLISH SHORT STORIES. Three Series. Selected by *H. S. Milford*. Introduction by *Prof. Hugh Walker* in Vol. I (193, 228, 315).

FRENCH SHORT STORIES. Eighteenth to Twentieth Centuries. Selected and translated by *K. Rebillon Lambley* (396).

GASKELL (MRS.). Introductions by *Clement Shorter*. Cousin Phillis, and Other Tales (168). Lizzie Leigh, The Grey Woman, and Other Tales, &c. (175). Right at Last, and Other Tales, &c. (203). Round the Sofa (190).

GERMAN SHORT STORIES. Translated by *E. N. Bennett*, with an Introduction by *E. K. Bennett* (415).

GHOSTS AND MARVELS and MORE GHOSTS AND MARVELS. Two Selections of Uncanny Tales made by *V. H. Collins*. Introduction by *Montague R. James* in Series I (284, 323).

HARTE (BRET). Short Stories (318).

HAWTHORNE (NATHANIEL). Tales (319).

IRVING (WASHINGTON). Tales (320).

PERSIAN (FROM THE). The Three Dervishes, and Other Stories: Translated from MSS. in the Bodleian by *Reuben Levy* (254).

POE (EDGAR ALLAN). Tales of Mystery and Imagination (21).

POLISH TALES BY MODERN AUTHORS. Translated by *Else C. M. Benecke* and *Marie Busch* (230).

RUSSIAN SHORT STORIES. Chosen and translated by *A. E. Chamot* (287).

SCOTT. Short Stories. With an Introduction by *Lord David Cecil* (414).

SHORT STORIES OF THE SOUTH SEAS. Selected by *E. C. Parnwell* (332).

SPANISH SHORT STORIES. Sixteenth Century. In contemporary translations, revised, with an Introduction, by *J. B. Trend* (326).

TOLSTOY. Nine Stories (1855–63) (420). Twenty-three Tales. Translated by *Louise* and *Aylmer Maude* (72).

TROLLOPE. Tales of all Countries (397).

¶ *Travel and Topography*

BORROW (GEORGE). The Bible in Spain (75). Wild Wales (224). Lavengro (66). Romany Rye (73).

DARWIN. Voyage of a Naturalist (360).

DUFFERIN (LORD). Letters from High Latitudes (158).

MELVILLE (HERMAN). Typee (294). Omoo (275).

MORIER (J. J.). Hajji Baba of Ispahan. Introduction by *C. W. Stewart*, and a Map (238).

SMOLLETT (TOBIAS). Travels through France and Italy in 1765. Introduction (lxii pages) by *Thomas Seccombe* (90).

STERNE (LAURENCE). A Sentimental Journey. With Introduction by *Virginia Woolf* (333).

INDEX OF AUTHORS, ETC.

Further Volumes are in preparation.

March 1934

PRINTED IN GREAT BRITAIN